DONALD HORNE

DONALD HORNE

Selected Writings

Edited by
Nick Horne

IN CONJUNCTION WITH BLACK INC.

Published by La Trobe University Press in conjunction with Black Inc.
Level 1, 221 Drummond Street
Carlton VIC 3053, Australia
enquiries@blackincbooks.com
www.blackincbooks.com
www.latrobeuniversitypress.com.au

Copyright © The Estate of Donald Horne 2017
Introduction © Nick Horne 2017
'A Public Intellectual: The Life and Times of Donald Horne' © Glyn Davis 2017
Collection © La Trobe University Press 2017
The Estate of Donald Horne asserts its moral right as author of the work.

Excerpts from *Dying: A Memoir* by Donald Horne and Myfanwy Horne copyright © Donald Horne and Myfanwy Horne, 2007. Reprinted by permission of Penguin Random House Australia Pty Ltd.
Excerpts from *The Lucky Country* by Donald Horne copyright © Donald Horne, 1964. Reprinted by permission of Penguin Random House Australia Pty Ltd.
'Mind, Body and Age' first published in *Griffith Review 4: Making Perfect Bodies*, 2004, www.griffithreview.com, reproduced with permission.
'The Metaphor of Leftness' first published in *Quadrant* vol. 6 no. 3, 1962, reproduced with permission.

ALL RIGHTS RESERVED.
No part of this publication may be reproduced, stored in a retrieval system, or transmitted in any form by any means electronic, mechanical, photocopying, recording or otherwise without the prior consent of the publishers.

National Library of Australia Cataloguing-in-Publication entry:
Horne, Donald, 1921–2005, author.
Donald Horne: selected writings/Donald Horne
biographical essay by Glyn Davis;
edited and introduction by Nick Horne.
9781863959353 (paperback)
9781925435757 (ebook)
Horne, Donald, 1921–2005.
Authors, Australian–Biography.
Pioneers–Australia–Biography.
Other Creators/Contributors:
Davis, Glyn.
Horne, Nick, editor, writer of introduction.

Design and typesetting by Peter Long
Cover photograph by Alec Bolton, National Library of Australia

Contents

A Public Intellectual:
The Life and Times of Donald Horne
by Glyn Davis ... IX

Donald Horne: Selected Writings

A Brief Timeline for Donald Horne ... 3

Introduction by Nick Horne ... 7

FORMATIVE YEARS

CHILDHOOD

1. The Education of Young Donald ... 17
   Making our own fun ... 17
   Country, King, God ... 28
   'Be yourself, Don' ... 45
   'It is my desire to do great things' ... 59

UNIVERSITY

2. John Anderson and the Andersonians ... 62

3. A Time of Sadness ... 66

4. You Made What You Liked of Me, Boys ... 70

RADICAL CONSERVATIVE

5. Some Cultural Elites in Australia ... 75

6. The Great Crisis of the Golden Age ... 79

7. Ambition ... 84

8. The Metaphor of Leftness ... 93

9. The Lucky Country ... 104
The Australian Dream ... 104
The Lucky Country ... 113

FICTION

10. But What If There Are No Pelicans? ... 129
The last interrogation ... 129

THE AUSTRALIA DISCUSSION

11. The Australian People ... 141
The orphans of the Pacific ... 141

12. Money Made Us ... 155
The secular faith of growth ... 155
The profit motive ... 162

13. Death of the Lucky Country ... 171
Landscape of disaster ... 171

14. Ideas for a Nation ... 180
Australia is ordinary ... 180

15. A Story of What Might Have Been ... 194

16. The Importance of Symbolism:
Australia Should Become a Republic ... 207

IT'S ALL ABOUT THE CULTURE

17. The Intelligent Tourist … 213
How to be real … 213

18. The Public Culture … 222
A national mirage … 222
A declaration of 'cultural rights' … 230

19. The Politics of the Australian Tribe:
A Confidential Report by an
Anthropologist from Outer Space … 236

20. It's the Culture, Stupid … 246

THE THOUGHTS OF OLD DONALD

21. Into the Open … 251
Knocking down a national edifice … 251

22. Looking for Leadership:
Australia in the Howard Years … 257
Putting on a show: leadership in
a liberal-democratic society … 257

23. 10 Steps to a More Tolerant Australia … 265
The pleasures of tolerance … 265

24. Mind, Body and Age … 276

25. Dying: A Memoir … 285
Faith … 285

Sources … 292
Index … 294

A PUBLIC INTELLECTUAL: THE LIFE AND TIMES OF DONALD HORNE

Glyn Davis

Australia is a lucky country run mainly by second-rate people who share its luck. It lives on other people's ideas, and, although its ordinary people are adaptable, most of its leaders (in all fields) so lack curiosity about the events that surround them that they are often taken by surprise.[1]

This tough-minded verdict by Donald Horne, central to *The Lucky Country*, lost its force over time. Speechmakers quoted the tagline but not the stinging judgement it introduced. Shorn of irony, criticism became affirmation.

More than half a century on, a new generation explores the work of Donald Horne.[2] So this timely anthology, edited by his son, Nick, provides a welcome selection from a long life of journalism and academic writing. Compiled with care and thought, it highlights the breadth and imagination of Horne's catalogue. It offers different glimpses of the same man – the enthusiastic chronicler of his life and times, poet and novelist, journalist, polemicist and, later in life, the academic keen to contribute to debates about public culture, economic rationalism, national identity.

Nick Horne adopts a 'hybrid chronology' for the collection, an astute arrangement given Donald Horne (1921–2005) worked his way through several careers and most of the political spectrum. After a memorable if incomplete education, Horne spent much of his professional life as a journalist and editor. He was known for fierce anti-Communism, his co-editorship of *Quadrant* and his condemnation of Australia's elites. Horne dismissed those who aspired to be intellectuals. This was a European term, ill-suited to an egalitarian nation. When it appeared in a publication Horne edited, 'intellectual' might be surrounded by quotation marks if Horne wanted to highlight or question the claim.

Yet in midlife Horne came to doubt many earlier convictions. The young Donald imagined his destiny as a poet or novelist, and his middle years were focused on journalism. It took the unexpected success of his first published book, written when he was forty-two, for Horne to begin to speak regularly in public about ideas. This Donald Horne was rarely a systematic thinker, since his undergraduate philosophy education made him suspicious of epistemological claims, as of any attempt to influence the world. It was the late-blooming academic Donald Horne who strived to order the set of ideas that had preoccupied him for many years, shaped by the question of how culture is formed and sustained.

By documenting changing preoccupations over decades, Nick Horne traces how his father became a familiar public intellectual in Australia, a man who helped the nation understand itself. His regular books and newspaper articles, his lectures and political activism, and roles such as chairing the Australia Council ensured a wide audience. By his death – characteristically chronicled for publication – Donald Horne embodied the Australian public intellectual he once found implausible. He learned that intellectuals can 'give shape to inchoate ideas already agitating the public mind'[3] by providing concepts and language that might travel.

To capture his experiences, Horne kept notes and letters, alongside the chattels of a busy life.[4] These Horne condensed into a series of popular autobiographical volumes, including *The Education of Young Donald* (1967), *Confessions of a New Boy* (1985), *Portrait of an Optimist* (1988) and *Into the Open* (2000). Each volume chronicles a phase of life, reading, conversations, friends, private and political passions. Perhaps it is the daunting richness of primary material that has discouraged any detailed biography of Donald Horne to date, and yielded only a modest list of secondary works touching on his life and writing.

Despite the inevitable lapses in reporting, there is an appealing openness in Horne's endless self-observation, a shifting world view nestled closely within the flow of his life. Taken together, his writings offer a portrait of a thinker who, as Horne acknowledges, is at his worst when ideological but at his best when curiosity and scepticism make him question conventional wisdom.

It is instructive to trace the characteristic ideas and public arguments that emerge from each stage of that life. Nick Horne identifies broad themes in the development of Horne's thought, captured in this anthology.

The first deals with the early enthusiasms of student years under the influence of the philosopher John Anderson, and the second a long period as a journalist and editor associated with causes of the political right. As a reporter Horne developed the approaches and subject matter that would influence an excursion into fiction, and a return to polemic in the study of Australia. His range broadened further with a move to academia. Horne the reporter had always written about the economy and national interests, but the tone changed as he favoured long-form books over earlier journalism. Here he could explore at length interests in reform agendas, politics and the implications of economic rationalism.

Two themes complete the anthology and the life. A long-time interest in how culture is formed and sustained produced some of Horne's later work, notably *The Public Culture* in 1986, which found an international audience. The closing decades were committed to political activism around democracy, cultural rights and representation. There was a final turn to the personal with reflections on ageing and faith, concluding more than fifty years of publications in a joint volume with wife Myfanwy with the provocative title *Dying: A Memoir*.

There are important continuities, notably Horne's libertarian beliefs and sceptical view of the state. There are also significant changes – not least, in recognising and promoting the possibility of conversation in a culture that once seemed hostile to public debate. As a public intellectual, Horne believed in independence of judgement. Diana Gribble noted that Horne was capable of 'startling moments' in which he would be persuaded by someone else's point of view and 'completely change his mind'.[5] This openness to new ideas makes it impossible to describe Donald Horne in conventional political terms. He was not simply a man of the right who moved to the left later in life, but someone who came slowly to a view about the role of ideas in society. The thinking and the journey are one.

Formative years

Donald Horne was born in Sydney in 1921, the eldest child and only son of a schoolteacher shell-shocked by service in the Great War and a mother who put aside work for family. He would later recall his early years in astonishing detail: the buildings and families of his early home in Muswellbrook, the books on the shelves, the ten houses in his first sixteen years, the social structure of the town, with its gradations of status and influence. When his father transferred to a new school in Sydney, the Horne family left the Hunter Valley for life in the suburbs during the Great Depression. It was a caring family, but a lonely life for a talkative boy with no siblings until a teenager, and few opportunities to discuss the books he loved.

Always a keen reader, young Donald found much to admire in the four volumes of *The History of the British Nation*, with their optimistic view of Empire and virtue. Yet he did not miss the subtext revealed amid glimpses of setback and defeat – the 'inhumanity, treachery, stupidity and meaninglessness' of history. His father's later breakdown may have reinforced a disturbing realisation that life could be disconnected, discordant, irrational and unpredictable. During his teenage years the family would move once again, this time to his grandmother's house, 'Denbigh', at 40 Arthur Street, Kogarah, to live on a war pension.

During high school Horne began to recognise some essential elements of his character – his love of reading, storytelling and joking, an eagerness to learn, a drive to invent things and disdain for 'serious people' who couldn't laugh at their misfortunes.

He also pondered the possibilities of a career in law, politics, literature, academia or perhaps journalism. In fact, journalism was already looming large in Horne's life. He recalls fondly the sympathetic world view of a new newspaper, the *Daily Telegraph*, a paper of serious writing and influence owned and run from 1936 by Frank Packer. The *Daily Telegraph* spoke to Horne's desire for modernity. Horne 'fell in love with it from the first issue' – its contemporary voice, the 'rebelliousness of spirit' in a newspaper of firm opinions. Through the *Daily Telegraph* Horne could take the 'side of Progress against Reaction or, perhaps more exactly, of Intelligence against Stupidity'. He became so immersed in the publication that one day while in the city he 'walked into the *Telegraph* building to see what it looked like'.⁶

Horne would spend much of his professional life as a journalist and editor in the Packer organisation. He found in the *Daily Telegraph* a voice that matched his own character – optimistic, impatient with artifice, allied to the new, occasionally brash.

The transition from enthusiastic reader to writer was not immediate. On finishing at Canterbury High, Horne enrolled in Arts at the University of Sydney. His study was supported by a Teachers College scholarship that would require him to follow his father's profession. Horne arrived at university in early 1939, just seventeen and thrilled to be there. Yet he felt quickly the gap between his background and that of the many privileged students. He found himself dissembling about his family origins. To modify his accent, Horne taught himself new diphthongs from an English textbook. He would reinvent himself in more important ways. Horne swiftly discovered talk in the quad was more rewarding than time in the classroom. Like many students, he was swept up by each new discovery. He used his time at university to try on a rapid series of identities: as poet; follower of aesthetics, psychology and Freud; as scientist, artist and laconic conversationalist – 'young Donald, mumbler of witticisms', as he later observed ruefully.⁷

Horne was determined to test himself with the challenging ideas of his time. He found these personified in the most famous man on campus, Challis Professor of Philosophy John Anderson.

> On the day I first arrived at the University I saw Anderson walking along the cloisters in the Quad: someone pointed him out as the Scottish radical who was the University's main rebel, a renowned atheist, not long ago a Communist, censured in the New South Wales Parliament and by the University Senate.

Anderson seemed the most important person at the University ... He was in his forties, very tall, stooped, gangling, striding loosely past in a brown suit and green hat with an upturned brim, usually sombre, with his pipe jutting out from between his teeth. He seemed an embodiment of what was grave and constant in human suffering, but sometimes he would wave an arm at a student, loosely, as if it were a puppet's, and smile, strong teeth bursting out beneath his full black moustache ... Recognition. Sunshine ... I was gripped by the need to know him.[8]

Horne began attending Literary Society meetings with Anderson in the chair. The professor's papers were heard in reverent silence. 'It took only an hour,' recalled Horne, but 'we felt that we had just witnessed an important new contribution to the theory of aesthetics.'[9] In the quad, Horne sought to master the argumentative style favoured by Anderson's many acolytes, with an emphasis on logic, grammatical integrity and precision. Horne found himself pounced on for many careless phrases – 'But what do you *mean* by that?' – and bewildered as his flights of fancy were critiqued by others more attuned to acceptable utterances.

The university education of young Donald ended abruptly. In late 1941, amid world war, Horne was conscripted by the army – first into a regiment hastily constituted to handle university conscripts, and then the artillery. Horne was not a natural soldier, though his usual powers of observation produced a fine running commentary on the social structure and organisation of the Australian military, which he shared with his university friend, the poet James McAuley, then a schoolteacher in Newcastle.

It had been a turbulent if engrossing engagement with university life. Horne did not graduate, and the anthology includes a eulogy to the years at the University of Sydney. 'You Made What You Liked of

Me, Boys' is a poem written in 1941. The background is Horne's activism, his emerging engagement with journalism. Donald Horne loved his time with the student newspaper – 'I could think of some new thing on the tram on the way to the university and, minutes later, I could hurry to the *Honi Soit* office and start doing it.'[10] Yet he recognised the costs of political life as a student. 'For I sold my soul to the devil/ In a temper, some time to go,/ For a pot of pride and mirror/ And I knew I'd have to go.'

Radical conservative

Donald Horne's war spared him combat and provided time for reading and reflection. Away from student life, Horne could ponder his embrace of John Anderson's politics, and think about his future.

That Horne struggled to process the essence of Andersonian thought is not surprising, for the Challis professor constantly reworked his philosophical position. During the 1930s John Anderson had been associated with the Communist Party, then briefly became a Trotskyite before breaking with organised Marxism to embrace a libertarian position.[11] This pitted him against authoritarian states and institutions, including the formal requirements of university life; Anderson led a campaign, for example, against the presence of a university regiment, only to see many of his students conscripted for the Second World War.

Anderson sometimes characterised his later views as anarchist, but eventually rejected political labels and any suggestion that meaningful change can be achieved through political action. He turned to exposing the illusions of progress and the need to promote freethinking in all spheres of life. Anderson's vehicle, in part, was the Sydney University Freethought Society, which for a while welcomed D.R. Horne as secretary.

John Anderson's striking influence on generations of students attests to his magnetism. When Anderson spoke 'in his urgent Glaswegian sing-song the room seemed stilled by significance', Horne said. Anderson could project certainty – Horne was 'thrilled by his implacable lack of compromise and the way he argued stubbornly and passionately against almost everything said by anyone apart from the Freethinkers at Sydney University'. Anderson 'led the Freethought Society with the distant assuredness of a prophet on a faraway mountain'. He appeared to the admiring young student an 'intransigent believer in the exposure of all illusions and a prophet of the ideal of a life lived in permanent protest'.[12]

The influence of John Anderson on young Donald would run counter to Horne's personality. As Horne later grasped, he was by temperament an optimist, but his intellectual training made him a pessimist. He took from Anderson an understanding that a freethinker should attack both right and left in politics, which Horne would do enthusiastically for decades to follow. But Anderson also encouraged Horne to disengage, by fostering a sense that people cannot influence their surroundings, which are shaped by social forces rather than individual agency. Hence attempts to 'reform' society are doomed to failure – 'one must *account* for things, not try to *change* them' – as Horne summarised a key learning from quad discussions.[13]

Above all, Horne was influenced by Anderson's article 'The Servile State', from which he derived an argument that 'the well-intentioned reformer always produces results which he did not anticipate'.[14] Like Hayek in *The Road to Serfdom*, Anderson resisted the claims of the state to order individual lives in the interest of better social outcomes. Anderson evoked the phenomenon of unintended consequences – the assertion that attempts at social amelioration produce results that undermine the intention. This insight justified

Horne's rejection of Labor politics as 'meliorist' and misguided, preferring a view of himself as a 'radical conservative'. In the Andersonian spirit – 'the servile State is the unopposed State' – Horne did not register to vote and delighted in attacking welfare and planning.

Yet maintaining ironic detachment was never Donald Horne's most plausible persona. He was by instinct an activist. Even while professing Andersonian beliefs about the futility of individual agency, the undergraduate Horne embraced university life with gusto. Student politics was unacceptable to the Freethinkers, but Horne launched an unsuccessful campaign against sex segregation in the university unions, before standing and failing to be elected to the student council.

Despite these failures, Horne found a sense of purpose and achievement through student politics. 'However trivial a source of power,' he decided later, 'it can provide the same pleasures as the greatest office ... this was my education.'[15] Finally, the activist Horne symbolically slayed the father – he organised enough votes to depose Anderson as president of the Literary Society and install himself as leader.

Still, for decades to follow Horne remained enthralled by Anderson's ideas, judging his own actions as inadequate against Anderson's more austere standards. As he worked as a journalist Horne 'could go on feeling that Anderson's sad, brown eyes were staring over my shoulder while I was writing a *Daily Telegraph* piece'.[16] Horne sought guidance on life decisions in Andersonian terms, and worked much of his life, in journalism and later academia, with others trained by Anderson.

Anderson's strong influence flows through the anthology, particularly his first political writing. This was a long phase in Horne's career – the first piece drawn from *Angry Penguins* in 1945, through to a critique of 'leftness' published in *Quadrant* in 1962.

In 'Some Cultural Elites in Australia', Horne is at his most scathing about intellectuals and what he calls the 'myth of cultural renaissance'. By the time Horne wrote this piece, his career had taken a new turn. Life in the army provided time to read new British literary magazines such as *Horizon* and *Scrutiny*. Horne also discovered the *Economist*, which introduced him to the new genre of 'current affairs', his first encounter with 'serious journalism'. Horne also began reading about Asia, as he pondered the regional post-war settlement to follow. In 1944 this interest was given practical expression when Horne was selected for the first intake of the new Australian Diplomatic Corps. Horne left the army with relief, and moved to the Canberra University College to train for overseas service. Thus the opponent of planning found himself recruited to the public service as part of a new generation 'coming to power to modernise Australia'.[17]

In the long college holidays, Horne headed home. He enjoyed the chance to read classics of political science and diplomacy as part of his course, but found Canberra 'offered nothing more than the stunted amenities of an Australian suburb or country town'. There were interesting encounters, such as meeting Lieutenant-Colonel John Kerr over drinks at the Hotel Canberra, but the escapes to Sydney became more lengthy.

Horne supplemented his cadet pay by writing as a casual reporter for the *Daily Telegraph*. He relished the world of reporters – his successor as *Honi Soit* editor, Murray Sayle, taught Horne the house style, the art of journalism in which 'the mysteries of existence would freeze into a few short, sharp and solid sentences'.[18] Journalism meant making the world understandable for readers. It was teaching of a sort, a way to communicate with an imagined audience. The lucid prose that emerged, even when dealing with complexity, would mark Horne's writing. It would prompt Hugh Stretton to describe Horne, among nonfiction authors, as 'the finest writer of our generation'.

Horne had been plagued with doubt about the prospect of becoming a diplomat. How could he speak for an Australian national interest when he had learned that 'society was simply an arena of conflicting forces'? So in 1945 Donald Horne quit public service for journalism, a boarding house in Kings Cross, and the 'general detachment from everyone's sense of reality' that defined the *Daily Telegraph* newsroom. He covered politics and city news and occasionally wrote features, including a two-page profile on John Anderson. He met legendary newspaper men in Sydney hotels, for a while shared a Potts Point apartment with a fellow scribe, was excited and disappointed in love, and developed an enduring fascination with the court politics surrounding his employer, Frank Packer. He lived, in short, the life of a journalist engrossed in his work, skilled at his craft, at home in the heavy-drinking male culture of newspapers, spending his income on books, hotels, taxis and restaurants.

Horne was also experimenting with new styles of writing. 'Ambition' is an unpublished paper from 1959. Here emerges the author who takes a common concept, breaks it down into differing shades of meaning, and asks about the cultural work done by the word.

The term 'radical conservative' is one Horne favoured, since it captured a welcome contradiction – activism in favour of limiting the state and discouraging government intrusion. Working in a newsroom, Horne found himself a conservative in a profession more often peopled by the left. Horne was out of sympathy with the era of post-war reconstruction, quoting Hayek or the *Economist* to fellow journalists. 'To be an anti-Stalinist intellectual as late in history as 1947,' he recalled, 'seemed a gallant and lonely stand.' It did not help that fellow Andersonians had split into rival camps, with some upholding the writings of the present John Anderson and others denouncing the current philosopher as 'reactionary', preferring an 'earlier and truer Andersonianism'. Horne found this disconcerting, particularly when he came under attack from former allies – 'here were Andersonians attacking me. Andersonians were not supposed to attack each other. They were expected to unite against the illusions of the rest of the world.'[19]

There is a chronological gap between extracts in this section of the anthology, for much else was happening in Horne's life. In 1948 he married Ethel, an Englishwoman living in Sydney. Within a year he and Ethel had abandoned life in Australia for a slow voyage to the United Kingdom and a new life as a novelist. Horne settled into an English village, became active in the local Conservative Party and began work on a novel. When funds ran short he pursued occasional journalism.

Eventually Horne could no longer live a financially haphazard existence. He moved to London, there to work with fellow Australian novelist George Johnson in the Fleet Street bureau of the *Sydney Sun*, before shifting to the *Daily Telegraph*. He reported first from London, then as an international correspondent. Finally he was recalled to Sydney by Frank Packer to establish a new newspaper closely modelled on a successful British publication of little repute. He returned to Sydney without Ethel, and the marriage, already failing, fell apart 'in an unexpected exchange of letters'. Arriving home in Australia was a shock. 'All of Sydney seemed second-rate and run-down: I saw myself as an exile from the old world – itself shabby, but with a shabbiness rich in meaning. Australia was mindless, I would say to myself. Where were the art museums and theatres, the intellectual debate?'[20]

Horne resolved to start a journal of ideas, to create in Australia the sort of reading he had enjoyed in Britain. But first he must learn to be an editor, leading a new publication with the less than promising title *Weekend: Australia's brightest newspaper*. A quick study, Horne grasped the essentials of working in the Packer empire, in the newsroom and executive offices overlooking Sydney's Hyde

Park – the need to generate profits, anticipate the whims of the boss and manage relations with current Packer favourites. Horne learned how to control costs and when to hire journalists.

It took longer to master managing a team. Horne's behaviour as editor could be 'monstrous'.[21] Unhappy with the quality of one article produced for *Weekend* he tore up the typed copy and threw it out the window.[22] His editorship was marked by bursts of rage, and he became notorious for his technique in sacking people, when he would lose his temper to give himself courage.[23] The alcohol-fuelled culture of journalism made such incidents the stuff of bar-room legend – the brother of one sacked employee poured a glass of beer over the *Weekend* editor in a local hotel. Horne would look back on these incidents with embarrassment, and later change his approach to working with colleagues.

Professional success did not mean personal happiness. Now in his mid-thirties, Horne worried about his life editing Australia's brightest newspaper and acting as court jester to Frank Packer. There were periods of depression and doubt for D.R. Horne the 'angry, ill-informed shouter', a failed novelist consumed by 'alcohol, rage and self-pity'.[24]

It also proved a time of hardening political identities. In the 1950s Communism became the defining issue, particularly following Khrushchev's denunciation of Stalin and the Hungarian uprising. Old friends, such as James McAuley, began to define themselves as anti-communists and established the Australian Committee for Cultural Freedom to publish a new journal, *Quadrant*, and build links with international anti-communist movements. Some fellow Andersonians followed McAuley into the committee. Others shared his opposition to repressive states but preferred to explore the 'anarchist potential of being'. They declared themselves 'libertarians' and became, in time, the Sydney Push, a subculture that lasted much of a generation.

Horne could not empathise with the Sydney Push. He disliked

its masculine and often anti-intellectual culture, and its 'romantic playing with anarchism'. Yet John Anderson could no longer provide reliable guidance – in his final years as Challis professor the philosopher had 'now assumed a position so inherently contradictory that it was no longer available for imitation'.[25]

As Horne pondered his political stance in his middle thirties, two important changes in his life would define the path ahead. The first was personal – he met Myfanwy Gollan, a journalist with the *Sydney Morning Herald* twelve years his junior, who, like Horne, had learned her craft on *Honi Soit*. They married in 1960. Family life became central to Donald Horne and a source of great joy. Their close partnership would endure until Horne's death, forty-five years later. They worked together as authors and editors, social commentators and political activists. An obituary would suggest Myfanwy Horne's 'enduring legacy is her work as Donald's editor',[26] but stressed the emotional and intellectual intimacy the couple shared. At Horne's memorial service Myfanwy recalled, 'We were very lucky that we were able to make such a life together. He was my companion and our companionship grew richer over the years.'[27]

The second change was an opportunity at last to edit an intellectual journal. Horne had come to believe an audience for ideas existed in Australia. It would be hard work, given the dearth of serious books and journals about Australian life. Still, Packer agreed to underwrite publication, so from 1958 Australians could read the *Observer* fortnightly, with commentary on local and international affairs. With Horne as editor there would be articles from academics such as Henry Mayer, and contributions from a cast that included Michael Baume, Robert Hughes, Bob Raymond, Bruce Beresford, Les Tanner and Desmond O'Grady. The *Observer* challenged the notion that Australia had 'long since been reduced to an essence, bottled and labelled'.[28] Through the pages of a journal he described as 'intelligently conservative', Horne developed topics and themes he would publish in December 1964 as *The Lucky Country*.

To assist with the new journal Horne hired Peter Coleman, a student of both Anderson and the English philosopher Michael Oakeshott. Coleman and Horne would work together on a number of Packer projects, providing space also for fellow anti-communists.

The *Observer* encouraged frequent parties and dinners at the houses of contributors, often including visiting British or American participants. These stimulating symposia were arranged by a new friend, Richard Krygier, the founder of the Australian Committee for Cultural Freedom, which published *Quadrant*.

Horne, ever social and interested in new ideas, sought possible *Observer* contributors among a lively group of political scientists and sociologists – his old friend Doug McCallum, now at the University of New South Wales, Brian Beddie, Arthur Burns, Sol Encel, Dick Spann and Hugo Wolfsohn, along with Henry Mayer. He was invited back to Sydney University to defend *Weekend* and found himself 'addressing an overflow lecture theatre in the same room in which I had made my first public appearance as a student, seventeen years ago, defending (as a poet) good verse against bad'.[29]

A further significant change would take some years to play out, but went to the core of Horne's longstanding political beliefs. As an Andersonian, Horne remained sceptical about the prospects for meaningful reform through the political process. So, despite his personal misgivings, Horne judged it pointless to attack too vigorously the White Australia policy. Australian folk roots, he observed, 'are in many ways among the most reactionary and racially bigoted in the world'. The prevailing political culture argued for a 'realist' approach: 'there was not yet a chance of surmounting the prejudices of the Australian people'.[30] The editor decided the *Observer* would not press the issue of institutionalised racism in Australian migration policy.

Horne was proved wrong. As he later observed:

> a year after the *Observer* got going, twenty or so young intellectuals, mostly from the University of Melbourne, began meeting in a suburban house in Camberwell to discuss the practicalities of reforming the White Australia immigration policy. In the liberal intellectual tradition they decided to publish a pamphlet … It was expressed conservatively, but it was a new way of looking at the practical chances of amending what was seen as one of the foundations of both the Australian state and Australian society and in only a few years it had practical effects, much bigger than those expected. As good intellectuals, they were negotiating part of the new sense of the possible in Australia.[31]

The campaign proved influential. By 1966 the Commonwealth Government announced it would assess potential migrants on skills and suitability rather than race. Horne recognised the Melbourne campaign called into question his assumption that social progress is an illusion. Further, it suggested that intellectuals could organise campaigns and challenge foundational tenets of the Australian settlement. Donald Horne the pessimist, carefully schooled in 'realism' by 'Anderson and a host of books', glimpsed the possibility of Donald Horne the optimist, someone who knew that culture can be changed, and government can rise above prevailing attitudes. Horne had always held as true that reform is overwhelmed by unintended consequences. Now he grasped the risk of inaction – failing to change might also be harmful.

Marrying, beginning what would prove a happy and stable family life, editing the *Observer* and watching a successful social movement all encouraged Horne to reassess his assumptions about the world. As a commentator with access to the pages of an influential national opinion journal, Horne discovered a 'new sense of the possible'. Ideas could matter; change was possible. And this could be led by people 'doing one of the things only intellectuals can do: good, bad or indifferent, they were providing new concepts of what was going on and new concepts of what could go on. Despite myself, I was an intellectual, if not in quotation marks.'[32]

In 1960 Packer acquired a venerable, if moribund, Australian institution, the *Bulletin*, in a deal designed principally to block the young Rupert Murdoch. The *Bulletin*, with its famous pink covers and proud slogan, 'Australia for the White Man', had a reputation for 'diehard reactionaryism, even among the conservatives'. Packer gave Donald Horne a choice: he could fold either the *Observer* or the *Bulletin*, and edit the remaining publication. Horne chose to reinvent the *Bulletin*, and set out to confound. He hired new writers, dropped the pink paper and slogan, removed the tired cartoons about Indigenous Australians. In hiring cartoonist Les Tanner, Horne changed the 'visual tradition' of the *Bulletin*, encouraging cartoons that were 'more visible and politically radical'.[33] Horne was determined to produce a *Bulletin* that included 'as fellow Australians women, city dwellers, young people, New Australians, Catholics, Aborigines, scientists, intellectuals, executives and dozens of other previously forgotten species; and that now accepted that Australia adjoined South-East Asia and that we lived in changing times'.[34]

Bulletin readers professed outrage, but for Horne it was 'one further step from pessimism'. In transforming the *Bulletin*, he was also rethinking his own views. When transferred to other projects, Horne decided to leave the Packer empire. He spent some time contemplating alternative careers – one colleague suggested he become a state Liberal MP – before settling for financial security in advertising. In quiet moments at Australia's third-largest advertising agency,

Jackson Wain, he began what would become his first published book, *The Lucky Country*.

As a young journalist in 1946, Horne had sketched a fifteen-page outline of a book about Australia. The project stalled but the idea of writing about the nation persisted. Horne observed the paucity of books about the country, with the architect Robin Boyd's *Australia's Home* and *The Australian Ugliness* and the historian Manning Clark's three selections of Australian historical documents rare exceptions. Beyond a few periodicals, such as the *Australian Quarterly*, Horne found nothing worth reading from the universities. So, drawing on his articles for the *Observer*, feature ideas for the *Bulletin* and the editorials he had been writing in his head since his teenage years, Donald Horne sat in a backyard deckchair on a Sunday afternoon after lunch in December 1963, next to his wife and sleeping baby daughter Julia, and 'began writing a book about Australia'.[35]

This was not a scholarly work. Horne did little original research, and relied instead on old clippings and some fieldwork, such as the visit to South Sydney Junior Leagues Club that opens the original edition. He had in mind a transient book, a collection of snapshots of Australia in 'The Age of Menzies'. The book would trace the 'innocent happiness' of Australians, the sense of national identity, the groups excluded from national conversation, 'government by imitation' and 'politics without ideas' in a 'second-hand culture'.

The project gave Horne an opportunity to address subjects that had been in his mind for some time. This included Australia's engagement with Asia: thinking about neighbours seemed essential when imagining Australia. The attention to Asia in the book, as in publications Horne edited, proved prescient – half a century later, he would be credited with 'grasping and synthesising sentiments bubbling to the surface of public discourse, and for envisaging how

Australia's neighbourhood and international relations could be reconstituted in a post-imperial age'.[36]

Horne wanted his book to be realistic about contemporary suburban living, avoiding the idealised landscape of Russel Ward's *The Australian Legend*. As his key theme, Horne developed the argument that Australia was fortunate rather than clever or innovative. It was Geoffrey Dutton, editor of the newly established Australian Penguin imprint, who suggested the title, drawing on the title of the final chapter. The work benefited from Max Harris and publisher Brian Stonier, who shared with Horne an aspiration: the 'articulation of what made Australia unique'.[37]

When the draft was complete Myfanwy 'went through the typed copy, nipped out unnecessary words and sorted out word jams – in a way that became characteristic of what, in the old-fashioned sense, is our partnership'.[38] This pattern would endure through more than twenty-eight books; towards the end of his publishing career Horne acknowledged that without Myfanwy's 'emotional and intellectual support I don't know that I would have "become a writer"'.[39]

Published in the closing weeks of 1964 as a Penguin paperback costing eight shillings and sixpence, *The Lucky Country* was serialised in the *Australian* and sold its original print run of 18,000 copies in just nine days.[40] Readers welcomed a book that 'expressed opinions' not previously 'put into words'; a later assessment suggests *The Lucky Country* 'had the effect Horne wanted – it shook Australians out of their complacency and started a national conversation'.[41]

Through multiple editions *The Lucky Country* would eventually sell more than 260,000 copies, and inspire television documentaries, school exams and a national slogan that profoundly misunderstood the irony of the title. Meaghan Morris recalled reading the book in one sitting: 'I had never struck anything like it; we had old Australian novels and a history or two around, but I did not know that you could write like *that* about our way of life.'⁴² Donald Horne found himself modestly famous, speaking to, and about, Australia. In urging government to encourage the innovation missing from public and business life Horne also found himself becoming 'unconservative'. For the rest of his career Horne would argue that a progressive state was possible. It would be some time, however, before the implications of this change of political view would be apparent to Horne or his long-established circle of conservative friends.

Fiction

When Donald Horne moved to England soon after his first marriage, a key goal was to pursue literary ambitions – 'reminders that I was now aged twenty-seven and had not yet written even one novel could strike me momentarily senseless with disbelief'.⁴³ Yet the fiction was slow to arrive. It would be nearly two decades before *The Permit* was published, in 1965, followed by *But What If There Are No Pelicans?* in 1971. In 1977 Horne published *His Excellency's Pleasure*, a satire inspired by the dismissal of Gough Whitlam, and two decades later *The Avenue of the Fair Go* completed the extended interlude with novels.

Writing fiction was important for Horne, but his novels did not achieve the same success as his writing on politics, economy and culture. Horne later imported techniques from fiction, such as describing tourists exploring new societies, into his writing. Yet the novels remained important to Horne, who hoped one day 'a few people might look at [*But What If There Are No Pelicans?*] more seriously' given its focus on 'the ephemeral nature of reality'.⁴⁴

Later in life, as chair of the Australia Council, Horne stressed that 'imagination isn't confined to fiction'. He was keen to 'get rid of the expression "nonfiction". Nonfiction to me made as much sense as non-gardening books, or non-philosophy or non-history. Why fiction? There was nothing particularly literary about fiction. There are some things which fiction can do that history can't do. There are things that history can do that fiction can't do.'[45]

The Australia discussion

In time a changing outlook on political life provoked a confrontation with conservative politics. Yet this proved a slow process. Horne remained close to many in Coalition politics. As an advertising man he was engaged by the Liberal Opposition Leader, Robert Askin, for the 1965 New South Wales election. Horne helped design the campaign 'With Askin You'll Get Action!'[46] In the closing days of the race, Askin put his arm around a staffer and said, 'I think we're going to win.' Then, with a laugh: 'And think of the money we'll make.'

As Horne said, 'I thought he was joking.'

In 1964, Horne agreed to become co-editor of *Quadrant* with James McAuley, and in 1967 was invited to return as editor of the *Bulletin*. Through these years Horne was closely involved in the Committee for Cultural Freedom, working with Sydney colleagues such as Richard Krygier, David Armstrong, Leonie Kramer, Jim McClelland and Laurie Short, and new Melbourne contacts such as Frank Knopfelmacher and Bob Santamaria. In their company Horne embraced a fervent anti-Communism that, for a season, marked his thinking and writing.

Of his career as an anti-communist, Horne later observed: 'I did fall into folly for something like a year and a half, mainly from ignoring one of the key maxims of sceptical conservatism, *Pas trop de zèle* – no excessive zeal.'[47] Horne concluded a too-passionate rhetoric sacrificed the civil tone that characterised his earlier writing.

As co-editor of *Quadrant* Horne was an advocate of the war in Vietnam, of close ties with America, and a familiar voice in the causes of the right. *Tribune*, the Communist Party newspaper, dismissed *The Lucky Country* as 'right-wing extremism'.[48] Horne used his editorships to pursue alleged communists – a 1961 *Bulletin* story included sensational, but little-substantiated, claims of red influence in the Faculty of Arts at the University of Melbourne.[49]

Though Horne would later regret the failure to manage his enthusiasm, this anti-Communism was shared by many former Andersonians within the Committee for Cultural Freedom. As an editor, said Horne:

> I was the full Andersonian ticket: I believed that liberty was the active part of democracy (flourishing most in opposition); that people should be allowed to pursue their own ways of life in all their diversity; that all censorship should be abolished; that homosexuality and abortion should be made legal; that restrictions on drinking, betting and other forms of amusement should be taken off the books; and that the state could be a particular enemy of freedom.[50]

Horne retained these libertarian values through his life. By the later 1960s, though, he found himself at odds with aspects of the outlook reflected in *Quadrant*, which he found conservative rather than libertarian. Horne was criticised by Leonie Kramer and Peter Coleman for advocating Australian republicanism in *The Lucky Country*. Richard Krygier took Horne to task for his regular lunches with the avowedly communist author Frank Hardy.

Still, it was some years before Horne and his long-time political allies parted ways. In 1967 he handed the *Quadrant* editorship to Peter Coleman, though he remained on the management committee for some time. Horne attended occasional seminars until the 1970s, by which time he found the Committee for Cultural Freedom 'a fortress defending cultural freedom against the threats of Whitlamism'.[51] When Horne published *Death of the Lucky Country* following the Dismissal, relations cooled sharply with colleagues of decades' standing. James McAuley, a friend since 1939, did not speak with him again. In his final public speech, the poet condemned the works of Gough Whitlam and his four beasts: Germaine Greer, Manning Clark, Patrick White and Donald Horne.[52] Horne was not mentioned at the 1981 celebrations for *Quadrant*'s first twenty-five years.

Horne had formed his political identity as a student, and contributed to public debate as a journalist, editor and author. He joined those former Andersonians who viewed Communism as the larger threat to human liberty, and promoted their arguments with characteristic vigour and enthusiasm. This was a cause shared for decades with prominent and engaging Sydney intellectuals. To break with such company must have been distressing, but Horne published little about his personal response. His new political opponents, though, made clear their views. Peter Ryan criticised Horne as 'the national know-all', a narcissist and showman.[53] Horne would later reconnect with some old friends, but for many the rift was permanent and bitter.

The Lucky Country proved the first of numerous books by Donald Horne about aspects of Australia. For some years, Horne combined this writing with editing the *Bulletin*. Through the final years of the long Liberal post-war incumbency, the *Bulletin* traced shifting preoccupations in Australian politics: the new priorities of Harold Holt, the 1967 referendum to recognise Indigenous Australians, John Gorton and his interest in a local film industry, the emerging nationalism Horne anticipated in *The Lucky Country*. He used the *Bulletin* to press causes such as republicanism, with the poet Les Murray designing a new national flag.

In 1975, the dismissal of Prime Minister Whitlam on 11 November triggered an intense engagement with public debate. For Horne

A PUBLIC INTELLECTUAL

it 'had the shock of an assassination'. He'd known Gough Whitlam distantly at Sydney University. Horne welcomed many Whitlam government initiatives, though neither aligned to the Labor Party nor slow to criticise specific government actions; the old suspicion of the state ran deep. But Horne was profoundly angered by Sir John Kerr's decision to dismiss a democratically elected government.

On the day of the Dismissal, Horne was lunching with novelist Frank Moorhouse and a number of political scientists at the UNSW staff club.[54] A young woman waiting on the table, and listening to ABC Radio in the kitchen, relayed reports the Governor-General had sacked the Prime Minister. The commentators at the table carefully pointed out that such things could not happen in this nation – the ABC must have 'got it wrong'.

When the truth of the matter became clear, the lifelong republican Horne sent a telegram to the Governor-General at Yarralumla, caustically welcoming the Dismissal as the end of the Australian monarch; Horne later learned it was placed in the pile marked 'congratulations'.[55] Kerr's decision inspired a burst of political activism – for Donald Horne Australia must become a republic, with a constitution to express the basic principles of democracy. In the weeks after 11 November, Horne spoke at rallies in support of Whitlam, wrote letters of protest and appeared in a television commercial with Patrick White. As Frank Moorhouse recounts, 'He discovered something else there and that was himself as an orator.'[56] Until 1975 Horne had prided himself on being a professional 'independent', neither Liberal nor Labor, but he surrendered this identity in his passionate response to the Dismissal.

After Labor's resounding defeat on 13 December, Horne sought to keep alive the issue of constitutional change. Working with Myfanwy, academic colleagues, friends and supporters, Horne was part of public meetings throughout 1976, culminating in a 'Citizens for Democracy' rally at the Sydney Town Hall and the creation of a new movement to press for a democratic, republican constitution. It was a time of intense political engagement. Alongside his speeches on constitutional change and *Death of the Lucky Country*, Horne produced a satire on monarchy and, with Sol Encel and Elaine Thompson, an edited volume, *Change the Rules! Towards a Democratic Constitution*.

Through Citizens for Democracy, Horne enjoyed a new kind of political engagement: town hall meetings, pamphlets, banners, resolutions and, most importantly, people. The campaign allowed Horne to draw on contacts from his long life in Sydney – fellow republicans such as Warren Fahey, Faith Bandler, Les Murray, Fred Daly, Eva Cox and Don Chipp. Yet the moment passed swiftly. Horne found himself, by default, the 'principal media face of republicanism … while the idea of a new Constitution faded like invisible ink'.[57]

Horne would be similarly disappointed in his involvement with the Australian Republican Movement from 1991, under the leadership of first Thomas Keneally and then Malcolm Turnbull. He found the committee frustrating, with an 'almost pathological sense of confusion and detachment'. So, apparently, did the leader – arriving for one meeting, Horne found Turnbull 'sitting despondently in an armchair, hands hanging down listlessly, brow furrowed with care'.[58] The campaign ended in defeat at a referendum in November 1999, though Horne would remain an active republican in the years that followed.

It's all about the culture

Culture was always important to Donald Horne. As editor of the *Bulletin* he recognised the emergence of the arts as definers of national identity, hiring younger writers such as Sandra Hall and

Sandra Forbes to cover film and books. When Frank Moorhouse failed to secure a Commonwealth Literary Fund Fellowship, Horne offered him a weekly grant through the *Bulletin* payroll to pursue his writing. 'It's a Frank Packer Fellowship,' explained Horne, 'but don't ever tell Frank Packer!'[59]

Moorhouse, in turn, would encourage contact with a younger Sydney literary life. He and Horne became friends as they participated in the many seminars, workshops and symposia of the period. *Conference-ville*, a Moorhouse novella from 1976, includes a character named Horne, whose first rule of conference diligence is 'miss nothing and take one of everything' – that is, be committed to the whole experience.[60]

Through his many years in journalism, Horne continued an established habit of long lunches and dinners with a shifting cast – his way to keep in touch with numerous worlds and associates. He enjoyed the company of fellow editors Adrian Deamer of the *Australian*, Graham Perkin of the *Age*, John Pringle of the *Sydney Morning Herald*, Vic Carroll of the *Australian Financial Review*, Bob Raymond of *Four Corners* and Richard Walsh of *Nation Review*. There were new associations with publishers, political friends such as Jim McClelland and Neville Wran, longstanding fellow journalists such as Patricia Rolfe, old Andersonian friends until the 1970s, and thereafter a number of younger female writers and academics, as Horne began to 'reset' his 'personal compass' after reading Betty Friedan's *The Feminine Mystique*.[61] Meaghan Morris remembers Horne as 'one of the great, old-school Sydney lunchers who could eat and drink for hours and go home clear-headed for work'.[62] These conversations and a regular supply of new reading from Sydney's Pocket Bookshop shaped the *Bulletin* and his own writing.

Going to lunch with Donald Horne, recalled Frank Moorhouse, 'was like being part of an endless seminar'.[63] Somewhere into the third bottle of red, noted Max Bourke, Horne would pause and say, 'I wonder what I meant by that?'[64]

Yet amid the conviviality, the long years of journalism drew to a close. Horne found editing the *Bulletin* 'tiresome' and felt out of place in the commercial machinations of the Packer empire. During a long walk through the city to think about the future, he decided to resign. Soon after the 1972 federal election, aged fifty-two, Donald Horne left the Packer building, unsure what to do next. The choice of academia was unlikely and unplanned; the suggestion came in a telephone call from Owen Harries after a newspaper column suggested erroneously that Horne had been fired from the *Bulletin*.[65] Though Horne had no academic qualifications, university colleagues had been impressed by his numerous books, in particular, *The Australian People*, published in 1972. The research fellowship he was offered in the Faculty of Arts at the University of New South Wales paid less than half his income at the *Bulletin*, but Horne welcomed the opportunity to think and write, and could supplement his pay by acting as a contributing editor to *Newsweek International*.

When Horne joined the Department of Political Science at UNSW, led by his friend from student days Doug McCallum, he had no experience as a university teacher.

> I had given less than a dozen lectures in my life; they had all been to small intellectual audiences and they had all ruthlessly exposed some form of intellectual folly. What was I going to do in preparing a lecture for an audience of 'real people'? I recognised that I must avoid gabbling into the maze of unfinished sentences, switches in theme, illustrative anecdotes, even doing imitations, that sometimes made up the way I talked, so I fenced myself in with notes set out in a simple, overall structure that I would be able to read easily with my bifocals. *Notes*, not a full

text. Notes would give me a chance to seem natural and look the audience in the eyes, if there *was* an audience.[66]

In practice Horne proved a talented educator, and would present 1500 or so university lectures over the next fourteen years. He could stand at the podium and transform the apparently dull – constitutional arrangements, the work routines of journalism – into keys to the wider workings of politics and the media. He kept students engaged through striking assertions, rhetorical questions, amusing asides, always remembering to restate and reinforce his central points. When all else failed, a supply of anecdotes – and the occasional impersonation of political figures – carried him through until five minutes before the hour.

In his first years at UNSW, Horne sought to master academic research. He abandoned long notepads for neat little index cards that could be arranged and rearranged, though he was never an enthusiast for the apparatus of footnotes and detailed references, or for learned journals over books. His writing would be criticised for relying too heavily on the telling story, though his apparently fluent and accessible style often disguised considerable reading and careful construction. Horne spent time working in the Mitchell Library in Sydney, and established a friendship with Manning Clark when they ate pink iced cake together in the upstairs cafe during breaks from writing.[67] On campus he watched with amusement the petty politics of academic departments: the corridor of closed doors; office space allocated according to academic rank; the empty common room and colleagues who never appeared, instead eating lunch alone at their desks.

We students would speculate about the man behind the podium, and scan his books – *The Lucky Country*, now in many editions, the novels, the discussion of Britain in *God Is an Englishman*, the polemics – in search of clues. The later autobiographies were not published until the career in academia was all but complete, though students sometimes received essay notes scrawled on the back of rejected-manuscript paper. 'He's describing a girl with blonde hair. There's a line through the page. Perhaps she rejected him,' suggested one fellow student.

As a new academic, Horne explored various intellectual approaches – behaviourism, elite theory and recent German writing in political sociology – before settling on political culture as his research topic of choice. 'Even if I hadn't known it,' he observed later, 'ever since *The Lucky Country* "culture" was what I had been talking all the time.' The concept of political culture reminded Horne of John Anderson's phrase 'ways of life', understanding culture as 'a repertoire of habits of thinking and acting that give particular meanings to existence'.[68] In an Australian context this meant the values, mythologies and shared assumptions that supported local social and political life.

Though appointed as a research fellow, from 1974 Horne began to lecture in first-year Australian politics. His staff seminars on contemporary issues drew interest across the campus, while his undergraduate courses included lectures with titles such as 'The coercive and conspiratorial apparatus of the state'. Horne looked for scholars interested in the same subjects. He found some in nearby departments such as History, and others away from campus, through his friendship with the film critic and later academic Meaghan Morris. An important friendship began when Political Science hired a new doctoral graduate, Elaine Thompson. She and Horne turned up to a departmental meeting with rival proposals for a new course, only to discover each had independently designed much the same curriculum.[69] They would team-teach for years to follow, and publish together on shared projects after 1976.

In the courses he offered by the start of the 1980s, Donald Horne focused on those mechanisms which build a culture. Whether discussing political parties or the mass media, he proved less interested in institutions than in the technology and operation of hegemony. He wanted to understand how ideas, conscious and unexamined alike, work through language to shape our view of the world. Often a new course was the first indication of an incipient book; themes and arguments would be developed in seminars and lectures, then flow through to the writing. Like many academics Horne used teaching to think through new concepts, explore examples for argument, and develop a structure for the text to follow.

When Horne began teaching a popular course on 'Politics and the Media' – then still a novelty in universities – he was made a senior lecturer with tenure. He would stay for the rest of his professional career, promoted first to associate professor and then to a personal chair, rising to be chairman of the faculty and a member of the UNSW Council before retiring as professor emeritus, aged sixty-five, at the close of 1986.

The thoughts of Old Donald

Donald Horne constantly reflected on experience and modified his outlook to incorporate the latest lessons. The young Donald Horne dismissed political activity as a misplaced belief in personal agency. An older man, tested by failed campaigns such as an Australian republic, might consider his original judgement amply vindicated. Horne drew the opposite conclusion. His period of intense involvement in constitutional debate led him to see possibilities for engagement in Australian life. Community-based politics showed Horne he could be a talented public orator, speaking in compelling phrases and commanding a large audience; the *National Times* even praised his 'pleasing baritone' when leading the national anthem at the Sydney Town Hall. Horne, in turn, discovered a love of neighbourhood discussion. For decades to follow he would accept invitations to speak at clubs and societies, Rotary gatherings, Liberal and Labor branch meetings, and other opportunities for civic debate. His later writing emphasised the importance of conversation and the necessity for democracy to be grounded in local, autonomous groups.

More broadly, the campaigns for constitutional reform confirmed for Horne a viable approach for a public intellectual in Australia. In his early years at UNSW, Horne had worried about whether his books were 'academic' or 'intellectual' – as though the only choice was to talk to other scholars or to a popular audience. Involvement in public debate convinced him he could address both simultaneously. Horne wrote admiringly of the 'high popularisation' favoured in France, where new ideas are made accessible by talented writers who together create a shared life of the mind.[70]

A public intellectual, by definition, seeks an audience. To sustain a viable conversation needs an informed community, supported by numerous publications, essays and critics. Horne concluded that sustaining intellectual life requires 'tens of thousands' of interested people, and a commitment by those in privileged places, such as universities and media, to be inclusive. Above all, intellectual life needs books that address contemporary issues for local audiences: such writing gives people 'new things to think about – or new approaches to old ways'. Without such writing about Australian topics, Horne asked, 'in what sense, as Australians, would we exist at all?'[71]

Horne would pursue his vision of a public conversation, conveyed through accessible writing, during the closing decades of a long and productive life. His search for a more inclusive agenda would find expression in a role as chair of the Australia Council from January 1985. Horne championed people creating their own art, and promoted the arts as a necessary broadening of a political culture relentlessly focused on economic questions.

At the Australia Council Donald Horne took particular pleasure

A PUBLIC INTELLECTUAL

in stressing his independence from government. When pressured by one government member about disappointed grant applicants from his electorate, Horne responded, 'Well, Minister, thank you for exercising your democratic right as a citizen to tell me your views.'[72] Horne delighted in the work of the Council and of its talented staff, though his impatience with 'bureaucratese' was widely understood. Colleagues in the Australia Council appreciated the 'plurality, eclecticism and boundless curiosity' of their chair. They found him the 'ultimate humanist, with a fierce sense of nationalism', who championed the idea that all Australians have cultural rights.[73]

As a new editor, Horne had struggled with leading others. He learned over time how to inspire a team, set an agenda and pursue multiple objectives. By the time he chaired the Australia Council, Horne proved an able and much-admired institutional head. He commissioned events such as the National Summit of Ideas at Old Parliament House in 1990 and encouraged the creation of the National Council for the Humanities. On stepping down as chair in 1991, aged sixty-nine, Horne continued the conversation through his involvement in Ideas for Australia, Arts Action and programs for the Centenary of Federation. He remained, as Australia Council colleague Andrea Hull recalled, 'intellectually curious, pixelated, curmudgeonly, charming, quick to laugh, and glorious luncheon company'.[74]

Horne had established a role for himself as a public intellectual, and believed the model could work for others. The skill, he believed, was to influence debate 'through language and discussion', alongside the quotidian tasks of writing and editing, sitting on committees and accepting invitations to converse, no matter how modest the occasion. A public intellectual, he observed, should coin a new phrase, set out the argument for change, develop rhetoric to support the ideas, and create events and opportunities for conversation.[75]

In 1997, Horne published an ambitious book, *The Avenue of the Fair Go*, explaining core political concepts to ordinary Australians through an imaginary theme park of ideas. *The Avenue of the Fair Go* employed the technique of fiction and the language of everyday life to distil a lifetime of thinking about Australian political culture.

Unfortunately, as John Button argued in his review, the 'persistent, seemingly tireless' Donald Horne, successful polemicist and public intellectual of 'a rare kind', struggled to capture the essence of an Australian identity. Instead, concluded Button, *The Avenue of the Fair Go* is 'an omnibus of the things that Horne has believed in, and the things which he dislikes'. The presentation of the argument as a series of conversations undercut the serious attempt to 'define and celebrate what makes Australia different'.[76]

Button's assessment proved a reliable guide to the wider reception. The book has its supporters, and attracted some warm notices, but most reviewers were puzzled or hostile, and *The Avenue of the Fair Go* sold fewer copies than any of Horne's previous volumes. The aftermath of a particularly hostile assessment by Peter Coleman ended his friendship with the Hornes.[77]

There were further publications after *The Avenue of the Fair Go*, but Horne was now speaking to a very different political moment. His themes of constitutional change, fairness and Australian character struggled to find an audience in the era of John Howard. With his public roles largely concluded, Horne continued to offer views through articles and interviews, the work of Ideas for a Nation and the Australian Republican Movement. He participated in centennial celebrations of the Australian Federation in 2001 and published *Looking for Leadership* the same year, a study of Australia during the Howard years. Only around 2004, when pulmonary fibrosis took a more aggressive turn, did Donald Horne wind down his public engagement.[78]

The final pages of this anthology survey these later works. It also marks a turn from the public to the private, as thoughts turned to lessons learned from a long life, and thence to mortality.

Horne remained an optimist amid the challenges of old age. He completed his series of autobiographical books and enjoyed some recognition: an Order of Australia, inclusion in the National Trust's inaugural list of Living National Treasures and a Sydney book launch at which Noel Pearson acknowledged Horne as an 'elder'.

Encouraged by Julianne Schultz at the *Griffith Review*, Horne began a new project writing about infirmity. Earlier work had chronicled difficult operations on his eyes; now, in the remarkable essay 'Mind, Body and Age', Horne described illness and decay with the same detachment with which he earlier reviewed his childhood homes and years as a student. The essay was launched at the 2004 Sydney Writers' Festival. It was the first time this prolific author had been invited to speak at the festival in his home town, and he appeared deeply moved by the affection of the hundreds of people who packed the Sydney Dance Theatre rehearsal studio.

Before he spoke, a small group took Donald and Myfanwy to lunch next door at Walsh Bay, with Sydney Harbour lapping below the window. Despite his frailty and failing voice, the 82-year-old Donald was sharp and engaged as he speculated on changes to the word 'culture' in recent years, the need for more civic identity, prospects for the next federal election and the foibles of former academic colleagues.

In late April 2005 Donald Horne, complete with oxygen mask, finally received a degree from the University of Sydney – not his abandoned Bachelor of Arts but an Honorary Doctor of Letters. His moving graduation speech praised the 'marvels of the intellectual life', with its opportunities for imagination, wonder, inquiry and criticism. He recalled his training under John Anderson, who emphasised the 'rich variety of approaches to ways of being human'.

Donald Horne died some months later, in September. To

commemorate his life, Myfanwy organised a memorial service at the State Library of New South Wales. Family and friends shared memories and reflections. In the spirit of the man, spontaneous contributions were encouraged. Frank Moorhouse recalled the aphorisms of Donald Horne. Deborah Mills remembered the 'cultural visionary, intellectual and enthusiast' who recognised the 'importance of culture in the lives of ordinary people'. Diana Gribble evoked the image of the 'clever little kid from Muswellbrook, the *enfant terrible* of Sydney University, the advertising man' and Chairman Donald of the Australia Council. Owen Harries talked of the gifted teacher, Peter Manning of Donald Horne as a fixture at the New Hellas restaurant beside Hyde Park, while Elaine Thompson remembered her university colleague with 'no degree, nor formal background, no "academic" publications', whose 'continued popular success and absolute refusal to use footnotes infuriated many academic colleagues'.[79]

Donald Horne's intellectual curiosity ensured he engaged with many of the great questions facing Australia through the twentieth century: identity, character, values and place in the world. He explored these issues with the same drive whether a student, soldier, diplomatic cadet, young journalist, editor, advertising executive or academic. He believed life has no objective meaning, only the purpose we give our existence. This meant living in, and interrogating, the moment. His writing is always informed by experience, and therefore by the particular circumstances of being an Australian. As Mungo MacCallum observed, Donald Horne was 'always a participant, never just an observer'.[80]

In his early years, Donald Horne disdained political processes, while being fascinated by political questions. Later in life he came to embrace political work – never within a party structure, instead through writing and public meetings that encouraged a vigorous polity. The scepticism – 'question everything' – learned from John

Anderson at Sydney University served him well, as did an emphasis on individual liberty and toleration. Anderson's hostility to the state proved less enduring, and Horne eventually broke with this part of the Andersonian program, at considerable personal cost to friendships and the settled patterns of his first half-century. But he found enjoyment in the unfamiliar challenges of academia, and a renewed sense of purpose through writing and political activism.

As Dennis Altman observed, by moving to a university Donald Horne 'continued the conversation with Australia he had started through his journalism'.[81] Late in life this critic of bureaucracy found satisfaction in leading organisations: as chair of the Faculty of Arts at UNSW, chancellor of the University of Canberra, and chair of the Australia Council for two terms.

In this timely anthology, drawn from across a memorable life, Nick Horne evokes once more a great Australian writer and activist. The selection celebrates the journalist, the teacher, the historian, gossip, chronicler and poet. We are welcomed back into the company of a man who asked ceaseless questions, and turned answers into the next inquiries of his endless seminar.

This introduction draws on, and expands, 'The Endless Seminar', commissioned by Julianne Schultz for Griffith Review *and published in Issue 10, 2010. I am indebted to Chris Feik from Black Inc. for the kind invitation to be part of this project, and to Julia Horne for numerous helpful editorial suggestions. My thanks to Gwil Croucher for excellent research assistance with the original article, and to Lisa Carson for her thoughtful and thorough review of subsequent material for this essay. Observation of Donald Horne as a teacher is drawn from time as a student at UNSW, where among much else Donald supervised my 1981 Honours thesis on the origins of radio station 2JJ.*

Notes

1. D. Horne, *The Lucky Country*, Penguin, Ringwood, 1964, p. 233.
2. A non-exhaustive list might include: D. Brandum & A. Nette, 'Police Fictions', *Overland*, Autumn 2016, 222, pp. 94–101; M. Clausen, 'Donald Horne Finds Asia', in *Australia's Asia*, edited by D. Walker & A. Sobocinska, University of Western Australia Publishing, Crawley, 2012, pp. 298–321; E. Felton, 'A F/oxymoron? Women, creativity and the suburbs', *Queensland Review*, Vol. 22, No. 2, 2015, pp. 168–78; M. Hunter, 'Who Really Rules Australia?: Donald Horne revisited', *Journal of Self-Governance and Management Economics*, Vol. 1, No. 2, 2013, pp. 54–89; I. Lowe, *The Lucky Country: Reinventing Australia*, University of Queensland Press, St Lucia, 2016; R. Phiddian, 'The Revolution in Political Cartoons and the Early Australian', *Media International Australia*, Vol. 157 (November), 2015, pp. 56–67; C. Reinecke, 'The Vanishing Point: The story of the publication of *The Lucky Country*', *Meanjin*, 2016, pp. 42–54.
3. R. Dessaix, 'Donald Horne' in R. Dessaix (ed.), *Speaking Their Minds: Intellectuals and the Public Culture in Australia*, ABC Books, Sydney, 1998, p. 217.
4. Julia Horne, personal communication, reports Horne and his wife Myfanwy left 227 boxes and two outsize portfolios of documents, now deposited in the Mitchell Library in Sydney. There are a few diaries, including travel observations, and a huge correspondence that informed the three autobiographies and two memoirs. As Julia notes, 'like any good journalist of the day' Horne kept a 'notebook for brief jottings, a couple of words only, usually of the sort that might later become a newspaper article, or, in later life, used as reminders about what the doctor said. Only problem was his hand-writing ... illegible not only to others, but often (as

NOTES

he used to joke) to himself.' The Donald and Myfanwy Horne room will open at the State Library of New South Wales in 2017.

5   Myfanwy Horne, personal communication.
6   D. Horne, *The Education of Young Donald*, Sun Books, Melbourne, 1967, pp. 131–33.
7   ibid., p. 304, see also p. 210.
8   ibid., pp. 204–05.
9   ibid., p. 206.
10 ibid., pp. 292–93.
11 With admirable understatement, Cole describes Anderson as an 'iconoclast'. C.M. Cole, 'John Anderson's Political Thought Revisited', *Australian Journal of Political Science*, Vol. 44, No. 2, 2009, pp. 229–43.
12 Horne, *The Education of Young Donald*, pp. 174, 239.
13 ibid., p. 214.
14 J. Anderson, 'The Servile State', republished in J. Anderson, *Studies in Empirical Philosophy*, Angus & Robertson, Sydney, 1962, pp. 328–39; and D. Horne, *An Interrupted Life*, HarperCollins, Sydney, 1998, p. 428.
15 Horne, *The Education of Young Donald*, p. 305.
16 Horne, *An Interrupted Life*, p. 575.
17 ibid., pp. 377, 406.
18 ibid., p. 450.
19 ibid., p. 564.
20 ibid., pp. 747, 752.
21 Frank Moorhouse, personal communication.
22 Horne, *An Interrupted Life*, p. 745.
23 ibid., pp. 745–46.
24 ibid., pp. 777, 779.
25 ibid., p. 776.
26 J. Horne and N. Horne, 'Myfanwy Horne: writer, editor helped foster national identity, *Sydney Morning Herald*, 2 November 2013.
27 Myfanwy Horne, personal communication.
28 D. Horne, *Into the Open*, HarperCollins, Sydney, 2000, p. 5.
29 Horne, *An Interrupted Life*, p. 808.
30 Horne, *Into the Open*, pp. 23, 41.
31 ibid., p. 35.
32 ibid.
33 Phiddian, *Media International Australia*, p. 57.

34 Horne, *Into the Open*, pp. 45, 51.
35 ibid., p. 128.
36 Clausen, *Australia's Asia*, p. 315.
37 Reinecke, *Meanjin*, p. 53.
38 Horne, *Into the Open*, p. 128.
39 D. Horne and M. Horne, *Dying: A Memoir*, Penguin, Camberwell, 2009.
40 Reinecke, *Meanjin*, p. 43.
41 Reader responses cited in Reinecke, *Meanjin*, p. 44.
42 M. Morris, 'Remembering Donald Horne', *Gleaner zine*, Gleebooks, Sydney, 2005.
43 Horne, *An Interrupted Life*, p. 586.
44 Quotes drawn from a January 1992 interview with Donald Horne by Robin Hughes for the Australian Biography Project. Accessed at www.australianbiography.gov.au/subjects/horne/intertext7.html.
45 ibid.
46 Horne, *Into the Open*, p. 98.
47 ibid., p. 103.
48 Though Nick Horne observes, in a personal communication, that *Tribune* also published a favourable one later and eventually a second review by Malcolm Salmon, who detected some interesting critiques from this 'right-wing radical'.
49 F. Anderson, *An Historian's Life: Max Crawford and the Politics of Academic Freedom*, Melbourne University Press, 2005, pp. 332, 346, 348.
50 Horne, *Into the Open*, p. 28.
51 D. Horne, *On How I Came to Write 'The Lucky Country'*, Melbourne University Press, 2006, p. 121.
52 Horne, *Into the Open*, pp. 125–26.
53 P. Ryan, 'Donald Horne: a self-made man', *Quadrant*, 1998, p. 29.
54 F. Moorhouse, 'The Professors' Lunch', in S. Nolan (ed.), *The Dismissal*, Melbourne University Press, 2005, pp. 86–89.
55 Horne, *Into the Open*, p. 304.
56 Frank Moorhouse, personal communication.
57 Horne, *Into the Open*, p. 322.
58 ibid., pp. 326, 330.
59 Frank Moorhouse, personal communication.
60 F. Moorhouse, *Conference-ville*, Angus & Robertson, Sydney, 1976, p. 21.
61 Horne, *Into the Open*, p. 175.

NOTES

62 Morris, *Gleaner zine*.
63 Frank Moorhouse, personal communication.
64 Max Bourke, personal communication conveyed by Andrea Hull.
65 Myfanwy Horne, personal communication.
66 Horne, *Into the Open*, p. 196.
67 Myfanwy Horne, private communication.
68 Horne, *Into the Open*, p. 217.
69 Elaine Thompson, personal communication.
70 Horne, *Into the Open*, p. 249.
71 ibid., p. 250.
72 ibid., p. 294.
73 Andrea Hull, personal communication.
74 ibid.
75 Horne, *Into the Open*, p. 323.
76 J. Button, 'Voices in the Park', *Australian Book Review*, October, 1997, pp. 13–14. Accessed at http://home.vicnet.net.au/~abr/Oct97/butt.html.
77 Myfanwy Horne, personal communication.
78 Julia Horne, personal communication.
79 Myfanwy Horne, personal communication.
80 M. MacCallum, 'Donald Horne 1921–2005', *Overland*, Vol. 182, 2006, pp. 91–93.
81 Dennis Altman, personal communication.

DONALD HORNE

SELECTED WRITINGS

A BRIEF TIMELINE FOR DONALD HORNE

1921 Born in Kogarah, Sydney, to Dave and Flo
1927 Moves to Muswellbrook
1935 Moves to Sydney
1936 Sister Janet is born
1939 Begins his degree at the University of Sydney
1941 Edits *Honi Soit*; conscription ends his studies; serves in the army for two and a half years
1944 Becomes diplomatic cadet in Canberra
1945 Works on Sydney's *Daily Telegraph* for four years
1948 Marries Ethel, a social worker
1949 Sails to England, the country of Ethel's birth
1954 Returns alone to Australia to work on *Weekend*
1958 Becomes the editor of the *Observer* for three years; meets Myfanwy, a journalist, and becomes engaged
1960 Marries Myfanwy after divorcing Ethel; edits the *Bulletin* for a year
1961 Daughter Julia is born
1963 Begins work at advertising agency Jackson Wain for four years

1964	Co-edits *Quadrant* with James McAuley for three years; *The Lucky Country*; son Nick is born
1965	*The Permit*
1967	Returns to edit the *Bulletin* for six years; *The Education of Young Donald*; *Southern Exposure*
1969	*God Is an Englishman*
1970	*The Next Australia*
1971	*But What If There Are No Pelicans?*
1972	*The Australian People*
1973	Becomes research fellow at the University of New South Wales; writes for *Newsweek International* for three years
1975	Becomes senior lecturer in Political Science
1976	*Death of the Lucky Country*; *Money Made Us*
1977	*His Excellency's Pleasure*
1978	*Right Way Don't Go Back*
1979	*In Search of Billy Hughes*
1980	*Time of Hope*
1981	*Winner Take All*; becomes associate professor at UNSW
1982	Receives AO for Services to Literature
1984	*The Great Museum*; becomes professor at UNSW; becomes Australian Society of Authors president for two years
1985	Serves on the Australian Constitutional Commission; becomes chairman of Australia Council for six years
1986	*Confessions of a New Boy*; is awarded an Honorary Doctorate in Letters, UNSW
1987	*The Lucky Country Revisited*
1988	*Portrait of an Optimist*
1989	*Ideas for a Nation*
1991	Serves as chairman of Ideas for Australia for three years

1992 Serves as Canberra University chancellor for four years; *The Intelligent Tourist*; *The Coming Republic*; *The Trouble with Economic Rationalism*
1997 *The Avenue of the Fair Go*
1998 *An Interrupted Life*
2000 *Into the Open*
2001 *Looking for Leadership*
2003 *10 Steps to a More Tolerant Australia*
2005 Receives an Honorary Doctorate in Letters, University of Sydney; dies in Sydney
2007 *Dying: A Memoir*

INTRODUCTION

by Nick Horne

I N CHOOSING PIECES FOR THIS BOOK, I HAVE TRIED TO give people a good read. When my father, Donald Horne, whom I called D, was pushed to answer the question in an interview about how he would like to be remembered, he replied: 'As someone who gave people something to think about.' This book is an attempt to give people something to think about.

The pieces of writing are listed in a hybrid chronological order, with the first section covering the early years of D's own life, and subsequent sections ordered with a relaxed eye on the date of publication. The book is a kind of discontinuous narrative: each piece can be appreciated on its own, and the whole comes together to suggest a portrait of one of Australia's most famous public intellectuals and the country he wrote about. This collection is not just 'Donald Horne's Greatest Hits' but a study of the journey of a curious Australian, a child of the Enlightenment, as he describes a changing world. It includes a few opinions that he later disavowed, but they are expressed with vitality and intelligence and are included as a record of D's thinking, if not as evidence that people can, in good faith, change their minds.

INTRODUCTION

The first section, Formative Years, gives insights into what made D tick. Born at home, in Sydney, in 1921, D grew up in the country town of Muswellbrook in a happy, secure environment where education was seen as growth. Dave, his schoolteacher father, encouraged D to think for himself; he used to proudly recite the tale of a young D who, when told by Dave that God had created everything asked, with a four-year-old's innocence, '... Who created God?' D turned to writing about his own life after finishing his first book, *The Lucky Country*, in part to test out some of *The Lucky Country*'s generalisations. In the foreword to the first edition of *The Education of Young Donald* he called the book a 'sociography', in which characters are shaped by social circumstance, and offered himself as a test case for 'what social history can look like when told through *people*'. The section starts in Muswellbrook and concludes (in a change of narrative pace) with pieces about his time at Sydney University, which he wrote well before *The Education of Young Donald*.

Having identified vaguely with the left as a student, the second section of this book, Radical Conservative, starts when D came out of the army and worked for a while under the iconoclastic Brian Penton at the *Daily Telegraph*. This period was one in which he called himself variously an 'anarchist' conservative, a 'radical' conservative and a 'liberal' conservative. Small-'l' 'liberal' as he was always in favour of abortion reform and the legalisation of homosexuality, and against censorship, racism, wowser-inspired restrictions on amusements and the like. 'Conservative' as he 'hated' Stalin and was a rabid anti-communist, and – under the influence of Sydney University's John Anderson – anti-planning and anti-'progressive' (his quotation marks) because, although things weren't perfect, due to the 'the paradox of unintended consequences', trying to plan them or change them might make them worse. He applied this idea to other people's attempts to change things, but struggled to put a

INTRODUCTION

lid on his own desire for change. Thus conflicted, he left Australia for the UK in 1949 to write fiction, happy if he never returned. Unable to get a publisher for his two novels, he returned to journalism and, before too long, to Australia in 1954, in what was supposed to be a brief stay to help set up Frank Packer's new easy-reading magazine, *Weekend*. Four years later he was still intellectually misemployed working on *Weekend*, but its success had prompted Packer to offer D the editorship of a new intellectual fortnightly, to be called the *Observer*, honouring a promise he had made. Without the *Observer* from 1958 (and then the *Bulletin* when it merged with the *Observer*), or something like it, D's life might have been very different. It enabled him to have a good, serious think about Australia, and it was around this time (when he had the means to be heard in a meaningful forum) that his 'conservative' world view modified to the effect that (as he rationalised it) yes, change can have unintended consequences, but not changing things can also have undesirable unintended consequences. He was moving towards a return to the optimism of his childhood.

1958 was also the year when D met Myfanwy Gollan, a journalist, whom he was to marry two years later; it is no accident that their long partnership coincided with D's productive years as a writer. When things seemed to be going well, D was sacked as editor of the *Bulletin* in an office power struggle – which eventually freed him to take up Penguin's offer to write the book about Australia that became *The Lucky Country*.

In the next section, Fiction, there is an extract from one of D's novels. He had always been an enthusiastic reader; as much as he was a writer and a public intellectual, he was, when left to himself, a reader. Particularly in his early days, he would immerse himself in novels and finish them a somewhat different person for a while. Charles Dickens was a special childhood influence, and Evelyn

INTRODUCTION

Waugh an early literary hero, D feeling that they shared the world view that 'life is absurd compared with the aspirations we have about it, but you may as well laugh as cry', as he wrote in the *Bulletin* upon hearing of Waugh's death. For a while D had seen himself becoming a novelist, and published four novels all up, but he grew to believe that the division between fiction and 'nonfiction' was a bit overplayed, nonfiction requiring creativity if it were to be done well (and the nomenclature a bit odd, like dividing people into men and 'non-men').

Much has been made of the fact that D became a university professor without any tertiary qualification, and the fourth section, The Australia Discussion, begins with an excerpt from D's history of Australia, which helped to convince the University of New South Wales that he was nevertheless worthy of an academic position. D hadn't been especially happy in journalism, didn't want to just write books for a living ('too much like living on your wits'), and his move into academia proved to be a happy and productive one. It was partly by chance that he found himself in the Politics rather than in the History school, and Don Aitkin, when later arguing the case for D to become a professor, suggested that he could easily have taught in half-a-dozen different disciplines, reflecting D's multidisciplinary approach (and interests). He wrote a lot about Australia in the belief that 'the place needed new theories of itself – new histories, new economics, new geopolitical concepts, new social, political and cultural definitions – so that it could go on working', as he wrote in a later memoir. He wrote about Australia, but he was never parochial, believing that Australians could achieve their potential with one eye on what makes us distinctive, and the other on what links us with the human condition more generally.

One of the common themes of D's work is that 'how we act depends on how we see things'. Meaghan Morris described D as the

INTRODUCTION

founding father of Australian cultural studies, and he achieved that status in an unselfconscious way, observing and reading widely, and then writing things down 'to find out' what he thought. Ever the autodidact, he read a lot of theory and incorporated it into his own world view, as shown in the fifth section, It's All About the Culture. *The Public Culture,* first published in 1986 and then extensively revised after the fall of the Soviet Union, can be appreciated both for its argument and as an exercise in reading complex texts, having a think, and producing a readable synthesis.

Fortunate to have his wits, D was still going strong until the end. The final section, The Thoughts of Old Donald, features work from the last years of his life. D died well and his last book, written on his deathbed, can partly be seen as a gesture of goodwill to the future.

Style was important to D. He once said in a radio interview: 'Once you've worked out your style, you've got it made.' When writing his outline for *The Lucky Country*, one of the first things he noted was the four styles he would use: 'intellectualised' with simple words; 'reminiscent'; 'philosophising-about-life'; and 'descriptive narrative'. Irony and a bit of humour were perennials. In his use of pronouns, his early work reflected the sexism of the age; he sometimes tried to redress the balance in later years by using 'she' in non-gender-specific generalisations. Max Bourke, who worked with D at the Australia Council, said that D talked 'in parentheses', and it was true that much of what he said and wrote was delivered with qualifications and caveats and sometimes counterarguments. A lot of his work, including *The Lucky Country* and *Money Made Us*, was fragmentary, 'a collection of essays with no overall theme', as he said in an interview. He never suffered from writer's block and, perhaps it was his training as a journalist (not to mention his enthusiasm), he liked to get things down on paper; perfection could wait for the next draft, aided by Myfanwy's skilful editing. He often

INTRODUCTION

wrote several drafts, sometimes discarding many tens of thousands of words in the process (there were plenty more where they came from). Readability was always important, and given as a reason for not using footnotes, a practice reproduced in this book. He wrote many hundreds of articles and papers for newspapers, magazines and journals, and at times produced a book – or even two – a year, often written after he came home from work, his two fingers tapping away at a typewriter.

D thought things through and wasn't afraid to speak his mind; Geoffrey Blainey's description of him as a 'buzzing bee', pollinating whatever he touched, is an apt one. For all his success and fame, his book sales, his status as a 'National Living Treasure', his long and respected career as a commentator on Australia, D had something of the outsider about him. The state-school boy from a country town and the suburbs at Sydney University; a radical among conservatives; an intellectual among journalists; a journalist among academics; an academic in the public domain; an ex–Cold War warrior with a poster of Antonio Gramsci in his office. He had a lot of friends and liked company but, truth be known, he enjoyed being somewhat on the outside, connected but independent, sustained by self-belief (and by Myfanwy), calling it as he saw it.

Thanks to La Trobe University Press for the suggestion of this book, which serendipitously came while I was completing research for my own book on D. It benefits from talking with a lot of D's friends and colleagues, re-reading all his books and many of his articles, and an extensive use of the voluminous Donald Horne Papers (first drafts, book reviews, letters, diaries, tape recordings, videos, etc.) at the Mitchell Library, aided by its helpful staff. Also thanks to Chris Feik, Stephen Garton, Julia Horne, Jo Rosenberg and Emma Schwarcz for reading the book and making some good suggestions, and to Glyn Davis for his kind praise of the selection.

INTRODUCTION

D wrote a lot, so there is much to choose from and, necessarily, a lot of good stuff that didn't make the cut. Others are welcome to go in to bat for their favourite pieces, or for pieces that reveal the Donald Horne they think should be recorded for posterity. To reduce the work of such a prolific writer to less than 300 pages requires a coherent view on why things are important, but I have kept editorial comment to a minimum in an attempt to let the writing speak for itself: too much electric light can block out the stars. I have done some minor textual editing, in line with the principles D had about editing, based on being part of the editorial process for all of his books from when I became a teenager.

It has been a very great pleasure compiling this selection and I hope that you enjoy it.

FORMATIVE YEARS

Childhood

1

THE EDUCATION OF YOUNG DONALD

D.H.'s first attempts at writing an autobiography were unsuccessful. It wasn't until he employed a somewhat detached style, presenting things as they seemed at the time, that he was able to produce what might be his most loved work, in 1967.

Making our own fun

In the summer at Muswellbrook, as in other country towns, it was considered not only cooler but healthier and more manly for boys to 'sleep out'. Since my bed was on a veranda beside the room where my parents played cards, this meant that, although I have more conventional memories of sounds that drifted into sleep – of the church clock striking the hours and the quarters, or of the rushing of water in the weir – my immediate and prevailing memory is of dutifully thinking the Lord's Prayer and then losing consciousness to the sounds of the card game of bridge. For Thine is the Kingdom. The Power and the Glory. Forever and Ever. Amen. One No Trump. Two Diamonds. Two Hearts. Your Lead, partner.

Our house was one of the centres of Muswellbrook's amusement and triviality. It was said of my mother that 'Mrs Horne entertains as much as a doctor's wife' and while my father took some of his pleasures more seriously my mother's delight in the diversions of the late 1920s and early 1930s had no limits – bridge, mahjongg, sing-songs, surprise parties, mini-golf, tennis, grand balls, car drives, the talkies, golf tournaments, picnics, afternoon teas and late suppers were all there to be enjoyed as she waited for the next new 'craze' to catch up the people we knew in Muswellbrook.

When I came home from school, walking across the big paddock where the horses were kept, I was likely to see the white dresses of my mother and some of her friends as they enjoyed their afternoon tea beside the tennis court. I would take a cup of tea and a slice of sponge cake coated in crushed fruit and whipped cream and walk across the smaller paddock where we ran the cow, then into the backyard and up past the fruit trees to the kitchen, where I would eat the cake and give the plate to the dog to lick. My mother arranged at least three of these tennis parties during the week, mostly for her women friends, although my father usually came home early enough to change into cream trousers and white silk shirt and play a set, and at the weekends there were sometimes all-day tennis parties when a couple of dozen people would gather on one of the verandas for lunch and we would run a sweepstake on the results. The kind of tennis played at our house created some scandal in Muswellbrook. The puritans who saw tennis as a matter of competitions and tournaments dismissed ours as 'chatty tennis': too much fun, not enough nation-building.

Although my mother liked her bridge as chatty as her tennis, my father gave a puritan sense of seriousness to bridge, analysing mistakes in play even if they won a game. He was not a good player, but he had learned some precepts from a book called *Teaching Iris to Play*

Bridge, and since he expected life to yield its rewards only to those who followed the rules, justice demanded that the player who most closely followed the precepts in this book should win. I had learned to play bridge at the age of six or seven, and during the weekends we would often play the three-handed game, or, if a bridge player dropped in for an hour or two, I would make a fourth. In these family games my father would run us through some of his simple bridge player's beliefs: *Through strength into weakness* or *Lead the third highest of your longest and strongest*. At moments of great exasperation (perhaps when he had gone down after being doubled) he would remind us that *The game in bridge is to score below the line*. My father's simple rules from *Teaching Iris to Play Bridge* provided some of the most memorable precepts of my childhood.

At the gala bridge parties, the spirit of chattiness prevailed. For these great occasions, bridge tables and chairs were brought in from all over town and there were great doings in the kitchen as my mother prepared cheese straws, sandwiches, savoury eggs, asparagus rolls, lamingtons and sponge cakes and then boiled water and coffee essence in our biggest saucepan, ready for reheating. (Coffee was coming in as a craze.) On the big night there was so much eating and laughing that only the most puritan players worried about their bridge. In our evening family games other than bridge we paid no tribute to conscience. Mahjongg, for example, which was 'all the rage' before bridge, could be played without moral concepts. The hospital matron's daughter had taught me mahjongg at the age of five when I was in hospital with congestion of the lungs, and I preferred it to ludo or snakes and ladders, although in our house it was easy enough to get up a game of either.

My mother had issued an invitation to her friends to 'drop in' at night when they felt like it. (Scarcely anyone had a telephone: we had abandoned ours when my father had to economise after his salary was cut as a sacrifice to the Depression.) After dinner there might be knocks on the front door. *Now who would that be? Merv or Rita? Bill? Irene?* If only one or two dropped in, they might have a singsong. On more formal nights there were solo performances by those who 'had voices' and had brought their music. My father was one of those who had a voice – my earliest memory of song was of him lying in bed, bouncing me up and down on his bent knees as he sang hit numbers from musical comedies. (Later his songs became melancholy, perhaps reflecting the beginnings of what later became a catastrophic shift in how he saw things.) But the music I most enjoyed were the singsongs, if I was able to be the one pedalling away at the pianola, pressing the pp or ff buttons when the instructions on the roll told me to, surrounded by all these singing grownups. When 'Mick', my Sydney cousin and greatest friend, stayed with us she and I would sometimes play 'Tiptoe Through the Tulips' or 'Painting the Clouds with Sunshine' after breakfast, before we settled down to a game of poker.

When there were Sydney relatives staying with us – my grandparents or uncles and aunts – there was always a lot of shouting and laughter over dinner. Sydney people were like that: they shouted at dinner. I became a shouter early. I remember once, when I was aged eight or nine, running off to the lavatory, which was 'down the back' at the bottom of the backyard, and sitting there unyieldingly while my grandfather stood outside and tried to persuade me to come back to apologise to my grandmother for shouting at her over dinner. It must have been a matter of some moment; usually I avoided going down the back at night because of the spiders, and peed under the quince tree instead.

On the nights when my parents were not entertaining, they might go out to night tennis (with the hard-shelled flying beetles bashing against the arc lights) or to mini-golf while it was the rage, or to the 'picture show', which was built after the talkies had come to stay. Occasionally we would go to the lending library of 5000 books at the School of Arts, where my mother would 'get a good book', a Warwick Deeping novel, or something like that, while I would borrow a *National Geographic* magazine or a *Pearsons* or a *Strand* magazine. (The names of the dozen or so books that were added to the library each month were printed as front-page news in the *Muswellbrook Chronicle*.) If we visited other people I always took a book in case I got bored. On Friday nights, when the shops were open until nine o'clock, we would sometimes walk up and down the main street, lit up with its electric lights, with much of the rest of the town, to look at ourselves. On the hottest summer nights we might go to the swimming baths (which had just been opened). My parents enjoyed themselves down at the deep end; I was left at the shallow end, until I taught myself to swim.

The most formal ways of having a good time were the most traditional – the Anglican Ball, the Masonic Ball and the Golf Ball. For these a band was brought up by train from Sydney, 180 miles away, arriving half an hour before a ball started and leaving on the 3.30 a.m. train, half an hour after the ball was over. When there was a ball I waited around until my mother had pinned a corsage on her long evening gown and my father had adjusted his white tie and put on his tailcoat, then I went off for the night to our neighbours, the Jeeveses. While Gwen and Gordon Jeeves and I were playing bobs (the 'poor man's billiards'), a couple of dozen of my parents' 'crowd' would assemble at our house and have a drink – which they called a 'spot' – and a singsong. Then they would sort themselves into cars and drive off to the ball, some of them singing. The next morning I would wake up in a bedroom in the Jeeveses' house, watched over (as one might expect in a Catholic household) by prints of the Sacred Heart and the Pope. When I got back home my parents would still be in bed, sleeping it off, their finery scattered around them. On the washstand, for me, in a paper napkin, there would be a piece of cake with silver cachous on its white icing, and I would eat it as my second breakfast. In the next issue of the *Muswellbrook Chronicle* we would read descriptions of all the dresses women wore at the ball.

My father's most serious diversions were golf and shooting. His interest in golf overwhelmed even our interest in bridge, mahjongg, mini-golf, tennis and ludo. Golf was more than mere pleasure, and a great deal of our conversation was necessarily concerned with it. Between hands of mahjongg, for example. Sometimes we would start the day with me sending golf balls back to my father as he practised putting into a glass tumbler on the veranda. He even had a few small clubs made for me, and from the age of six I spent many tedious hours going around the course with him, or with my mother, who was a 'chatty' golfer. When he won a cup, his one trophy in seven years of golfing, it was put in the place of honour on top of the pianola, replacing a cut-glass vase. I looked at it every night when I was practising my piano scales. The inscription said: MUSWELLBROOK GOLF CLUB. D. HORNE. 'B' GRADE CHAMPION, 1931.

The Muswellbrook golf links was a 'sporting' course, with eight creek crossings during a full game. For me, crossing the creek provided the main relief in the tedium, along with watching the crows that circled restlessly above the clubhouse as if they were waiting to pick it clean; sometimes one of them would swoop on a ball lying in the brittle yellow grass of the fairway and carry it off to a nest in a gum tree. A few cows grazed on the course; occasionally a ball would land in a fresh cow pat.

Although most of them took their actual golfing seriously, the four dozen men and two dozen women who made up the Muswellbrook Golf Club allowed some social gaiety, when the golfing itself was over. When my father went off on a golfing expedition to one of the other country towns he would come back very jovial, with a pound of chocolate gingers or a jar of stuffed olives, or a pewter pot souvenired from a hotel. (For years I drank my milk out of a pewter pot on which was inscribed the name of a Singleton hotel.) I was taken on several of these expeditions. Once I sat on someone's knee in a car on the night ride back from Denman; for a while they sang songs or told jokes about the aviatrix Amy Johnson and the Prince of Wales; then one of them suggested a game of ring-a-ring o' roses. Beside the road, men in plus-fours and women in sensible shoes pranced around in a circle in the moonlight. I was told to stay in the car.

After golfing in his plus-fours on Saturdays, my father usually got into his grey flannels on Sundays and we went for a picnic, with rabbit shooting before and after lunch. There was the same dry grass as on the golf course, the same cow pats, the same crows with desolate cries, the same dazzling skies, but on the shooting picnics the carcasses of dead cattle were to be found, or their bleached bones, whereas on the golf course someone carted the cows away if they died. On the way home the man who acted as our host would ask me to recite poetry. As we drove along in the dark on this Australian country road I would recite from the works of the nineteenth-century English romantics, perhaps six or seven poems. My favourites were 'I wandered lonely as a cloud', 'Roll on, thou deep and dark blue ocean', 'I come from haunts of coot and fern' and 'Oh, to be in England, now that April's there'.

We spent about a fifth of the year in Sydney, holidaying there on each of the school vacations. My mother's first city sport was hunting down new things to buy in the shops. Apart from foodstuffs and small household requirements, she bought nothing in Muswellbrook, saving the pleasures of purchase for concentrated indulgence in Sydney. (I did not realise the risks she ran in this diversion until one night back in Muswellbrook I sat on the veranda and listened to my parents argue about my mother's having run up such a big bill at David Jones department store that they had cut off her credit and she had to open an account at Hordern Bros, a store down the scale from David Jones.) To me, the particular delight of the city was to enjoy the latest city crazes – pure orange juice served from green and orange coloured kiosks shaped in the form of huge oranges; then milk-shakes, in milk bars of black and white tiles, with a lot of glass and chromium plate (chromium was the latest thing); then, not long before we left Muswellbrook, the hamburger sandwich, the new American delicacy.

What Sydney really meant to us was enjoyment of the natural and the primitive. The demanding bustle of pleasure that occupied my parents in their country town was replaced in the metropolis by the simplicities to be enjoyed in the bushland on the outskirts of Sydney and on Sydney beaches. It was in Sydney that we beheld the delights of nature; in the country (so brown and bare that it seemed unnatural) we enjoyed the pleasures of society. There was a reserve of bush less than a mile's walk from my grandparents' house, which was much more pleasant than anything available at Muswellbrook (where the trees were stripped away so that animals could eat dry grass and make money to reduce their owners' overdrafts). Sometimes my father and I would walk there to eat our sandwiches, drink our thermos tea, sail my model boat and chat about topics such as the Roman conquest of Britain; but the real bushland extension of my grandparents' house was Yowie Bay, an inlet of Port Hacking, then almost deserted, though now a suburb of Sydney, where my grandfather had his weekender. To get to the weekender, we would walk along a sandy bush track (keeping an eye out for snakes) and then climb down the steep stone steps my grandfather had built to the little house that jutted into the bay on stone stilts. We would put the stores in the cupboard and get into the dinghy and row out and fish; or scramble over the boulders picking oysters; or dig around in the mud looking for worms for bait; or, if it was high tide, jump off the veranda into the water. There was a lot of shouting over lunch; in the afternoon we might sit on the veranda, look across the quiet bay and talk until afternoon tea. I would then go to sleep to the light of an oil lamp and to the sound of the water lapping around the house; I might listen for a while as my grandfather discussed getting up before dawn to catch the tide. At Yowie we were simple-hearted fisherfolk, taking our milk condensed in cans like true primitives, and ignoring golf handicaps and bridge scores and the other demands of the high-pressure living that was already considered to be one of the great problems of the age.

The motor car, the most fundamental of all new crazes, also aided our communion with the natural. Two or three carloads, with everybody's children and dogs, would occasionally go for a bush picnic, the men in their cream trousers and blazers and ties and motoring caps, the women in tailored 'suits'. We would go to the National Park, a large bushland reserve south of Port Hacking, or down the Bulli Pass (where somebody's radiator usually boiled over on the steep climb back), or up to the Blue Mountains or the Kurrajong Mountains. At any turn in the road, if a particularly beautiful view revealed itself, we might park for a while and admire it. For lunch we would build a fire of dry leaves, twigs and small dry branches, and grill lamb chops over it on a wire frame until they were black outside, the blacker the better: while we ate the burnt chops, holding them in our hands, a billy of tea simmered on the fire. We were true Australians. If we heard a kookaburra laugh during a picnic we felt even more Australian.

The climax of the year's pleasure was the most traditional. For a week before Christmas Eve my mother would go into the city every day to do her Christmas shopping, while my grandmother prepared for the feasts of the Christmas–New Year festival. She would ice two Christmas cakes, bake dozens of fruit-mince pies, boil three Christmas puddings in the laundry copper, bake two hams, and get ready the dozen or so chickens she had fattened for Christmas: after chopping off their heads, she would pluck their feathers in the garden, draw their entrails in the kitchen, truss them, stuff them with sage and onion, then roast them in the oven, two at a time. On Christmas Eve these delicacies would be packed into boxes and we would go off to the house we had rented that year at Cronulla, then a beach resort isolated from the suburbs by bush, but now, like Yowie, part of them. About ten of us would stay in the house; others would drop in for the day during the four weeks we stayed there. We would decorate the house with balloons and paper streamers, then I would put out an empty pillowcase at the end of the bed, with a note to Father Christmas (I did not believe in him, but kept up the pretence for my mother's sake). When I awoke at dawn the pillowcase would be crammed with purchases from the department stores. Instead of the usual mid-morning tea and scones in the kitchen we would all enjoy a glass (in my case, a sip) of port and a slice of fruit cake in the garden before we went down to the beach, sunned ourselves and had our first surf for the season. Boasting of our appetites, we would come back to find that the day's extra guests had arrived, and when we were seated around the tables, we would cram in all we could of our feast, washing it down with beer. When the last nut was cracked and the remains of the last dried fig extracted from the last set of artificial teeth we would rest for a while, then go for another stroll down to the beach, and another surf. In the evening, after eating exactly the same meal, we would take down some of the balloons and form sides across the table to play balloon handball. On Boxing Day and until the day after New Year's Day we would go on eating

Christmas dinner, supplementing it with fish netted near the beach and sold alive. Then it was all gone, and the bones of the exhausted hams were used to make stock for a delicious split-pea soup, which also lasted for several meals.

For the whole four weeks, unless there was something wrong with the weather, we would go to the beach morning and afternoon. On the beach there was always the feeling of being part of a friendly encampment; people would drift off into the surf and, when they came back and dried themselves, describe what had happened to them; then they would sunbake for a while and again drift off to the surf. We would discuss the kind of surf it was that day, what the seaweed, bluebottle or sunburn problems were, how the weather looked. Some days 'Mick' and I spent the whole time either on the water's edge, building sandcastles and then tunnelling water into them so that they fell down, or jumping around in the surf. There were other days when it was the sun more than the surf that attracted us, and we could enjoy more sun. We would lie on the beach, our backs turned up, our cheeks pressed down into the sand, to achieve the mahogany stain that marked the true White Australian. We would go crimson quickly, then so quickly brown that the scorched skin came off in long white strips. We would peel it from each other with delight, enjoying the gentle tickle and congratulating ourselves on getting out of last year's skin.

It was at Cronulla every summer that we bore witness to a truth that was self-evident to us every day of the year: the most important part of human destiny was to have a good time.

Country, King, God

IN THE BOTTOM RIGHT-HAND DRAWER OF HIS SIDE OF the dressing-table Dad kept the symbols of his most important beliefs. When there was no one in the house I sometimes took them out and wondered at them. There was his Masonic apron, his Bible, his war medals, a Bedouin's knife he had brought back from the Palestine campaign, an army revolver, his spurs. One day I put on the Masonic apron and the medals. Holding the revolver in my hand, with the Bedouin's knife at my waist and the spurs on my feet, I looked at myself in the mirror and saw an Australian.

In the photographs he kept in this drawer columns of horses marched along the desert; Dad, in his hat with the emu plumes, rode down a desert wadi; a desert plain was studded with Australian bivouacs; in Cairo there were men in sun helmets and Sam Brownes or fezes and galabeahs; there was a background of mosques, minarets and British lions; in Sydney the troopship was leaving for Suez, its paper streamers billowing up in the air. There was also a newspaper clipping of pictures of Dad and four of his brothers in their uniforms – a private, a sapper, a trooper, a lance-corporal, a sergeant – and a photograph of the grave of one of them.

The Great War and the ethos of the Australian soldier cast a bright light over our house. We lived not only with clear memories of the past war but with thoughts of the wars to come. It was assumed that when my turn came I would also play my part. One night, when we came home from a pacifist movie, as we had our cup of tea in the kitchen Dad was silent. Then he looked at me anxiously and said: 'You'd fight if you had to, wouldn't you?' Often there were rumours of war in the Sunday papers and, home from a day's rabbit shooting, we might discuss the prospects of war before I went to bed.

The only day of ceremony in our year was Anzac Day, the day we commemorated the Australian landing at Gallipoli in 1915, seen as the occasion when Australia 'came of age'. On Anzac Day Dad would put on his three medals and join the other returned men who were forming up in the main street behind the Muswellbrook brass band, the Boy Scouts and the Junior Red Cross. They would march up and down the street to the music of wartime marching tunes, then bifurcate – the Catholics to St James's Church, where the priest would remind his congregation that life was eternal and that they should pray for the souls of the dead soldiers; the Protestants to St Alban's Church, where as the rector processed, with the gold cross held before him, and the choir sang 'Onward Christian Soldiers', we knew that soldiers like Dad and his brothers, by volunteering to sail across the Indian Ocean to fight the Turk, had given the word 'Australia' meaning. The rector would remind us that Australia was young in the company of nations but that its nationhood had been earned in the glorious epic of Anzac bravery. 'The history of Australia begins with a blank space on the map and ends with the record of a new name on the map, that of Anzac.' While we sang 'Fight the good fight with all thy might' the returned men would move in procession to the Soldiers' Chapel, where in front of the flame of remembrance the roll of the Muswellbrook dead would be called. The Last Post would sound, then the Protestant returned men would march to the war memorial, where the mayor would preside over another ceremony and we would sing 'O God, our help in ages past, our hope in years to come'. One of the Protestant clergymen would then remind us that Anzac Day was a solemn sacrament of mateship, commemorating our heroes as a band of brothers who for the first time in history had shown a final understanding of the essential humanness of mankind. However impatient they were of saluting and ceremony, they could rise to the occasion, do the right thing and never let down a mate. We would observe two minutes' silence in honour of the men who had escaped calculation and ambition by dying blameless and young, in the simple act of men following their destiny. The Last Post would be sounded; wreaths would be laid; we would sing Kipling's 'Recessional'; then the bugler would blow Reveille and the ceremonies would be over until the reunion dinner at night, when the rector would again remind his audience that Anzac Day was the birthday of our nation, commemorating forever the nobility of men who took something on and saw it through without whingeing; other speakers would remind themselves that Australian soldiers were uniquely independent-minded and adventurous, uniquely able to display initiative, uniquely healthy in body and bold in spirit, uniquely *men*. Australian soldiers were the greatest men in the world.

Dad had fought in the desert with the Australian Light Horse. It was not on the Western Front and with the infantry, but only in the desert and with cavalry, that war seemed fully to assume the heroic meaning we gave it, that things renewed themselves when young men went off to risk death. Dad had not reached Gallipoli; he had got sick on the island of Lemnos and by the time he was better the Gallipoli campaign was over. When he campaigned in Palestine he was so reduced by the sicknesses of the desert that at the end of the war it was noted on his discharge certificate that his physical condition was one of 'general debility'.

Much of the Australian history we learned at school, particularly the record of exploration, seemed to concern itself with virtues similar to those of the Anzac spirit – endurance, commitment, the expression of will. (The school syllabus spoke of liberating the child's life force.) As men struggled across deserts of stone or sandy wastes Australia seemed the dead frontier, the land of the dogged gesture. Even the Gallipoli expedition, the savage act of national self-recognition, had failed.

We were living through a run-down time. I was seven when prices fell in Wall Street. The worst the Depression did to our own family was that Uncle Loy, who had been an agent for Borsalino hats and a few other Italian lines, was put out of business by high tariffs and for a while worked as a floorwalker at a city department store. But the Depression seemed to drain the whole country of its spirit, and for some years most of what I was likely to hear was pessimistic. There was an occasional glint of sardonic wit: merely to say 'Prosperity is just around the corner' could set a roomful of people laughing. But despite the happiness with which I was immediately surrounded, there was nothing invigorating to hear about Australia. Australians may have been the best people in the world, but the best, apparently, was no longer very good. The Depression had a sense of inevitable calamity about it, like floods farther down the valley, or bushfires on the coast.

The main contemporary enthusiasms lay in admiration for our sportsmen and aviators, particularly the cricketer Don Bradman and the aviator Kingsford Smith. Even here it was their will that was most admired. Bradman was the boy from the bush who had battled his way to the top; he was a calculating, implacable batsman; a granite idol. Kingsford Smith showed more dash. As he and other Australian aviators crossed continents and oceans in their improvised aeroplanes we marked their positions on maps and pasted their pictures in scrapbooks. This was 'exploring' – very Australian. When some of them died, lost with their planes, no one knew where. This also seemed very Australian. They were great men, capable of iron-willed Australian failures.

Perhaps the most human thing we felt at school for our newly established nation was an admiration of our plants and animals. We were proud of kangaroos and platypuses and koala bears, gum trees and flannel flowers. These were ours. The waratah seemed a proud symbol; we celebrated spring by festooning the classrooms with wattle; at Christmas we decorated the table with Christmas bells and put a sprig of Australian Christmas bush on the plum pudding instead of holly. Along with the English nature verse we also learned poems that boasted that our Australian seasons and countryside were different from those of England. The Anzac spirit had its place in the school syllabus, but it did not carry conviction at school; you needed a father at home with a secret drawer to do that. And it did not finally carry conviction anywhere. It was just belief. We believed in the Anzac spirit. But we didn't believe it *existed*. Not any longer. The Anzac spirit was a failure, too. On the evening of each Anzac Day the daughter of one of the old families subsidised the attendance at the reunion dinner of any 'old diggers' down on their luck who were passing through town. After their free dinner they could go back to sleep under the bridge or in the pig pens.

*

As well as being Australians we were also British, first-class citizens of the Empire, and at school this was what we were most taught to admire. One of the themes of the history curriculum was 'The growth of an empire based on liberty'. In this growth the campaigns of Clive and Wolfe, the Indian Mutiny and the Boer War led up to the climax of the Great War, in which the imperial dominions joined the mother country in fighting for freedom. A large part of the geography curriculum was given over to the theme of 'Australia and the Empire'. Jute in India, huskies in Canada, geysers in New Zealand, springboks in South Africa, rickshaws in Singapore. We learned the names of the British naval stations, the principal sea routes that linked them, the names of the great imperial cities, and we learned nothing about the rest of the world. That came later – in the newspapers when, nation by nation, year by year, the rest of the world demanded that we pay attention to it.

On Empire Day we would assemble in the school playground, clattering the tin mugs we were taking to the picnic. Arranged in classes, we would stand easy while some of the children gave Empire Day speeches. We stood to attention while Dad, the deputy headmaster, conducted us in singing patriotic airs, and then we would march to the Strand picture show, where we were joined by the boys and girls of the convent. Here we would sing 'Land of Hope and Glory', 'Rule Britannia', 'Three Cheers for the Red, White and Blue' and 'Advance Australia Fair', a song between each speech. When the three Protestant clergymen and the headmaster spoke to us they would suggest that the empire held together only because of some particular moral virtue. To the Presbyterian minister it was truthfulness; to the Methodist minister, the belief that if a thing was worth doing it was worth doing well; to the headmaster, love and good feeling; to the rector, unswerving loyalty and devotion in our sacred duties to King, God and Country. The rector would also tell us the story of the Indian prince who poured his tea into a saucer and blew on it when he visited Queen Victoria at Windsor and how, to put him at his ease, the Queen then poured *her* tea into a saucer and blew on it too, thus showing that the empire was a commonwealth of peoples. We sang 'God Save the King', then the convent children marched off to their picnic and we marched off to ours – sandwiches, jellies and lemonade provided by the Parents' and Citizens' Association. If we had tried pouring tea into our saucers when we got home we would probably have got a clip over the ear.

On Empire Day, 1933, I was one of the schoolchildren who gave a speech in the playground: 'When we speak of the British Empire what do we mean? We mean all those countries that are ruled over by our King, George V. They are scattered all over the world. There are tiny islands like pinpoints on the map, and great stretches of land, such as India, South Africa, Canada and Australia. It is a mighty Empire. All the people who live in our Empire are not white; yellow people, black people, red people and brown people own King George as their King. They do not all speak English as we do; but there is room in the Empire for men of all colours and creeds. Now, think of the heart of this mighty Empire! It is away to the north in a little country called Great Britain. There lives our King, and from there come the men who have made our Empire what it is. They were brave, those men who left Great Britain to come across the seas. Some carried the flag of Britain to places always hot under a burning sun; some went to lands held fast by the frost and snow of the icy north. In lonely stretches of desert country, in great forests, amid the hum and buzz of great cities, they raised the flag of Britain, and thousands have died to keep it flying there. Why were they ready to die for it? What does the Union Jack stand for? First of all, it tells us that we are free. No one is allowed to keep slaves under the British flag. It was not always so. Less than a hundred years ago, all slaves in the British Empire were set free, and, one by one, most of the other nations have done as Britain did. That was a great achievement for our Empire to lead the way in doing the right thing by making all her peoples free. Our flag, too, stands for right. Of course we all make mistakes, and our country has made mistakes: but we do our best to be honest and fair in all we say and do, and to help the weak against the strong. In a few years we will be men and women, and we will have to keep up the fame of our Empire. Upon us rests the task of keeping the flag flying high. How can we do this? We must lead a good and noble life; we must be honest and fair; we must do what is right; we must do unto others as we would like them to do unto us; we must work while we work and play while we play. These are some of the things that will help.' I was very proud of this speech, particularly the phrase 'the hum and buzz of great cities', which I had taken from an essay about city life I had written at school. I rehearsed myself for days before delivering it, sometimes to my parents, sometimes to the dog.

In Muswellbrook, out there in the brown grass of the Hunter Valley, we had never seen a ceremonial parade, or even a uniform, except the khaki of the 16th Australian Light Horse, the Hunter Valley militia regiment. In every classroom, however, there was a world map, with much of it covered in red. We lived in an empire on which the sun never set. That seemed a good kind of empire to belong to – the biggest. We always stood up for King George V when his image appeared on the screen at the beginning of the program at the pictures and we often saw this remote and taciturn monarch, to whom we owed our loyalty, in the newsreels, dressed as an admiral or a field-marshal or in morning dress. King George did not laugh in public or display a personality. This more modern requirement of royal persons was met by the Prince of Wales, who came through as someone who knew how to make his own fun, just as we did in Muswellbrook. One could not imagine sitting down to mahjongg with King George V or joining Queen Mary in a singsong around the pianola. But Mum spoke of 'Teddy' as if he were someone who might drop in for a spot before they all went off to the Masonic Ball. Perhaps our most demonstrably British period was when Noël Coward's *Cavalcade* came to Muswellbrook. It ran for a special season, and many of the shops in the main street carried Union Jacks in their windows. The father of a girlfriend at school considered the talkies immoral; but when *Cavalcade* came to town her whole family went to see it, dressed as for church.

*

As well as being Australians and British we were also Christians, but the formal practice of Christianity ran a bad second to Anzac stoicism. Apart from on Anzac Day the church seemed to be in the grip of elderly women. On the rare attendances we made there I could not make head nor tail of the form of service, being unable to follow the intricacies of the prayer book. Before we took up shooting on Sundays I went to Sunday school, but it seemed to be just a place you went to: there were songs to sing, there was money to collect, there were words to say, and then they handed out coloured pictures of Christian saints which I would throw away as I walked home to afternoon tea. I could not understand why I was supposed to be there. There was nothing to learn, no exams, no esteem for being clever: the kind of children who were esteemed at Sunday school seemed to be those who at school were remarkable neither for physical dexterity not for cleverness. There was about all this some mystery I could not comprehend. I made my protest by joining the delinquent set: before the bell rang we would gather at the back of the church hall, where nobody could see us, and throw stones at it, as if it were a martyr. At home Dad sometimes suggested that I should read the Bible, but the print was too small, the pages too thin, and the archaic language repelled me. The most meaningful religious instruction I received was from a textbook on the main anecdotes from the Bible read to us at school in scripture lessons – by our Catholic teacher.

From my earliest memories I had recited the Children's Prayer to Dad or Mum every night. *Gentle Jesus, Meek and Mild, Look upon a little child, Pity my simplicity, Suffer me to come to thee. Amen.* To this was later added the Lord's Prayer and the Creed. As I got older I was allowed to recite these to myself silently. ('Have you said your prayers, Don?' 'Yes, Mum.') After a certain age I dropped the Children's Prayer in these silent recitations, as being beneath my years. There was one brief stage in my boyhood – somewhere around the age of eight – when I practised a great deal of private prayer. *Please God, don't make it rain today. Please God, don't let the teacher find out. Please God, don't make this cup of tea too hot.* This period passed, although I went on reciting the Lord's Prayer and the Creed to myself until I went to high school.

Such personal addresses as I made to the divinity were to God the Father, never to God the Son. There seemed no point in praying to the simple man called Jesus to stop the teacher from finding out; his weakness and goodness made him seem an unlikely recipient for pleas for action. When he felt inclined to discuss religious matters with me it was the man Jesus that Dad always spoke about. Perhaps this gentle Jesus reflected Dad's own simplicity, put aside so that he could become an Australian and suffer in the war. When he spoke of the meekness of Jesus he spoke of a man who had failed, a simple, good man whom everybody had set upon. For a while we would contemplate our compassion, then retreat into the banality that was such a treasured part of our lives. The creed of this meek, gentle Jesus, Dad would say, was that you should do unto others as you would have them do unto you – or, as Mum would sometimes translate it: 'You should show more consideration for other people, Don.'

When, in fantasy, instead of imagining that I was the unknown elder son of King George V or the true descendant of Bonnie Prince Charlie, I would decide that I was Jesus Christ returned to the world, this time determined to win, it was as the throne-sitting Christ the King rather than Jesus the Man. But we Protestants knew little of the triumphant Christ at Muswellbrook; it was not only Dad who saw Jesus as the unfortunate sensitive man who failed: this was the prevailing concept. While we might pray to God to break a drought it was Jesus' name that was invoked if we were asked to spare a thought for the unemployed. He wasn't supposed to *do* anything about them, except to join us in sparing them a thought. God, the father of this decent-minded son, was unimaginable. Dad deprecated the idea that God was an angry, bearded old man dressed in a long, white sheet. So if I addressed him or tried to imagine him, all

I saw was a big glow. However, I maintained a belief in the anger of this unpredictable and powerful God of Destiny, Lord of his own far-flung battle line. The Bible anecdotes, and for that matter the prayers for rain, suggested an arbitrary God, laying about him right and left. This was a puzzle I did not often take up, except in an occasional spasm of fear. But the general rules, as revealed to Dad and passed on to me, fitted most civilly into the context of our life in Muswellbrook. If I showed consideration for other people, and was obedient, truthful, diligent at my lessons and neat in my personal habits (taking my castor oil every Friday night), I would probably pass muster with God. Dad was punctilious in his own neatness. Perhaps more than anything else it was his sense of tidiness that was affronted when he gave me my biggest belting – for writing 'shit' in indelible pencil beneath the red roses on a white box of chocolates. I was aged eight and I did not know what the word meant.

*

Both our Australianness and our Christianity involved us in some doctrinal affirmation of human brotherhood although this was not necessarily a matter for our daily lives and it existed in contradiction with other things we believed or were supposed to believe. Brotherhood was, of course, a matter for men and it reached its most ambitious moments on Anzac Day, when we attempted a formal synthesis of Australianness and Christianity, but the image of the Rev. Mr J. Christ, the sincere clergyman who served as a chaplain in the Australian Light Horse, was not convincing. The meekness of the man Jesus made him un-Australian: he was obviously not tough enough for the Light Horse, and toughness was one of the most important parts of brotherhood. God was the essential deity for Anzac Day: he would always see to it that we won. Our attempt to mix brotherhood with Britishness on Empire Day also failed: we did not really see ourselves as the mates of all these foreigners in the empire, least of all the English, who were notorious as stuck-up snobs: opposition to people who asserted their superiority over us was also one of the important parts of brotherhood.

At Muswellbrook, where invitations to the Picnic Races Ball made it clear that bank managers had something that schoolteachers couldn't get, and membership of the golf club showed that schoolteachers could enjoy something that shop assistants couldn't, the sense of social position as something that divided our parents was nevertheless an oddity that had nothing to do with children, and even among their parents it was something that one was supposed not to talk about or to display in personal relations. Although recognition of social difference was almost universal, and when it was asserted it might be with considerable crudity, there was a bad conscience about it. Open affirmation was rare. When pharmacists' wives openly showed their contempt for schoolteachers' wives at the golf club by expecting them to clear up the ashtrays it was breaking the rules. At my grandparents' home, Denbigh – which I loved and saw as a kind of family temple – we would often laugh over Sunday tea at the snobberies of Muswellbrook and wonder that people could divide themselves in this ridiculous way. There was my mother's father, Pa, a hero to me, who was both a member of an old family and a retired sleeping-car conductor. There was Uncle Alf, dentist, mayor, and once almost selected by his party to stand for election as a senator, who sometimes dropped in on us and displayed the wit of the big world, amusing us with anecdotes of power in Manly. And there was Uncle Tom, so poor that he lived in a one-room shack in a paddock on the outskirts of Sydney which we called 'Uncle Tom's Cabin'. Life was just a gamble. Australianness was what mattered at Denbigh, and we reserved our snobbery for mocking people who claimed to be better than us: governors-general, for example.

I do not remember being sustained by any of the explicitly stated beliefs of Australian 'mateship', or even hearing the word regularly used outside Anzac Day. Mateship had meaning for me only as a greatly admired relationship existing between Australian soldiers when they went off to war. When I became a soldier and went to war I would find out about mateship. From the Australian short stories we read at school we realised vaguely that mateship was also something practised in the old pioneering days in the bush, but we were not specifically taught anything about it at school: as a term used in civilian life 'mate' was simply a slang word and if you used it you would lose marks in an English composition. According to the official syllabus the virtues that were to be inculcated into us were not mateship but courage, prudence, perseverance, self-control, self-respect, cleanliness, orderliness, obedience, kindness, gentleness, fair-mindedness and truthfulness. One of the ways in which this purpose was to be achieved was through instructing us during history lessons in the fables of 'noble persons', such as Leonidas, Cincinnatus, Haroun-al-Raschid, Richard the Lion Heart, St Francis, Joan of Arc, Sir Thomas More, Sir Philip Sidney, Captain John Smith and Helen Keller. We learned about such people and passed examinations in their nobility, but they were all toffs and the only one of them who cared about his mates was that proto-Anzac, the wounded Sir Philip Sidney, who gave his drinking water to another wounded soldier and died.

At Denbigh we believed that one should not talk about politics or religion, and so far as religion was concerned, since we were all agreed the Catholics were up to no good and the wowsers were a menace and we should all be kind to each other, there didn't seem to be much to say. But we sometimes talked politics – several times with a bitterness that proved temporarily disastrous to our amity and when we did there was a division between those of us who held the world view that the workers were the salt of the earth and those who considered that money was what mattered. Most of us temporised, but when the extremes were stated brutally most of us supported the workers. The two greatest extremes of our view of the struggle between Capital and Labour were represented in my Uncle Ted (for Labour) and (for Capital) Aunty Lil and her husband, Uncle 'Candy' (an abbreviation of his proper name, 'Alcanda', an odd name we wondered about). In the early days of the Depression Aunty Lil and Uncle Candy had travelled New South Wales in a car, with their dog sitting on the running board, and, strapped to the luggage rack at the back, and on the roof, the trunks containing the women's dresses that they sold in country towns. When they decided to make their own dresses in Sydney and send travellers out to sell them they rented rooms in a city building and installed machinery and workgirls in it, and thus became capitalists. My Uncle Ted, in contrast, was an electrical fitter at the Chullora railway workshop who saw something splendid in his relationship with his workmates; to dramatise his contempt for money grubbers he kept the few shillings of his savings tied in the corner of a handkerchief so that if people started talking about money he could bring out his handkerchief and show us his entire capital, demonstrating that he was a worker. There was a shouting match one night when Uncle Candy talked about the mugs who rode to work on their bicycles while he rode by in his car. The rest of us were scandalised: we knew that Ted rode to the railway workshops on a bicycle. On another night the capital-versus-labour controversy was expressed in such cutting and directly personal terms (one of our richer relatives shrieking a defence of labour) that Pa told everyone to go to buggery.

A form of division on which we were nearly all agreed was that Australians were better than foreigners. Not that we knew much about foreigners. Only 140 of the 4000 people of Muswellbrook were born overseas, and of these 130 were British, and at Denbigh we knew no foreigners apart from Uncle Loy's wife, Aunty 'Jan' (short for Jeanette). Aunty Jan, Nouméan-French as we were Australian–British, and perhaps married by Uncle Loy because on the Western Front he had picked up a taste for things French, with her uncertain temperament, sometimes generous, sometimes grumpy and always smelling of very strong scent, was all we could handle in the way of foreigners. Like the English, we saw ourselves superior to 'continentals'. The Germans were the traditional enemies of Australians, and our fathers and the many war stories in the boys' comic books told us that the Hun made a tough enemy and it took us to beat them. As proof of this, there was the captured German machine-gun beside the school tennis court and the many German field guns in the parks of Sydney. We knew that in beating the Hun (which we might have to do again) there was not much help to be expected from our allies. The Belgians were all right as a gallant little ally, but the French (whom our fathers called 'the Frogs') were too excitable and the Mediterranean peoples (whom we all called the 'dagoes') were only good for running cafes or fruit and vegetable shops. The Yanks were all right in their own way, almost as good as Australians perhaps, but too boastful and upstart; the Yanks still had a lot to learn from us.

Insofar as we thought about it, our principal concern was to distinguish ourselves from other white peoples. We did not take Asians or Africans into any kind of account, or discuss them in any way, except when my father, in the course of an anecdote about the war might refer to 'Gyppos', whom we saw as rascally street beggars, or the nomadic Bedouin, for whom we had a certain respect. I do not remember being told that there was a White Australia policy. It simply seemed part of the natural order of events that we should be 'white'. My feelings towards 'Asiatics' were drawn mainly from books. Some 'Asiatics' were important people – maharajahs, mandarins, sultans and Hurree Jamset Ram Singh, the Indian boy at Greyfriars in the Billy Bunter stories – but they seemed more like English toffs than Australians, stuck-up snobs who treated their own people badly. Apart from these few toffs, all the inhabitants of Asia were called 'coolies', a class of person for whom I felt vaguely sorry. Both the Chinese and the Indians seemed very old-fashioned peoples, colourful, picturesque, living in the past: they had had their day. The Japanese were a different matter: their warships had visited Sydney Harbour; their manufactured goods were on sale in the shops; and we read in the papers about what they were doing in some distant place called Manchuria. Apart from sultans or ships' crews, the peoples of South-East Asia were almost unimaginable, and I was only vaguely aware of New Guinea and other Melanesian islands around us; these were inhabited by 'kanakas' who, as a result of our British love of liberty, were no longer exploited by blackbirding expeditions. Central Africa was all jungle and its native residents, the niggers, were happy savages, harmless to anyone except themselves, not as exploited and unfortunate as coolies, but even more remote from Muswellbrook. I did not see any Australian Aborigines, or give them any thought. At the front of our school atlas there was a map of Australia showing it as all black before the British arrived (meaning that it was 'undiscovered') and then a series of maps showing the spread of civilisation as a golden advance, ending with a map of Australia in which all the black had turned to gold. I was taught at school that since we were all brothers the empire was a giant co-operative run by the fortunate for the benefit of the unfortunate. Sometimes, as in the Indian Mutiny or the Boer War, disloyalty had to be put down, but most of the maharajahs, mandarins, sultans, coolies and niggers were loyal, and some day, in some way, they would move into equal partnership with us. Meanwhile we bought their jute and the English rode in their rickshaws.

Our intolerance was directed in effect almost exclusively towards the English, the 'Poms'. We looked down on Poms almost as much as we looked down on Catholics. At our house, where how men shaped up to the tests of battle was what counted, the Poms were considered too deferential to their officers and lacking in initiative, physically puny compared with Australians, and inadequate in personal hygiene. Their officers, of course, were effeminate, incompetent and dictatorial. The Poms did not make such good soldiers as Johnny Turk. Of all the peoples of the world living outside Australia, those we held in the highest regard in our house were the Turks.

'Be yourself, Don'

I HAD NO DOUBT THAT ACQUIRING KNOWLEDGE WAS ONE of the most admirable of human activities and that the institution in which I acquired much of my knowledge, the Muswellbrook District Rural School, provided that service efficiently. One of my favoured rooms – equal to the rooms of our house at Muswellbrook and even the sacred rooms of Denbigh – was the school classroom where, all around us, were reminders of knowledge, order and the virtues of improvement: the main dates in British history, maps of Australia and of the world, lists of principal exports, botanical specimens. On the wall alongside the 'model block' where the cleverest boys and girls sat (more girls than boys) were printed in black ink on white cardboard the names of those who came first, second and third in each subject in the written tests set each month throughout primary school. What divided us in this room was not our sex or the social standing of our parents, but cleverness – which seemed to me the only fair division among human beings. The daughter of the chook thief was one of my closest competitors in the monthly tests.

The Muswellbrook District Rural School consisted of a brick main building and half a dozen prefabricated wooden classrooms, called 'portables', that were placed around the playground, three of them along a bank of the creek. Here the inculcators of knowledge were the primary-school teachers, the second or third generation of the bearers of compulsory education, briefly trained in teachers' colleges and controlled by a Department of Public Instruction that moved them arbitrarily from one town to another, perhaps hundreds of miles apart; they were people on the move, living in boarding houses when they were single and rented houses when they were married, their furniture being carted all over the state; they were controlled remotely but in detail from Sydney, tyrannised by annual visits from inspectors; in whatever town they settled they were never part of the permanent scene. In old photographs, posing under the trees in a school playground, their very clothes seem to say: here we are, upholding standards. Whether I would have liked them so much if I had met them only at school I do not know, but as it happened some of them were in and out of our house much of the time and I saw them not only as the purveyors of facts and upholders of standards, but as part of my mother's 'crowd', delighting in bridge, mahjongg, golf, or singsongs around the pianola.

It was they who taught us (or failed to teach us) how to write cursive at a slope of seventy-five degrees to the line, how to divide 1.08 by 12, or 22 by 5½, how to multiply 4½ by 24 or to work out what was left when 2s. in the pound was taken off 7s. 6d. We were instructed in the person, number, gender and case of nouns and pronouns, in the tense and voice of verbs, in the use of the past participle, how to identify a principal clause or a relative clause or an adverbial phrase. We were given poems to learn and 'compositions' to write. Our teachers campaigned against usages such as *ain't, brung, drownded, drawed, would of, uster, says I*; they distinguished between *may* and *can, don't* and *doesn't, lie* and *lay, rise* and *raise, teach* and *learn, shall* and *will*; they fought against what they considered inelegant uses of *start* and *got*, and tried to dissuade us from redundant pronouns and misplaced modifiers. It was on these questions of speech that we began to divide among ourselves; there were the boys who went on using *ain't* and the other forbidden words and usages defiantly and with ideological fervour (they were proclaiming their independence not only of grammar and arithmetic but from Leonidas and Joan of Arc); and there were those of us who said *aren't* instead of *ain't*.

Whatever I lacked in loyalty to sporting teams was compensated for by loyalty to the Muswellbrook school. The school returned my loyalty. Each month, from third class to sixth, I came top of the test in every subject, except for the month when I went down in arithmetic. Any information that anyone cared to present was taken with pleasure. I was several times called into a senior class and asked to read something or answer some problem on the blackboard, not realising that this was to show up the slowness of my seniors, and I was encouraged by my parents and my teacher and all the Carpenters at Denbigh to cultivate my cleverness. To be myself was to be clever. As other boys delighted in being good at running I delighted in being quick-witted. Without feeling either vain or guilty, I enjoyed exercising a talent. We learned at school that *life was mostly froth and bubble, two things stood like stone, kindness in another's trouble, courage in your own*, and that one should *be good, sweet maid, and let who would be clever, do noble things, not dream them all day long* – but we also knew that it was prudent to have a good head on your shoulders. I had a good head on my shoulders. When he heard of this clever boy at the public school the principal of the town's merchant family took the trouble to urge my father to make sure I had a good education and even hinted that he would give him the money to see me through.

In the dining room, as well as the sideboard and the traymobile there was a bookcase with a frosted and lead-lighted front, where we kept the mahjongg set and all the pianola rolls, and also three sets of books – the four-volume *History of the British Nation*, the eight-volume *Cassell's Book of Knowledge* and the two-volume *Dr Vertue's Household Physician*. This meant that my devotion to learning wasn't confined to school. I could read and re-read *Cassell's Book of Knowledge* with its more than 2000 articles and 10,000 photographs and drawings. Sometimes I would supplement *Cassell's* with Arthur

FORMATIVE YEARS

Mee's *Children's Encyclopaedia*, borrowed from the school library. I kept on returning to favourite bits and reading them again, passing from 'Caesar, the Man Who Crossed the Rubicon' to 'Strange Hats of Many Lands' to 'Brave and Thrifty Belgium' to 'Kinematograph, the Wonders of Moving Picture Land' to 'Marx, the Originator of the Modern Internationalist Socialist Movement' to 'Mighty Russia's Rise and Fall'. There did not seem much more to learn.

The world as it presented itself in *Cassell's Book of Knowledge* was more diverse than the simple ideas we used at home or at Denbigh or on Anzac Day or Empire Day or the more complicated but still highly patterned ideas introduced to us at school. I passed from the language of one world to the other without thinking about it. I did not speak to anyone else about the world of *Cassell's*. It was my own. It was a matter of private knowledge, personal to me, that 'Strange Empires Had Flourished When the World Was Young' or that 'The Protoplasm Was the Beginning of the Wonderful Story of Evolution'. It was only I who admired pictures of 'The Basilica of St Anthony at Padua' or of 'The Curious Striped Bacilli Which Are the Cause of Dreaded Tuberculosis'. I thus began a habit that was to remain with me: some of the things in which I was most interested were matters that I could discuss only with myself. I did not then consider that I was any better for this kind of special knowledge nor even different. It was simply a secret delight that could not be practised publicly without embarrassment. While Mum and Dad and their friends talked about their golf scores, who was to know or care that, as I sat there with them, my nose in a book, I might be reading that 'if we could discover a means of making atoms break up at a fast rate we should discover the key to unlock enormous stores of energy'?

The principal pattern of events we learned at school was one of inevitable and desirable change. Year by year we learned the history of change. Month by month we sat for examination in it. (When did

Hargreaves invent the spinning jenny? When did Vasco da Gama sail to India?) Our teachers taught us change out of a book, from a syllabus of instruction that – if some of its principles had been expressed in the British Isles earlier in our history – might have led to transportation in chains to New South Wales. We were offered a view of life based on an optimistic belief in inevitable improvement that would proceed of necessity, without our doing anything in particular about it. It was the officially expressed belief of the New South Wales Department of Public Instruction that there was a natural 'sense of growth and development' in human affairs, and that 'the human race ... was developing towards better and happier conditions of life'. This meant that one of our schoolroom views of mankind was optimistic, progressive and radical. We were on the side of revolution, exploration and innovation. We were for the barons against King John; for Wat Tyler against Richard II; for Sir Thomas More against Henry VIII, and for Henry VIII against the Pope; for Cromwell against King Charles; we supported the Bill of Rights, the Declaration of Independence, the Declaration of the Rights of Man, the Toleration Act, the Catholic Emancipation Act, the Factory Acts, the Reform Acts of 1832, 1867 and 1884. (Many of the dates that we had to learn by heart commemorated the passing of famous Acts of Parliament.) Some of the greatest people in our pantheon were explorers, inventors and reformers: Prince Henry the Navigator, Columbus, Magellan, Hudson, Cook, Livingstone, Scott; Galileo, Copernicus, da Vinci, Caxton, Newton, Watt; Lincoln, Plimsoll, Howard, Nightingale, Damien, Wilberforce. Human history was a story of discovery and reform; innovation served the welfare of the ordinary people in a sure evolution from serfdom to having a good time playing tennis at Muswellbrook.

The sense of inevitable improvement taught at school was tempered by the many hours I spent at home studying the four volumes of *The History of the British Nation*, a work that offset the sense of reason in *Cassell's Book of Knowledge*. This work had come to us first in weekly instalments from the newsagent. Then it was bound into four volumes, each of 600 pages. Its special appeal was that it had 3000 illustrations – the whole range of paintings of English history along with hundreds of illustrations 'specially painted for this work'. Its text told the history of progress, but I did not read much of the text; I read the lines beneath the 3000 pictures, and these told a story of inhumanity, treachery, stupidity and meaninglessness. I was as familiar with most of these 3000 pictures as if they were cigarette cards, so that, along with the optimism of school history, I taught myself another view of life: of disconnected, discordant, irrational and unpredictable events, and the possibility of failure.

Sometimes, while Mum was chatting with her friends over afternoon tea, I might fill in my time reading *The History of the British Nation*, my imagination excited by the procrastinations, incompetence, favouritism, murders, depositions, superstitions and dishonesties that had gone into its making.

The view of the world I obtained from the pictures in *The History of the British Nation* was confirmed in some of the discussions on politics I had heard at Denbigh. We liked to tell stories demonstrating the venality or the stupidity of Australian politicians. In fact, we delighted in any stories of misbehaviour, often swapping yarns about the high jinks of Kingsford Smith, or the girlfriends of the Prince of Wales. Nanna, my grandmother, gave historical depth with tales of Sir Henry Parkes ('Oh, he was a real old devil!'). This cynicism combined with our despair at the calamity of the Depression to lead us to the view that, so far as politicians were concerned, none of the buggers was any good.

I remember reading newspapers, but it was from a weekly news magazine called the *Sydney Mail* that I seemed to get the most coherent impressions of what was supposed to be happening in the world outside Australia. At first the main use of the *Mail* was to provide pictures of great events, to be cut out and pasted in a scrapbook – Kingsford Smith flying somewhere, Don Bradman scoring a century, Uncle Alf as Mayor of Manly greeting a visiting duke at a surf carnival. But the *Mail* also ran regular commentaries on foreign affairs that gave more connected and interpretive accounts than appeared in the newspapers. Some of this was what any student of *The History of the British Nation* might expect: assassinations in Eastern Europe, for instance, or the Japanese invasion of Manchuria. But what seemed improbable was Adolf Hitler. A piece I read on Hitler when I was aged eleven seemed meaningless: it explained the *Führerprinzip*. How could that be true? How could people deliberately believe in one man absolutely, and surrender all their liberties to him? Accidents could happen so that people lost their liberties. But to develop a principle of surrendering one's liberties voluntarily seemed very unlikely as late in history as 1933.

The sense of accident and of the indifference of events to human values that I learned from *The History of the British Nation* were strengthened by reading Dickens. Apart from a children's version of *The Christmas Carol* I first came across Dickens at the age of ten in an extract from *Oliver Twist* in the school magazine. I turned the extract into a play, adding it to the repertory I had written for classroom performance. That Christmas I came across the full text, in a shelf of cast-out books in Nanna's laundry. (This assortment of volumes, which consisted mainly of books picked up by Pa from sleeping-cars when he was a conductor, was my grandparents' library.) I was so fascinated that I read it through twice, and daydreamed about its characters for days. I wondered whether to risk asking for it, or whether I should simply steal it. Thereafter my moneybox savings were invested heavily in Dickens, who more than took his place among the *Chums Annuals*, pirate novels and Billy Bunter stories. This was a *History of the British Nation* view of life: things were unpredictable, catastrophe was always imminent and the existence of evil and horror was a matter of course. I had to summon Australian manliness to withhold my boyish tears whenever I re-read the description of Oliver's farewell to Dick. I asked Dad to buy me a notebook and I began writing a novel about a little barefooted boy who ran away from Muswellbrook by hiding in a freight train. After some pages were done I read what I had written to Mum and Dad. Mum did not think the subject was very nice. I was scolded for writing about a boy whose parents couldn't afford shoes. It was wrong to draw attention to boys who were worse off than I was. I brooded about this misunderstanding and lost confidence.

What seemed to me most 'lifelike' about Dickens was his sense of grotesquerie. The people in his books were as grotesque as the people in *The History of the British Nation* or the people I knew in Muswellbrook and Sydney. I had a child's sensitivity to the self-caricature and repetitiveness of most external human behaviour. Most of the people I knew seemed static representations of a few simple and predictable 'characters'. Human society consisted of people whose characters were unchangeable and obvious. They would go on being the same: the interest was in the wonder of the display of what they were, and of their relations with each other. It was like a game of cards. This feeling for character was most intense when we were staying in Sydney: there were the people who visited Denbigh to stimulate it then. I would sometimes sit in the sun on the front steps of Denbigh and make out lists of characters – Dickens people combined with Denbigh and Muswellbrook people – and then imagine stories in which they were all shuffled together.

The melodrama of Dickens and *The History of the British Nation* left me at times with the fear that I might end up in the workhouse or on the executioner's block in the Tower of London, but it was Dickens's sense of the comic that most affected me: in what usually seemed the certainty of my own life, to make a joke of things was what seemed of supreme importance. To talk about the things one respected most it was sometimes necessary to make fun of them. Thus if I wanted Mum to take some interest in *The History of the British Nation*, I made a joke of it. We giggled at these peculiar people in their old-fashioned clothes making this ridiculous fuss – beheading people, burning them and the like – all over nothing. If you could make a joke of things everything seemed more comfortable. At school I preferred the boys and girls who liked to have fun; at home I liked to do imitations of people to amuse Mum and Dad; and at Denbigh I was so surrounded by jocularity that an important way of distinguishing between one person and another was to categorise their sense of humour. Most of the Carpenters were laconic in their humour: Uncle Loy, for instance, was a master of the wry humour of the trenches, front-line wit, clipped like his moustache and cropped as close as his hair: but the people they married and our other relations practised other types of humour – chiacking and leg pulling, sardonic anecdotes, jolliness and exuberance, wise-cracking, cheerful vulgarity, ruminative humour, crazy inconsequence, and gentle observations of absurdity. We abhorred whingers who could not laugh at their misfortunes. I detested all serious people, seeing them as strait-laced sobersides who had nothing to say.

Except when I feared the workhouse I had as strong a sense of my past and my future as anyone could have in even the most static society. I saw myself as being happily just one of the smaller people stitched into a huge tapestry that on my mother's side was so crammed with figures I could not see them all; although on my father's side it was almost bare, with only a couple of younger cousins stitched in. Behind me, where the tapestry stretched back beyond sight, the first people I could see were Great-Great-Great-Grandfather Mileham, who arrived in the colony as a surgeon in 1797, and Great-Great-Great-Grandfather Sellar, who worked at the convict settlement at Norfolk Island. With a face of granite, Great-Great-Grandmother Howell, 'hard' in the family fashion, was sitting at the head of a table; Great-Grandfather Carpenter was leaning back in his chair with an insolent smile; Great-Grandmother Carpenter was on her knees in prayer; Great-Great-Aunt Lloyd was discussing the Western Front with generals and bishops in London; Great-Aunt Lila was galloping her horse across the paddock; a host of Sellars were on their building sites, constructing bits of Sydney; Grandfather John Horne was founding a co-operative society in his Hunter Valley mining town; my unknown Uncles Horne were in their new uniforms, off to the war; and closer to me all my Denbigh relations and Muswellbrook friends were laughing at my jokes.

*

My life was to be a matter of moving from classroom to classroom. I had moved from first class in the main school building to second, third, fourth and fifth classes in the 'portables' that surrounded the playground. At the age of eleven I was now back in the main building, in sixth class, preparing for the Primary Final examination. To go to high school I would leave all my friends behind me (they would leave school at fourteen) and accept a new continuity in which for five years I would again move predictably from classroom to classroom. Then I would go to Sydney University, take an Arts degree, spend a year training at Teachers' College, and become a teacher like my father, although, being a high-school teacher, of a higher grade. There was nothing unpredictable about this, since there was no doubt that I would pass the necessary examinations.

However, this sense of progress was to be disturbed. Dad tried to conceal his sensitivity by irony and wit, but somewhere in the process of pulling himself up into the world he had come to express belief in truth and in knowledge for its own sake. He was not learned and he had little natural curiosity of his own. But his life would have lost some of its meaning if he had not believed that he was encouraging curiosity in me and encouraging me to speak 'the truth as I saw it'. He had chanced to read an article on modern education in the *Cassell's Book of Knowledge,* and when he began to think of writing the thesis that might gain him promotion he copied it into an exercise book. He did not write his thesis, but in his handling of me he had decided that what they said in *Cassell's* was true: education was growth. None of us knew what this meant, but the practical effect of this belief was that while I was still expected from various quarters to pay respect to God and the King by obeying orders, dressing neatly, writing neatly, talking neatly, thinking neatly, and emptying my bowels daily after breakfast, and to pay respect to Jesus by showing some consideration for other people's feelings, and to pay respect to the Anzac heroes by not whingeing and by always doing the right thing, along with this I was also expected to *be myself* ('You have to be *yourself,* Don,' my mother would say), read, ask questions, tell the truth, and always say what I thought. (But if I wrote 'shit' on a chocolate box I would get a belting.)

Dad's admonitions to me to express myself meant that I was encouraged not only to enjoy exercising my wits by regurgitating on demand what I had learned: I was also encouraged in my eagerness to invent things of my own. Like my mother, I could bounce around, impatient to find out what I might do next. I liked to air my views in school lecturettes, at Sunday teas at Denbigh and the like. Then there came a new opportunity: with my teacher's co-operation I was able to run a drama club, with its headquarters at our house and its principal performing space at school.

Several years earlier, before my piano lessons had begun, I had taken a year's elocution lessons from Miss Alma Doepell, who, with a name like that of a character in a novel, and a supply of exotic shawls and fans and an assured and professionally modulated voice, seemed the most 'cultivated' person I knew. I would visit Miss Doepell once a week in her 'studio' (a large room at the top of one of Muswellbrook's oldest stone houses, which she also used as a living apartment) and there I would be trained in posture, gesture and how to speak with expression; I would recite the special exercises she gave me (full of tongue twisters) and when she thought I was ready for it, she began giving me a new 'piece' every week, which I was to learn and then recite to her the next week, with the appropriate gestures and expressions. After a year it was considered that elocution lessons had nothing new to teach me and I was put on to piano lessons. But now I had a whole repertoire. 'Don's recitations' became one of the regular turns at Denbigh, when at one of the large gatherings I would be asked to stand up and 'recite something'; 'Mick' and I put them into concerts; they were used at children's parties at Muswellbrook; and once a year, at the annual concert of Miss Doepell's students (piano, violin, elocution), as well as doing a very uncertain turn at the piano I would put on an assured performance as Muswellbrook's best schoolboy reciter, enjoying the uncertain delights of applause.

This assurance made me feel the star of the few plays we put on at school (seen in the syllabus as an encouragement of 'self-expression') and gave me the idea that I would produce a show on my own. I decided to turn Charles Lamb's *A Dissertation on Roast Pig* into a play. My friend Rosemary Hart would be my collaborator and we would rehearse in the large space under the house. Our mothers made our costumes and we made the scenery at home, lugging it in several journeys through the streets of Muswellbrook to the schoolroom for an after-school dress rehearsal before the great day of the first performance. The show was so successful that we put it on for other classes – with such praise that the girls who were my two main competitors in the tests joined us in forming a drama club to produce other shows. Later, even a couple of boys joined in, although usually, since we had so few boys, girls had to play some of the male parts. Our plays became part of the school's routine. When we put on a special performance for the annual visit of the school inspector our teacher's obvious talent for cultivating self-expression helped gain her promotion.

As entrepreneur, author, producer and chief character actor of our group I could see a clear road ahead for my own 'self-expression'. It was not about my cleverness but about our drama club that I was vain. I was bossy with the members of it, a show-off who wanted to get things right so that the audience would applaud, but wondering whether they meant it. But sometimes I could feel afraid that as an only child I might be 'spoiled'. When I looked around me it could sometimes seem necessary to ask if showing off was what God, King, Jesus and the Anzacs expected of me.

The audience reaction about which I became most vain, however, occurred when one of the teachers, as punishment for my making fun of the way he said 'Left, right, left, right' in the playground, told me to stay in after school for three consecutive afternoons. I was to write on the first afternoon a page composition beginning with the word 'left' and ending with the word 'right', on the second afternoon another composition which began with 'right' and ended with 'left' and on the third afternoon a third composition that began with 'left, right' and ended with 'right, left'. I wrote all of them in the one afternoon and he was so pleased with them that he took them home and kept them. This was really holding an audience.

To Dad the world of action, with its necessary calculations and assessments of the use of fraud, was a mystery. We would often compare him favourably with Uncle Candy as our materially most successful relative who had made a whole philosophy based on being sharp-witted. The result was that from an early age I was to regard business, politics, success and the whole conduct of affairs as the discreditable side of human activity. There were the ordinary decent people, making their own fun; and – with an occasional exception like Cincinnatus or Harun al-Rashid – there were the rogues and survivors, the expediency men, the con-men, the cheats. Disinterest was what mattered – doing things as a service for others or for their own sake, with no reward. Although Dad believed that the men who had volunteered to fight the Hun or the Turk were the only real men in Australia, he also despised ex-soldiers who tried to cash in on their war service. Volunteering to fight was simply doing the right thing: it was not done in any sense of reward. The simple innocence of his theory of outspokenness, independence and utter honesty appealed to me so much that by the time I had reached adolescence in Sydney I argued with him most of the time, saying what I thought. Finally it was almost impossible for us to have any conversation about anything.

'It is my desire to do great things ...'

The family moved back to Sydney and D.H. attended high school. D.H.'s father, afflicted by deafness and a nervous condition linked to his war service, spent some time in a psychiatric hospital. This piece, reproduced in The Education of Young Donald, *is from a diary D.H. kept at the time.*

Friday, 7th January 1938

TIME HAS PASSED SINCE LAST I TOOK UP PEN TO this book – much of it has been unhappy time – time without hope some of it – and I look to the future with hope in my heart that this year, at least, I shall be spared misery. To relate my personal experiences through the year would be tiring and difficult and unnecessary. Therefore I shall busy myself with the present. This year I sit for the Leaving Certificate and I see a year overcrowded with work ahead of me, too much work. It is my aim to get an 'A' pass in Latin, French, Chemistry, Maths I & II and First Class Honours in English and History. Whether I shall accomplish this the future alone can tell. And then, after this, my last year at school, what? It is my desire to do great things, but I have not yet decided what great things. At present I tell people my ambition is the law – but hardly anyone is enthusiastic. My ambition is not the law; it is to use the law as a stepping-stone to Parliament. I regard lawyers as useless things, for what good is ever done for civilisation in a law court? But then I have other positions in mind. If I knew I could write well, I should write. But I am afraid that, if I wrote, the stuff I should write might not bring me much in the way of money – on the other hand it might. If I write I want to write literature. I want to write for Australian Literature too. But by that, I do not mean copy Henry Lawson or this piffle-monger Thwaites or such people as Idriess (he has never written Literature). And then I may become a university lecturer or a journalist. And so the list goes on.

D.H. finished The Education of Young Donald, *describing himself as a 'rebellious and (so it seemed to most people) entirely objectionable university student' and, at times, 'D.R. Horne, angry shouter' ran rampant. He would later write more volumes of autobiography. D.H. had called* The Education of Young Donald *a 'sociography' but, as he later said on the ABC, 'If you take writing an autobiography seriously and make it more than a mere memoir it can have a strong personal effect on you. I found all that sifting around into the hopes and fears of my own past had a final effect curiously, like confession and absolution.' Manning Clark, his ears perhaps still ringing from an angry review that D.H. had done of his* Meeting Soviet Man *wrote, in* Overland, *'He, who managed somehow to survive possession by that evil spirit, must now get back to the roots of his life which, one suspects, he rediscovered while writing this deeply moving account of his early days.'*

University

2

JOHN ANDERSON AND THE ANDERSONIANS

The Education of Young Donald was written at a time when D.H. was a successful author, having published two books that did very well, but it wasn't always like that. This piece was written at age thirty-six, and published in the Observer, *1958, when D.H. saw himself as a 'failure' because he had not yet published a book. He wrote himself back to the kind of life where, to use the language of the optimistic teenager, he might do 'great things'. Here he writes about the influential philosopher John Anderson, without using the detached style of his autobiography.*

SOME PEOPLE HAVE RECURRENT EXAMINATION NIGHTmares; I have a recurrent John Anderson nightmare. I am an undergraduate again, addressing the Sydney University Literary Society, opening a discussion with a paper of unparalleled brilliance that appears at last to have solved a great problem in aesthetics and pushed the immense frontiers of truth forward an eighth of an inch. The meeting is, of course, being held in the Philosophy Room. Behind me on the wall on either side of the blackboard are murals of Socrates, Plato, Aristotle, Descartes, Spinoza and Bacon. Beside me, as chairman, is John Anderson; he is taking a lot of notes. The paper is finished and Anderson opens the discussion; he attacks with a full blast; he detects idealist confusions in every second line of what I have said; I have probably even committed the fallacy of the undistributed middle; I am routed. The violence comes. Oliver Somerville attacks me with a knife; Jack Lynn has a revolver; Bruce Nield is laughing.

The violence wakes me up. But it is not fear but the immense sadness of exclusion, expulsion from a group and the resulting derision that stays with me for a few moments until I come properly to my senses. The dream can take other forms; indeed I suffer from other kinds of expulsion nightmares, but this is the strongest. It was certainly the first, because before I belonged to the Freethought Society (to which the Literary Society was a kind of ladies' auxiliary) I had not, with the exception of a brief schoolboy flirtation with the British Empire and the Communion of Saints, ever belonged to anything. To someone who was rebellious, but still craved to 'belong', Anderson and the Freethought Society were Anarchy's own gift.

I was considered with distrust by Lynn, Nield and Somerville, who at that stage constituted the quadrangle wing of the Freethought Society. Lynn still had a touch of The Revolution and used to browbeat us by proclaiming himself a Leninist; Nield was given to psychoanalysing anyone who professed an interest in literary matters; and Somerville had an intuitive distrust of me as a person of petty bourgeois inclinations (clean shirts and that kind of thing) that did credit to his intuition. I remember attending a discussion group on anarchism that was held by Somerville in the University Park in which I did not understand a word that was said; I must have attended a few (more orthodox) Freethought Society meetings, but I do not remember them; I remember volunteering with some effrontery to address the Freethought Society myself, then, realising that I had nothing to say, getting drunk instead of attending the meeting.

But there was a great deal of talk about Anderson among the fringe Andersonians with whom I seemed to find it easier to mix; I spent large parts of the summer vacation reading Joyce, Trotsky, Freud and back numbers of the *Philosophy Journal*; I began my second year in Arts by joining the Philosophy One classes and becoming secretary of the Freethought Society (perhaps because there was no one else who would paint and put up notices of meetings).

Memory now becomes clearer. There was the feeling of fearlessness (opinion must follow its own rules and damn the consequences); of pure truth untouched by human hands; of power (transmitted from a Glaswegian voice, passing temporarily from pencil to paper, and then being absorbed into the body for ever and ever); of being accepted (but I was scared stiff that I would put a step wrong one day and become disaccepted); and of exclusive revelation (it was impossible for non-Andersonian statements to be accepted seriously).

For one seeking the feeling of belonging the rewards were Spartan. Within the group there was a hardness in social relation that reminded me sadly of playground bullying; the principal younger Andersonians seemed to use their beliefs as protective weapons. Friendship did not seem to exist. There was such an artificiality and restraint that it was an impossibly brittle intellectual community; when it did relax it just broke down into badinage or suburban vulgarity. Anderson himself says he has no small talk. His most wholehearted younger supporters at this stage went further than that; they had no conversation. This was too much; I began to feel that I would never make the higher grade; that I was essentially the sign-writer and notice-hanger; I began to drift away into a group of our own that was fringe Andersonian, but liked to talk, too. The next year I had very little to do with the Freethought Society, but managed to take over the Literary Society.

All the same, I still considered myself an 'Andersonian'. (I don't know whether Anderson shared this belief; I did not speak to him often and I was too overawed when I did to make much sense), and I now had a set of beliefs and an approach to questions. This was probably my university education; I cannot even now believe that a better one was offering. All the other alternatives seemed incoherent, compromised. It was its complete lack of compromise that made Andersonianism – and by this one means the whole complex, of course, not just the philosophy lectures – both so attractive and so valuable. The intellectual attitude does not grow on trees in Sydney; for three decades Anderson has been Sydney University's conscience. It was here that the lack of compromise was good. To all matters one learned that the intellectual approach was to override every consideration with the simple questions: what are the facts about this? Are these arguments valid?

He is a philosopher, but it is as an educator that Anderson has perhaps had the most influence – not only on the Andersonians themselves, but on the many other people to whom his intellectual attitude meant the break from suburbia and their entry into intellectual life. I can think of dozens of people – and I do not mean academics – who are busy applying to affairs or problems some of the attitudes that he liberated in them; he would probably despise them for it. In his own university there is hardly a professor in the Faculty of Arts who, however little he knows of Anderson's philosophy or his radical beliefs, has not been affected by his long struggle for the maintenance of academic standards. Anderson would certainly not have had any of this influence if he had learned the art of compromise; so many other people know that.

3

A TIME OF SADNESS

From the Observer, *1958. Poet James McAuley and D.H. had a long association, which included McAuley reading some of D.H.'s manuscripts, including* The Education of Young Donald. *Their relationship became frosty at the time of the 1975 constitutional crisis shortly before McAuley's death.*

IT WAS DEPRESSING TO READ THAT A.D. HOPE, JAMES McAuley and Judith Wright are now part of an Australian Establishment. That is the kind of statement that makes you glance desperately at the mirror as you realise how quickly time is running out. I still think of McAuley, for example, as a brilliant old man of twenty-two (I was seventeen) whose overwhelming genius was acknowledged by only a small privileged group who had spent much of their university days sitting in the quadrangle. In so far as he was known to the literary elites then prevailing, he was considered by them to be too troublesome, too intellectual, too experimental, too young. Orthodoxy ('Establishment' did not exist with a capital 'E') then spelt out those three aged and respectable characters Kenneth Slessor, Robert Fitzgerald and Douglas Stewart. These three were, of course, already in their decline, exhausted by their many years; one used to linger slightly over each syllable of their names with delicate derision. It was felt that McAuley's talents would perhaps never be recognised in Sydney but that, as soon as he was published, London, New York and Paris would buzz with his name. To think of him as part of the Establishment reminds one that this was nineteen years ago, not now. Things have worked out differently since then.

It is a little difficult for me to recall what McAuley was like then. I was too young, too impressionable and too much under his spell. The impression of a spell certainly remains. To the susceptible, McAuley was a charmer; he even had the hypnotist's mannerisms – a significant stiffening of the hand, the careful gesture, lowered eyelids raised for the piercing stare, face muscles well controlled to register significant emotions. The belief in his genius was universal among those with whom he mixed; and he did not mix with the others. To the shrewd observer those were already signs that if McAuley possessed genius it was likely to be a restricted one – his range of interest in human activity and in literary forms was narrow although his stamina in the business of being a poet was already evident; but who is a shrewd observer at that age? We believed in genius and it was nice to know one. This setting apart of McAuley as a person of exceptional talent has probably done him great harm.

Another thing one looks back on is the feeling of exclusiveness that surrounded McAuley; it was a privilege to be 'in', to receive the right encouragement and the right smile. This was a rather subtle thing; any form of organised overt groupishness was out. There was a general (but usually unexpressed) distaste for the meretricious cultural activity that other people engaged in; this distaste could be taken merely as preciousness, but it was in fact contempt for the second rate and a loathing of pretension, a questioning of motives and a suspicion that most people who engaged in cultural activity were impostors. It applied not only to Australia; Eliot was taken to have betrayed poetry for Anglo-Catholicism and Auden and Spender were considered to be literary spivs. It was a kind of literary puritanism;

its strength was one of the reasons why McAuley had made the grade. It was, perhaps, narrow-minded, implacable and ruthless, but those are the characteristics of young men or young reform movements on the way up; what was being reformed is, nineteen years later, no longer clear. I can no longer remember what all the fuss was about; it merely left me with a distrust of all cultural activity, good or bad.

Hope and Harold Stewart were McAuley's only equals in this group that was afraid even to recognise its existence as a group because to do so might seem pretentious. They were three Major Poets and that was all that was important. To be a poet was somehow everything. Novels were crude, unimportant stuff; so, indeed, was all prose. You could resort to prose if you weren't a poet, perhaps, but it was not a significant medium of communication; this attitude probably accounts for the fact that when these three try to say something outside verse they usually write rather badly. They write prose as duchesses help with the washing-up. But their attitude to poetry did more than foul up their prose; it restricted their lives by giving to poetry an overwhelming importance that just could not be sustained. At this distance I can no longer remember why poetry was so important.

To those who now regard McAuley as a clerical fascist hyena it may come as a surprise to know that he was then a fairly orthodox liberal as, indeed, on some important issues, despite the fierce face he now pulls, he still is. But even at that stage the enthusiasms of the 1930s had turned sour. John Anderson was there to protect everyone from the illusions of Stalinism and was already developing that rebellious scepticism towards progressivist doctrines that has given a distinctive mark to generations of Sydney graduates and made them such troublesome people for everybody else to understand. It is fundamentally Anderson's attitude to progress, not the Pope's, that marks McAuley's present attitude to politics; that is why he is now so generally misunderstood and why even the sincerity of his motives are questioned. But the weird ways in which Andersonianism has produced so many different results merit a study of its own. All that need be said here is that we just did not accept the proposition that because a thing is new it is good. And when you think of some of the new things that have happened in those nineteen intervening years I do not think we were wrong.

Despite the parties, and the jazz and the jokes, the prevailing memory of that time is one of enervating sadness. In much of what he wrote McAuley was very sad indeed; his love's beauty would fade, the house next door was burned down, everything was change and decay. Even about McAuley himself there was a suggestion that at twenty-two his best days were over; I suffered from the perennial undergraduate sense of having just missed out on a Golden Age; that if I had only been a few years older I would really have learned what it was like to live in those far distant days of three or four years before when McAuley was really in his prime. One suffered endlessly from a sense of loss; 1939 was too late, Australia was too remote, nothing happened anymore; we just lived out our middle class or lower middle class lives and soon we would all die. But at least great things might come from Jimmy McAuley. Being sad was not in my nature but for three years I did the best I could to be as sad as I could about everything I could think of, talking wistfully out of the corner of my mouth in a low voice so that no one could hear what I had to say. It took some time to get over the idea that one had to be sad about things. Even now one feels the temptation to feel sad that one is no longer seventeen and no longer believes quite so fundamentally in McAuley. Perhaps the thing to be sad about is that McAuley has now become rather modest and is always these days so infernally bright and cheerful.

4

YOU MADE WHAT YOU LIKED OF ME, BOYS

D.H. wrote this poem in 1941 after losing the editorship of the student newspaper, near the end of his time as a student; within a month he was conscripted into the army.

> You made what you liked of me, boys,
> But you didn't make me your friend
> For I lived in a world full of toys
> And discontent, played without end.
>
> My style was to reach for the moon
> In a poem or two full of death,
> Or talk for an afternoon
> Until I ran out of breath,
>
> To make my friends by the dozen
> And talk to them late in the night,
> To eat all the food in their pantries
> And never turn out the light.
>
> My life was a half-tone screen,
> Dotted and broken at heart.

People could make nothing of it,
It wasn't significant art.

Make who you like of me, boys,
Make what you can of me, do.
You'll get no reward for your trouble.
My father's not in Who's Who.

I made my friends by the dozen
And talked to them late in the night
And all they got for their kindness
Was a bill for electric light.

For I sold my soul to the devil
In a temper, some time ago,
For a pot of pride and a mirror
And I knew I'd have to go.

I put on a show for you, boys,
That cannot be put on again
For now they've packed up the toys
That I used, in default, for a brain.

RADICAL
CONSERVATIVE

5

SOME CULTURAL ELITES IN AUSTRALIA

From Angry Penguins, *1945, pp. 133–34. An early piece by the future chairman of Australia's main government-funded arts body.*

Selling us the Australian cultural renaissance seems to be one of the conditions of existence of 'cultural' magazines in Australia. Max Harris, for example, wrote in the last issue of *Angry Penguins*:

> In my opinion, up to this time a surge of literary vigour and cultural ferment was taking place in this country without parallel before in its history. Literature was developing with an energy and fervour of which the country might well be proud – *Meanjin Papers, Poetry, Comment, Southerly, Jindyworobak, New Writing* all forging ahead along their particular lines of development. *Angry Penguins* was a part of an advancing national culture.

According to *New Writing* a new period of 'social awakening' was on – a 'ferment such as we have not known for 50 years'. The final comment on *New Writing* was provided by a review of it in *Education*, the organ of the NSW Teachers' Federation: 'A vigorous and lively collection – not only a valuable contribution to Australian literature generally, but to the war effort in particular.'

Lloyd Ross says: 'The Australian cultural scene shows many signs of bursting into bloom as glorious and adventurous as the hopeful days of the nineties.'

And so it goes on.

The shoddiness of this renaissance comes out in the statements of its supporters. Some think it provides a fresh hope for the nation's future. Since when have intellectual movements had anything to do with the nation? What a simple view of society this reveals! Would Arthur Calwell give James Joyce a job? Intellectuals and artists have nothing to do with governments or nations except at very rare moments in history. Sometimes they can successfully swindle the State, get a good job out of it on their own conditions, but usually it is their greatest enemy.

Max Harris says 'the country' might well be proud of the current renaissance. Why so? Any worthwhile movement in Australia is almost always attacked by the powerful pressure groups that constitute 'the country'. Why worry anyway? Don't try to pander to the 'country'. Please yourself. If what you write happens to be popular – good. If it doesn't – too bad. 'An advancing national culture,' says Max. Really! A culture of the horseracing-going public perhaps. Max also speaks of all of these wonderful publications 'forging ahead on their particular lines of development' as if somehow they all belonged to the same thing: it doesn't matter much what you publish so long as you publish. But it isn't activity which matters. Activity describing itself as cultural is worthless unless it really does belong to the great cultural traditions.

Along with the myth of cultural renaissance we find the myth of service. Writing in *Meanjin*, Clem Christesen seems to have a functional theory of the artist. The artist has a given role in the organism of the state, e.g., 'Now is the time for re-creation, the rebuilding not of the city or town but of the nation. Towards the achievement of that end, the artist can make his significant contribution.'

It reads like a politician's speech, but there it is. In answer I should say simply that the artist has his own responsibilities. He has responsibilities to his own work. 'The Nation' can go to the devil – that is not part of his business. (It is about time that someone told Christesen that a word such as 'nation' has no clear and exact meaning and that anyone using such a vague word falls under suspicion of being a charlatan. It is a politician's word – as meaningless and as dangerous as 'the common good'. All of these words are completely discredited in social theory, surely.)

In so far as the artist has anything to do with those matters of re-creation and rebuilding (note the simple-minded rationalist, voluntaristic character of much of Christesen's reasoning) his 'role' is that of the demolition expert. This place doesn't need any more builders and creators among its intellectuals – there are enough of those, God knows – you can see them falling over each other trying to get the sweet jobs. What this place needs are some WRECKERS. Wreckers of shoddy thinking, religious prejudices, polite claptrap, colonial provincialism and all of the unlovely, unlovely slums on the local landscape.

In *Meanjin* Christesen lets his hair down and really lets us in on what has already been 'achieved'. 'Proposals', he says, for Commonwealth, state and municipal co-operation in a number of social projects have been 'placed' before the Prime Minister. But that is not all. No! We are beyond the proposal stage, us. Preliminary meetings have been called by the Department of Post-War Reconstruction with the object of establishing a Commonwealth Cultural Council and a National Films Board. And even more: departmental handouts have been issued to the press. The public spirit, he concludes, has been aroused.

John Anderson in an excellent article on 'The Servile State' in a 1943 issue of the *Philosophy Journal* (and here is a magazine from which *Meanjin* might well learn a lesson in proper intellectual responsibility) points to the weakness in the kind of case that Christesen presents, in one sentence: 'Planners in general miss or conceal the fact that planning can advance only what can be *planned for* – and that is not culture but commerce.' He then shows how planning for education can only mean commercialising education despite all the demagogic claims made for a body such as the Universities Commission.

Who really thinks that you can plan a literary movement? It just grows up. Certainly certain conditions are necessary for its survival – and one of these is free speech. Complete free speech – that's what we want here. A guarantee that nobody can be prosecuted for saying anything. That will do more than five hundred committees. Don't rely on governments and preliminary meetings – rely on yourself. This country is becoming a nation of bludgers and time servers – and its intellectuals are showing the way.

The cultural elites of this country are hot with the culture. So hot that they are keen to give it to the masses. Yet their social theory is, I think, even more primitive than that of the masses if for no other reason than that they lack the elementary cynicism that the masses have. If Australia is about to have a cultural renaissance it certainly won't be in the field of social theory.

What is needed is a complete and thorough debunking of all these 'leaders'.

6

THE GREAT CRISIS OF THE GOLDEN AGE

From the Daily Telegraph, *1948. Actors' Equity was arguing that too much hardship would be inflicted on announcers by asking them to press the buttons on the new fans that had been installed in the studios of a Sydney radio station. The following piece of satire connected that item of recent news with Ben Chifley's vision for a planned 'Golden Age' for Australia.*

It was the 110th year of the Golden Age and the Government was facing a great social revolution.

This is what had happened:

Even before the Trade Union cult became the state religion, the complicated problems of who should push what button had disappeared from industry.

In the early days many serious inter-union disputes had arisen about which union's members should start or stop electric gadgets. These disputes came to a head when a member of Politicians' Equity objected to the hardship of pushing buttons to open irrigation schemes, underground railways, child guidance clinics, wars – and other symptoms of civilisation.

Faced with a complaint from so distinguished a quarter the Conciliation Commissioner to conciliate Conciliation Commissioners made a final ruling. This Conciliation Commissioner didn't fool around. He got right to the root of the evil. He abolished all privately owned buttons as a wicked relic of the long-discredited system of private enterprise, and ordered that all button-pushing was to be centralised – in the common good, and to preserve the rights of unionists to confine their activities to their duties as legally defined.

In his wisdom, this Conciliation Commissioner later extended his ruling to cover electric switches, gas and water taps. The order in which he gave this boon to humanity began:

> With all reference to all buttons, switches, levers, taps, and all other instruments and contrivances whatsoever used for the purpose of inaugurating or terminating the passage of electric and/or other currents, water and/or other liquids, gas and/or other vapours, and of all other forms, categories, sub-categories, or types of publicly reticulated services it is ordered that all such buttons etc. and all such other instruments and/or contrivances whatsoever as are privately owned or controlled or privately caused to be controlled shall henceforth be declared to be forbidden implements and shall not be manipulated or caused to be manipulated in any manner except by the Public Authority (henceforth known as 'The Authority') hereunder constituted.

This order later became famous as a perfect example of the bureaucratic literary style, the language of progress, which had been evolving in Australia since 1940 A.D. Children memorised it as they once memorised Shakespeare and Henry Kendall; the Speaker opened Parliament with it instead of prayers; the *Government Gazette* (the only paper, of course) reprinted it in full every Nationalisation Day.

But the inevitable grumblers, in whom the Satanic doctrines of liberalism died hard, attacked this historic order. Typical of their trivial arguments:

'It is inconvenient to have a remote official turn our fans on and off when he feels like it rather than when we feel hot or cold.'

'It isn't much trouble to turn a fan on anyway.'

These subversive wretches failed to realise the important principle at stake.

They even sneered when officials patiently explained that to have a public authority turn the gas supplies on or off at its discretion was better than to leave this job to the Gasworkers' Union, which had turned supplies off pretty regularly in the first years of the Golden Age.

But these saboteurs soon gave in.

They realised that the Golden Age was not going to produce much gas or electricity, anyway, and the question of who turned non-existent supplies on or off was only an academic quibble.

The Great Button-Pushing Order initiated a general revision of all industrial awards to eliminate the possibility of a unionist doing anything except his strictly defined duties. Some of these new orders were so successful that they eliminated the possibility of a unionist doing anything at all.

Other orders were not so successful. It was difficult to define exactly the duties of workers in some rather complicated industries. Disputes arose in these industries. Finally the Government intervened with a brilliant solution.

It abolished the industries. That put an end to the problems of definition.

In thinking up this solution the Government had followed its basic economic rule: 'It is better to forbid a complex activity than to leave it partly uncontrolled.'

Even this solution failed in the troublesome primary industries.

Economic purists insisted that if the strict division of labour could not be applied to the primary industries, then the primary industries must go.

But there was an unreasonable uproar at this suggestion, and reactionary, conservative influences protected the primary industries from the abolition they deserved.

These primary industries, despite their ephemeral economic importance, had always been a hotbed of reaction.

So the Government had another brilliant idea. It had many criminals on its hands – carpenters who had painted, floor sweepers who had scrubbed, surgeons who had prescribed medicine, Philosophy professors who had studied history.

It decided to dump these undesirables in the country.

And it worked out perfect forms of punishment for them.

It would leave them to their own resources, completely unprotected by the state. Nobody would save them from working more than twenty hours a week, nobody would save them from doing more than one kind of job.

This meant that they might find themselves in the horrible position of milking a cow one minute and mending a cowshed the next, of passing from fence-mending to rabbit-poisoning in the one day.

They were to make their own arrangements about paying doctors' bills, and seeing themselves through their old age. As youngsters, if they wanted education, they would have to study for it.

But even this brilliant government idea did not succeed as it deserved.

When the Government decided to make rural areas a penal colony, all kinds of malcontents, renegades and disruptionists hastened to get convicted of shocking offences – working in their leisure, absconding from Community Centre meetings, giving cheek to union bosses.

This produced a constant rush of people from the cities – the religious citadels of unionism – to the savage backblocks. By the 110th year of the Golden Age this flow had become so great that some of the unions had lost all their members except the paid secretaries.

7

AMBITION

From an unpublished paper, probably delivered in Sydney in 1959, possibly to the WEA, an adult education group.

I WAS ALWAYS BROUGHT UP TO CONSIDER AMBITION AS A dirty word; I never received any sane, healthy Ambition Instruction; I used to furtively envy the sons and daughters of enlightened parents who had enjoyed Ambition Instruction, and who were able to display their ambitions naturally; of course I could not openly praise them – I projected my own ambition frustrations, anxieties and guilt into the form of condemnation of their ambition displays. This repression was, if anything, accentuated in my early adult life when I mixed exclusively with puritan groups who condemned ambition even more severely than my parents had done. But already by this stage two horrible truths were beginning to make themselves evident to me and they both suggested that everywhere the filthy practice of Ambition was raising its ugly head. The first was the growing suspicion that, although no one talked about it, some of my friends were engaged in secret ambition fantasies and were even beginning to practise ambition privately. The second was that – try as I might – I could not quite keep my hands off it and I was having ambition fantasies myself.

My innocence of ambition was not altogether strange. There is something of a conspiracy of silence about ambition in modern literature. Ambition is a theme of some of the older writings but to the innocent young it seems to be a characteristic of a special class of human being. Ambition is part of the subject matter of history and biography but it often gets rather rough treatment; it becomes too black and white because historians and biographers tend to judge personalities by the effects of their actions, giving them much more rationality than they possess; or it is excluded altogether in the kind of approach that takes a purely social, or even economic, view of events.

Yet people are always making judgements about what other people are doing with their lives in relation to what they want to be doing with them or 'ought' to be doing with them. The judgements are often quite nonsensical because they are not based on any detailed kind of observation at all, but merely on gossipy generalisations. Indeed, this kind of thing can be one of the preoccupations of the intellectual classes although it is usually carried out in a nonintellectual way. The nonsensical nature of it is due more than anything else to the fact that there is no recognition of the multiplicity of ambition. Yet one can talk only of kinds of ambition. One man is not likely to be describable in terms of only one of the kinds of ambition. His overt conduct may seem to make this possible but experience suggests that a man is usually a battleground of conflicting ambitions. Certainly he cannot necessarily be described by the kind of ambition that seems to have been satisfied. The satisfaction of ambitions rests partly on the fluke of opportunity. Hitler would have been quite happy if he had become an architect of houses rather than the dis-architect of Europe. Reading his endless intellectual blather in the book *Hitler's Table Talk* one can just imagine this successful architect of violent intellectual opinion boring his after-dinner guests with his crack-brained ideas of what he would do with the world. This is worth remembering next time you have dinner with an architect who has views about the world. I have made this point not to suggest that Hitler cannot be described by what he did to the world but to suggest that lots of other people could be described in the same way, except for the fact that their success as something else has obscured the point.

Ambitions are closely connected to fantasy structures. When the fluke opportunity means that the wrong ambition wins this does not necessarily tell one much about the person concerned. Successful men in their forties are often characterised by a deep sense of failure and frustration which puzzles unsuccessful men in their twenties. The explanation often is that the wrong ambition won and they don't know what to do about it.

One confusion into which one can fall when talking about ambition is this definition of people's ambition structures in terms of what they have become. Another common confusion comes from the use of the word 'power', which is often used in a blanket sense to discredit men at the top. An examination of possible meaning for this word assumes final significance only in regard to the fantasy structures of those who use it. Instead of this one word I have prepared a pretty rough and ready list to cover the range of ambitions; not all of them are mutually exclusive; perhaps some of them are just different aspects of what is probably the same thing. But they are not all the same; some of them are in contradiction with each other. It would be a very frustrated and neurotic man in whom they all flourished in equal degree; it would be a superhumanly successful man in whom only one of them flourished. The list consists of Bigness, Manipulation, Money, Security, Comfort, Prestige, Acceptance, Excitement, Independence, Dominance, Leisure, Perfection, Achievement and Destruction.

[D.H. wrote this sketchy think-piece at a time when he was reviewing a number of books for the Observer *on how people*

AMBITION

become 'great'. It's of especial interest as a rare foray into the examination of psychological motives. By the time he wrote his autobiographies he had adopted a more behaviourist model, which didn't speculate on the inner workings of the mind. He is not writing about himself in this piece but, of the fourteen types of ambition described in the paper, here are listed four types that D.H. himself, in some respects only, might be said to have had.]

Excitement

[DH was not a 'practical man' in the sense used in this excerpt, nevertheless he said that his life had partly been a story of the management of his enthusiasms. When he started the Observer, *he used 'On s'engage et puis on voit' as a rallying cry.]*

The importance of excitement in practical affairs and the seeking of excitement as an ambition is often ignored by intellectuals when they speak of successful men. Yet the love of risk taking, of gambles and sheer recklessness is so obviously a characteristic of some top people – and not only that but one of the main reasons why they were able to get to the top in the first place – that one wonders if some people become intellectuals partly because they are terrified at the thought of taking risks. Perhaps one of the real differences between certain kinds of intellectuals and certain kinds of practical men is their quite different attitude towards excitement; to an intellectual who does not know the thrills and uncertainties of trying to pull off a difficult practical achievement practical activity may seem senseless, except in terms of power or prestige – which may be despised. Yet the whole excitement of trying to pull things off by making decisions that involve risk is one of the stimuluses of creative ambition (that is to say ambition that is concerned with achievement and not mere position, or the rewards of position).

The Napoleonic maxim '*On s'engage et puis – on voit*' (You commit yourself, and then – you see) is very much at the basis of a lot of practical decisions. It is the waiting to see what happens after one has committed oneself to action that provides the excitement. In the preface to his translation of Sukhanov's *The Russian Revolution, 1917* Joel Carmichael says of Lenin:

> It must be clear that while having had a wholehearted faith in the general inevitability of a European and for that matter worldwide revolution, Lenin's actual seizure of power was essentially an act of boldness performed out of sheer high spirits. For there can be no doubt that ... he never thought socialism could possibly be realised in isolated, primitive Russia. Nor for that matter did anyone else ... The title of Lenin's last work was *On s'engage et puis on voit*. Fundamentally that is what Lenin did: he committed himself, and his party and his country, and perhaps the world, and then – but he died before seeing. As a man of action in a situation that demanded action he was bound to commit himself – and see.

Or as I said in the *Observer* when reviewing Brecht's *The Threepenny Novel*:

> Powerful men in capitalism, socialism, liberalism, fascism, communism and all the other 'systems' that provide struggles for power can be competitive, ruthless, frivolous and given to the thrill of the chase; they trample all over everybody else in the course of it but they do have a good time. From afar it probably all seems the same kind of thing, the same kind of people

galloping around in the same kind of way, the only difference being that different words come out of people's mouths according to whatever ideology has put them into the saddle. It is the failure to realise the great sense of fun that power can provide that makes most biographers such anaemic failures ... Anyone who has ever started anything can recapture in *The Threepenny Novel* all the brilliant improvisations, sleepless nights, cheerful doggedness, black despair, unexpected triumphs, sudden disasters and endless restless tossings and turnings of the difficult business of trying to pull something off.

Dominance

The drive for dominance is the desire to win arguments, to be combative. It can sometimes force those it drives towards independence because it is only from that position that the Dominance Man can survive. There are cases of people who battle their way up without even necessarily intending to get there simply because they are belligerent and have become good at winning when there are disagreements. The drive for dominance can be combined with most of the other drives (most obviously with bigness, manipulation, prestige, excitement, independence, achievement or destruction); but it has no necessary partners. The one drive with which it is impossible to see any connection with dominance except a neurotically ambivalent one is the drive for acceptance. Dominance *is* connected with the great desire to be the boss so that you can win all the arguments.

Achievement

The fact that some people are ambitious because they have an urge to get things done, that it makes them happy to achieve things they want to do and desperately unhappy if they fail (until they think of something else they want to do), is almost ignored in some intellectual discussion of ambition: this is carrying cynicism to the point of blindness. It is really rather ludicrous to have to say this, but one must point out that lots of people are ambitious because there are things they want to get done. These are all external things and they have nothing to do in themselves with securing power, prestige and all the rest of it although the securing of these other things may be necessary to getting things done, or may follow from getting them done, or a man who externalises his ambitions may nevertheless be intensely interested in money, acceptance, and some of the others.

Practicality is the way of going on of the Achievement Man. It is the matter of trying to get done certain external things you want to do – and judging yourself by your success or failure. It is a comparatively rare human characteristic. It is not concerned with the performance of set, routine tasks; anybody can do those if they set their minds to them. Nor is it to be confused with the ordinary idea of 'practical affairs' or of 'being practical' that some people use to describe what goes on outside their own fields of activity. In fact there are as many impractical men inside the field of what are described as 'practical affairs' as there are in the field of what are described as 'non-practical affairs'. It is here that one sometimes meets man at his most irrational and fanciful. People pick up telephones and put them down, write things on bits of paper, make journeys across the world, talk to each other across tables, fuss around with their papers until late in the night, work themselves up into nervous breakdowns and they can spend a whole lifetime engaged in these expressions of anxiety without achieving anything. It is only the Achievement Man who tortures himself by setting up objective standards of comparison, who needs some proof that he has got something done. All the rest are merely following established administrative formulas (that may lead to disaster because the conditions that originally generated the formulas have changed) or engaging in the satisfaction of ambitions other than achievement. For this reason much of the activity that goes on in organisations has nothing whatever to do with their declared purposes. Organisations are often carried on by a momentum of their own that gives an illusion of practicality. People think they are being practical because they are actually doing something – spending expenses, dictating memos, answering telephones, flying in aeroplanes – and because the organisation that pays them is in fact doing something. Only the Achievement Man cannot be content with mere activity.

But Achievement Men have their dangers and their idiocies. They have their idiocies because the drive for congratulations of oneself by external performance can mean that one performs anything at all or – and this is more likely – that one operates in whatever field it is that fate happens to bring along. The quality of achievement can be strained by its availability. Also, as innovators, Achievement Men have all the dangers of innovators as well as their blessings. They are likely to do any old thing at all because they happen to believe that it is connected with the thing they want to do; the thing they want to do may be impossible so that the effects of what they do are unpredictable. Lenin and Clement Attlee would be examples of Practical Men of this kind; their urge to action overwhelms their judgement. In politics Achievement Men can be conservatives but unfortunately it requires a very considerable sophistication to pull off this double; usually they are idealists – and that can mean trouble.

Destruction

An Achievement Man of the most blockbusting kind is usually associated with what has been called 'a creative gale of destruction', that constant dynamic upheaval, that élan vital which is the essential contribution of enterprise as distinct from management. But there can be as many equations between achievement and destruction as there can be between love and hate. Not only is destruction sometimes necessary for achievement but the man who employs the one to aid the other can enjoy both equally. Men who build up firms or parties or nations can enjoy the destructive side of competition and struggle – the weakening or eliminating of opponents – as much as they can enjoy the achievement to which this destruction may or may not be necessary. Some men feel it necessary to destroy their achievements once they have made them, making a great funeral pyre of them; others at least do so at times in desperate fantasy. But not only is the ambition to destroy linked – and sometimes necessarily linked – with the ambition to achieve, it can be an overriding ambition in its own right. In that sense Hitler, for example, enjoyed the perfect end; he destroyed others; then he destroyed himself. Sheer delight in destruction has flickered in all the left-wing movements of the century and has sometimes burst into terrible flames.

8

THE METAPHOR OF LEFTNESS

From Quadrant, *Winter 1962, as part of a* Quadrant *series, 'What is to be done?'*

It is typical of how tightly the phrase 'the Left' holds so many of us intellectuals that when *Quadrant* wanted to choose something that something should be done about, it chose the Australian Left. The thing I should like to see something done about is the Australian Right, because I am afraid that in due course it may keel over, submerging all the good parts, still perhaps staying afloat, bottom up and dangerous.

But since it is more fashionable to discuss the Left I must begin by saying I hope to heaven that some day it is destroyed. I mean this both metaphorically and literally. Metaphorically because it is going to continue to be an ideologically dangerous factor until it defines itself more exactly to exclude policies both of the enemies of humanity and freedom and of those conformists who wish to preserve pricked illusions as children sometimes save the flabby, wrinkled skins of burst balloons. And literally because such a redefinition of the Left would mean that some sections of the Left would destroy other sections of it so completely that it would become something different.

Short of this political slaughter we are left with a completely false metaphor in which the Left is an exclusive symbol of progressiveness, humanity, radicalism and freedom (when, in fact, some members of the Left are fundamentally enemies of all that the Left is supposed to stand for) and in which the Right is considered somehow to be the opposite of these standards (when, in fact, some members of it are more practically concerned with progress, humanity, radicalism and freedom than their opposite numbers).

There accrues to members of the Left, including many of the crooks, fools, opportunists and proto-assassins, some part of an aura of holiness, sincerity and historical inevitability; whereas members of the Right are assumed to be evil, insincere and mere obstacles to be swept away by the forces of history. If an intellectual is finally disgusted by the bad element of the Left and disgusted to the point of rejecting all the Left, he may do so – but according to the rules he should do it in private. He may become disillusioned, take to drink, make money, become cynical, or in some other way display himself as a victim of the system. But he is expected to give up politics altogether, to believe in nothing of any major practical import, to be a 'left-liberal'. To attack the Left publicly, or to support the Right as his choice between two evils, is to be insincere and corrupt. The following truth must be considered to be self-evident: one never attacks the Left except from self-interest.

The holiness of the Left comes from its generally unchallenged claim to attract to its aura all the liberating, humane or progressive movements in history. Historically, one could put up a good case for Mr Menzies being the heir of Pym and Hampden, Voltaire and Rousseau, Russell and Wilberforce. But the Left grabs the bourgeois reformists along with Spartacus and Wat Tyler because it claims to be the exclusive party of reform – even at times like the present in Australia when it has no agreed and immediate policy to reform anything.

It has acquired the reversion of the whole liberating movement of history, because until recently there were great economic and social problems inherent in emergent capitalism to which only the

THE METAPHOR OF LEFTNESS

Left paid any coherent ideological attention. These problems have produced the reform movements of our era, and since it talked about them incessantly the Left was the reform party. These problems have now been solved.

By solved I do not mean completely solved, but that they no longer appear to be grossly insoluble; we no longer feel hopeless about them; and such great reforms and changes have occurred, and such other great problems have emerged, that the problems of capitalism are no longer the great problems of the age.

I believe that the contribution of the Left to their solution has been greatly exaggerated. In some ways the Left was merely a symptom of the problems, a dramatisation of them rather than a solution. But even if this is not so, even if we gave the whole credit to the Left, this still means that the Left, generated and shaped by a set of problems that are now solved, may become peculiarly dangerous if it continues to behave as if these problems have not been solved and it still holds a copyright on the images of freedom, humanity and progress, when the problems of freedom, humanity and progress have changed in a way the Left will not acknowledge.

The two main problems that emergent capitalism presented are well known. There was the social problem of semi-starvation, exploitation and tyranny that was the workers' lot as the rich got richer and the poor got poorer. And there was the economic problem: capitalism looked as if it wouldn't work. Crises would become more frequent, greater and greater, until finally there was one crisis too many. Both a sense of humanity and a sense of efficiency called for a solution.

Some hoped for gradual amelioration and moderate government intervention; some wanted drastic state action; nearly all nailed on their platforms the inheritance of bourgeois freedom-loving. There were dreams of something called 'socialism', which it was unscientific to define, but which was inevitable. It was inevitable because, as inequality and crises increased, situations would emerge in which the 'working class', which was taken to possess semi-magical properties, would establish a classless society which would then establish a heaven on earth.

To most of us the latter half of this dream now seems so improbable that we may sometimes forget that Marx was right in his diagnosis. Things could not go on as they were. It was in his solutions that he proved to be wrong. He was right in seeing that the growing inequalities and crises of the early capitalist form of modern industrial society would destroy it. They did. Our present kind of 'mixed economy' or liberal-democratic state, or whatever it is, is not capitalism. It is the product of the social clashes that destroyed capitalism and its problems. The redistribution of wealth, combined with fast-growing productivity and accompanying social changes, have made inequality (unless by a sense of inequality you mean envy) a minor problem – still a problem, but a minor problem. And state intervention has so controlled the business cycle and softened risk that we can no longer speak of capitalism digging its grave, although we can disagree about methods of control. Even national business rivalries are dissolving, in Europe at least, in the Common Market; and in its nineteenth-century form capitalist imperialism has vanished. If it were not for the fact that we may be destroyed by the tyrannies that claim to be Marx's heirs, a miraculously prosperous and human life would lie ahead of us (which could involve its own problems).

Now if the Left is not socialist it is nothing. Whatever their actual performance may be, all of these people who are lumped together as the Left are supposed to have a unique relation to something they still call the working-class movement. They are supposed to be about to reform something they call capitalism, and what they are supposed to stand for is something called socialism. And this narrow range of discussion is supposed to be their primary distinguishing characteristic. Although they may clothe themselves in the mantles of the Pyms and Hampdens, and of every other liberating figure in history, they are supposed to be something more than that; they are supposed to be socialists.

What do they mean by that? The communists, crypto-communists, proto-communists, communoids and pro-communists mean something like the Soviet or Chinese regimes, that is to say that in effect they support systems of rigid inequality, inhuman subjection and economic hardship. In a crisis they stand for starvation and economic hardship. This may not mean that these people do not admit many criticisms of Communism. But they feel it has destroyed 'capitalism'; it talks of the 'workers'; they hope it might work some day; and their boredom and frustration with the existing order drives them to brutal dreams.

If these totalitarians did not exist the Left would still have a crisis, but it would be more a crisis of boredom and disillusion than of moral suicide. As it is, the existence on the Left of supporters of socialist tyrannies befouls the whole Left and destroys much of its moral vigour. It is in the slogan 'No enemies on the Left' that the metaphor of leftness runs mad. The maintenance of the myths of socialism and of a working-class movement which has mystical properties in its relations with 'capitalism' and the maintenance of the verbal armoury of the Class Struggle mean that anti-Communism, which (usually) is to say the upholding of the standards of humanity, freedom and economic progress, becomes unrespectable on the Left. It can be attacked as boss's talk, as anti-working class, as right wing and Rightist, viz., treacherous to the 'real' Left. It does not deploy the terminology of the Left. It seeks a new language and is suspect.

It may not be its practice, but socialism is the conscience of the Left, and those who express its principles in their most classical and pure form possess the mystical and honorific status of 'militants'.

Since the Left perpetuates the myth of itself as a radical movement of the dispossessed there is still regard for 'militancy'; militants, even if misguided, express in pure terms principles that are supposed to be held by all. Those who privately reject these principles in toto cannot afford to be too open about it; others, though more or less rejecting them, feel guilty when the old words come out as the voice of conscience. As long as the Left is officially entrapped in socialism, 'militants', whether pro-communist or fundamentalists, can set a significant part of its tone.

This may seem a quibble but it is not. In the two numerically most significant sections of the Left in Australia, the union movement and the ALP, there is a non-communist section which sometimes supports communist policies and does it in the name of working-class unity, of the struggle against capitalism, etc. In itself this may not finally matter, but there is a *dominant* section that, although a wake-up to Communism and indeed socialism, can at times be prepared to play along with it, or denigrate the attackers of it, or at least keep up with the boys by insisting on the formula that both Communism and capitalism are evils.

This kind of formula destroys anti-Communism and it is the kind of formula that also, because of its cynicism, helps destroy the Left as a force for reform. The men who put it up do not really believe in it; most of them know that even nineteenth-century capitalism was better than twentieth-century Communism, but they are being dishonest. A politician can be dishonest from time to time for special purposes and still maintain standards of morality. But the typical 'moderate' of the Left can become hopelessly and corruptingly and permanently dishonest; he uses socialist words but he believes in nothing; he is finally demoralised and he is likely to do anything. He may 'go right', he may 'go left'. Sometimes he may move out of the Labor Party altogether; or he may stay in it and feather his nest. He is dangerous because even in good times he is so meaningless; he takes the heart out of the reform movement and fills the gap with a consideration for his own career and verbal ritual. In bad times he could possibly be fatal. At a time when the Left of the Left is in the ascendant, it can sweep through the dried, sapless timber of the 'moderates' very quickly.

Before moving on to be more positive about the Left and find some good in it I want to examine socialism from another direction. I have already said that there are two dangers in binding the Left together with nineteenth-century working-class movement dogma and believing that there can be something in common between all elements of the Left even if, in the case of the 'moderates', it is only opposition to a common enemy called, for the sake of ritualistic observance, capitalism. The first danger is that under some circumstances this process aids the communists, which is to say, the foreign policies of Russia and/or China. The second danger is that it takes the heart out of the reform movement because so many of the high priests of the ritual do not believe what they are saying. The third danger is that some of them still believe in what they are saying.

There are those who still believe in the objectives of classical socialism, the ownership by the State of the means of production and distribution. That men can still believe in this when regulated capitalism so clearly operates so well for the ordinary person, and totalitarian socialism in Russia has not yet pushed per capita agricultural output above the pre-revolutionary figure, is simply a tribute to the power of belief. But there are others who reject classical socialism but still believe in something they call socialism.

In a recent *Partisan Review* Arthur Schlesinger Jr had this to say about them:

> So far as I can see, the so-called 'democratic socialists' have … become proponents of a mixed economy. If they derive emotional

satisfaction by calling this 'socialism', this is an act of rhetorical piety which has little relation to reality – and is, indeed, as absurd as those who insist on talking about the American mixed economy as if it was an example of unfettered 'free enterprise' ... Calling State action 'socialism' is only one more example of the use of words to conceal realities – and this time an example cherished alike by old-fashioned socialists and old-fashioned capitalists. The hard fact is that the world has moved beyond both classical socialism and classical capitalism, and addiction to the old words is an expression of arrested development.

In what is supposed to be a movement of reform it is this traditional addiction that is dangerous. Helped on by dreary nonsense from the Right it makes the standard of economic discussion in Australia very boring, when it should be lively and informed. It perpetuates the myth that the great problems of the day are economic; and, to keep some feeling for tradition, it leads the Left to look for methods of direct state intervention, of 'physical controls', where there is some reason for believing that economies run better when businessmen are left to settle the details, with the Government doing the general direction and setting the climate.

In the field of economic planning in Australia there is a market wide open for a radical and progressive approach, nothing as exciting as the musty barricades-talk of the Trades Halls perhaps, but something that might provide genuine reform. Unfortunately, the 'planners' of the Left often seem more concerned with extending power than with getting results and they tend to ignore opportunities for reform that stray outside their orthodoxies.

The problem so far as it concerns right-wing manipulators of the economy is, as I once put it in the *Bulletin*:

Those (on the Right) who know that the economy has to be manipulated ... are far too modest about it. Their approach to planning is reminiscent of the Victorian approach to sex: it's all right in its place, but you mustn't become expert at it, or even talk about it, or – as far as possible – think about it. Or in a few words: we already have many planning devices; let's co-ordinate them and use them.

Or as Professor Wilson put it in *Crossbow*:

The manifold activities of the State already affect the country's economic life in all sorts of ways. If growth is to be fostered, the Government should subject these activities to urgent and critical scrutiny with little regard for the sacred cows of social and economic life. What is required is a comprehensive survey ranging from the structure of taxation to educational policy, from tariffs to the training of apprentices, from Treasury control to the location of industry ... In some cases it might be thought right to extend the State's activities, for example, by the granting of more developmental contracts in order to help forward highly risky innovations ... in other cases the State might reduce the scale of its efforts, for example, by granting few subsidies to decaying industries in order to postpone a little the date of their decease. Finally, the policies approved should be reasonably consistent with one another.

To those who are used to discussing economic problems in terms of ideologies, what Professor Wilson says may sound pretty uninteresting. But if carried out in Australia it could lead to enough change and excitement to challenge all of the boldness and vision of the Left.

Boldness and vision of the Left? That group of cynics or formula-mumblers? It is not altogether untrue. There are men of radical conviction in the Australian Left. Most of them are active anti-communists, some of them perhaps a little tired of the strait-laced, conventional, old-fashioned atmosphere in which they have to live. But in a different environment they could be displaying that restless, ingenious, practical urge to make some things better that marks the reformer. They could even still make the bosses (or many of them) one of their targets. Not in the socialist v. capitalist old-time dance sense, but because there are many examples of Australian businessmen who are too highly protected by the taxpayer, too lazy and unimaginative to survive, too greedy and self-interested to think of their country's interests as well as their own.

The trouble with the Left is that left-wingers are supposed to be radical, or even rebellious about new things, and our Left is going on and on being radical on old patterns about problems that have passed. It has become a conformist movement. Perhaps a Left, like history, has a double run-through, once as tragedy, once as farce.

Once the thing to be most radical about was the economic problem. Now it is the survival of freedom. There is still plenty of need to be radical about economic problems, but part of being radical about them now is to admit that things have changed and to be more detailed in approach.

I don't often engage in this kind of thing, but here is a contribution to the literature of dreams: let us make a bonfire of the metaphors of Left and Right. The friends of totalitarianism could go up in flames, and the dreary ashes of the demoralised conservatives of Left and Right could be mingled together in one party and put on the mantle shelf. Here would be the chance to form a Radical Party, its policy determined not by the problems of the nineteenth century but by the problems of today.

Dedicated to a sense of humanity, a love of freedom and a desire for general prosperity and continued national independence, its first task would be to ensure that Australia played its part in fighting the Cold War not as an ideological racket or as a defence of 'free enterprise' or of any particular religious creed, but because we opposed the inhuman cruelties, tyrannies, miseries and degradation that we would be fighting. We would recognise this as the great issue of the day. It would not be socialism against capitalism, but kindness against cruelty, independence against subjection, prosperity against poverty, life against death.

This would involve sacrifices for most of us, but most of them would be trivial. The serious sacrifices could be reserved for the totalitarians and their supporters in our own country, and those others whose private greed endangered the national good.

Otherwise we would happily accept the widening horizons of a prosperous and free liberal-democratic state based on a policy of directed and regulated capitalism. Welfare for the unfortunate would not be a matter for election tub-thumping but for a day-to-day detailed concern; industrial relations would be left to unions and businessmen impelled by a new spirit; innovation would be stimulated; stagnation would be allowed to stagnate itself out of existence – but not to the injury of innocent wage earners. Progress would be the keynote of economic approach, and tolerance – except of totalitarians – of social life. Old wrongs could still be righted – Aborigines, crooked elections, and other legacies of history – but we would also see that the problems of freedom within our present kind of society include the twentieth-century problems of affluence, bigness, 'mass culture', 'alienation' and the general effects of mass education, on the one hand, and massive technological advance on the other; and we would try to do something about them.

I wonder how much support there would be for such a policy from the Left, still shrouded in its own dusty dreams.

9

THE LUCKY COUNTRY

The Lucky Country, *published in 1964, described Australia as the first suburban nation; suggested that there were diverse kinds of lives being led in Australia, while making intelligently superficial generalisations; called for Australia to become a republic; pointed out that Australia was geographically close to the different countries that made up Asia; looked at the multifaceted answers to the question of who ran Australia, and more. It also raised the concepts of a 'nation without a mind' and a 'lucky country'.*

The Australian Dream

[The first chapter begins with a snapshot of how Australia seemed in the 1960s.]

Innocent happiness

The South Sydney Junior Leagues Club, 558a Anzac Parade, set in a suburb of what may be – in certain senses – the most democratic city in the world, would still be described in some countries as a working men's club. It has a membership of thousands of men and women of only average weekly wage who arrive by bus, taxi or private car to play its 'pokies' – the poker machines before which members stand or sit, their glasses of beer beside them, and pull levers to win an average of several thousand dollars a day. The club makes a *profit* of hundreds of thousands of dollars a year from its pokies after expenses are allowed for, and puts this money into bars, restaurants, a swimming pool, squash courts, steam rooms, gymnasia, bowling alleys, a roof garden (glassed in, with $120,000 worth of air conditioning), a small library, and a nursery. There are dances four nights a week (two are held simultaneously on Saturdays), $52,000 worth of floor shows a year, a car park, six tennis courts and 'the most beautiful billiard room in the Southern Hemisphere'. The general tone is of suburban good taste – vases of gladioli, goldfish tanks, parquet floors, pastel colours, light wood furniture and an Aboriginal mural pay tribute to the cultural standards of the women's magazines. People dress as they please, men in shirtsleeves and shorts, or suits; women in party dresses or stretch pants. The club represents the Australian version of the old ideals of equality and the pursuit of happiness: that everyone has the right to a good time.

In outward form, and as far as ordinary people know or care, Australia is the most egalitarian of countries, untroubled by obvious class distinctions, caste or communal domination, the tensions of racialism or the horrors of autocracy. Taxi drivers often prefer their passengers to sit with them in the front seat and sometimes tip them the small change. A person who doesn't like ordinary people to think they are as good as he is, or to enjoy some of the things he enjoys himself, will not like Australia. The spirit of fraternalism permeates the nation. Sometimes the substance of an accompanying equality is missing; there are still inequalities of wealth, power and opportunity, but the ordinary people have won – or had delivered to them – a profound and satisfying ideological victory. Australia is a nation that for a large part accepts the ideology of fraternalism.

There are underground tensions of snobbery or power but these are almost unknown to the mass of the people. Whatever kind of bastard the boss might be, he usually rolls up his sleeves and looks like one of the boys. Usually he does not outwardly contest the belief that those who work for him are as good as he is. Ordinary Australians no longer envy their bosses, although they may hate them or pity them. They attribute success to good luck or sharp conduct (thereby providing a more accurate view of success than most) and to them the economic advantages of getting ahead (they do not detect any social advantages) sometimes seem too slight to be worth the trouble. Ordinary Australia is not a society of striving and emulation. Ordinary people are not concerned with the ways of the rich or the highly educated. What they want they can usually get – a house, a car, oysters, suntans, cans of asparagus, lobsters, seaside holidays, golf, tennis, surfing, fishing, gardening. Life assumes meaning in the weekends and on holidays. In the ocean cities Australians can live the life of the Mediterranean or the South Seas. To some they seem lazy. They are not really lazy but they don't always take their jobs seriously. They work hard at their leisure.

Australia has one of the highest per capita national incomes in the world; there are more cars and TV sets for its population than almost anywhere; there is the largest rate of home ownership in the world; there are more savings accounts than people. Even these figures do not give an idea of Australia's economic equality. Not only are very rich or very poor people rare, the average income is not just a simple average, it is also close to the typical income.

As Australians line up at the polling booths in schools and halls at election time most of them do not know that Australia, which has been enjoying manhood suffrage and the secret ballot since 1860, was one of the first to show that society could survive what was then attacked as the triumph of 'selfishness, ignorance and democracy'. There are less than a dozen countries like Australia that, throughout the century, have been ruled efficiently by stable democratic governments that have been accepted by a vast majority of the people as legitimate. As in these few other countries, the opponents of a government in Australia (except for the small Communist Party) are not prepared to use any except democratic means in their attempts to replace it. And there is so *much* political democracy in Australia. Less than 13,000,000 people, but there are six State Governments and a Federal Government – altogether thirteen legislative chambers (including the upper houses), more than 700 politicians, about eighty Government ministers. And the system of compulsory voting at elections, with fines for non-attendance, makes the 'donkey vote' – the vote of those who just vote down the list from top to bottom – a factor in political planning. And the system of preferential voting (in which every candidate for the one position must be voted for in order of preference with preferences being distributed until one candidate has a majority) encourages a 'fair go' for minority parties that pesters the bosses of the two major parties.

Social stability is high: Australians are too easy-going to become fanatics and they do not crave great men. People count on orderly reform to right whatever they consider to be their wrongs. It is part of the nature of Australian government to juggle things around, to avoid sharp issues so that questions of final judgement do not suddenly arise. Even Australian nationalism – once strong – is now so hesitant that it no longer achieves self-definition. No one any longer tells Australians who they are, nor do they seem to care. They have their families, their leisure, they know what to do with their lives. *They* seem to know who they are but their easy-going definitions of themselves do not meet the fashions of intellectual or political rhetoric so that when Australian writers or politicians speak of their own people they often speak falsely, or with contempt. Whatever opinions Australians express personally, ordinary Australia is now a more tolerant country than it used to be. The mass of the people have available to them as full a range of civil liberties as a mass of people usually want except, paradoxically, in the field that interests them most: having a good time. Generally, authority is despised. Politicians and government officials are distrusted and the police are often hated, although there is more unconscious acceptance of authority – perhaps indifference to authority – than Australians recognise. There are displays of aggressive individualism, although fewer than there used to be. But the aggression often springs from the feeling that someone else is being aggressive. Normal friendliness can be quickly resumed.

The remarkable openness of manner impresses – and sometimes appals – those who are used to social stiffness or deference. Truth is sometimes blurted out with a directness that can disgust those who come from more devious civilisations. A cult of informality derived from a deep belief in the essential sameness and ordinariness of mankind reduces ceremony to something that is quietly and self-consciously performed in a corner. Australians are self-conscious if they have to take part in ritual. Their wartime armies must have had the lowest saluting rate in the world. The only really national festivals are Anzac Day, Christmas and New Year. Anzac Day is the Festival of the Ordinary Man; Christmas the Festival of Family; New Year the Festival of the Good Time. Other holidays are just days off – except for people of religious conviction. On Anzac Day, commemorating the landing of Australians at Gallipoli in 1915, in every town in Australia ordinary veterans in very ordinary clothes march down the streets (many out of step), go through a brief ceremony and then many of them go and get drunk. There are themes of death and sacrifice: but the appeal of Anzac Day is an expression of the commonness of man (even death is a leveller), of the necessity for sticking together in adversity. It is not a patriotic day but, as Peter Coleman said in the *Bulletin*, 'a tribal festival', the folk seeing itself as it is – unpretentious and comradely.

Australia is not a country of great political dialogue or intense searching after problems (or recognition of problems that exist). There is little grandiose ideology and politics is usually considered to be someone else's business and a dirty business at that. For many Australians, playing or watching sport gives life one of its principal meanings. The elements of loyalty, fanaticism, pleasure-seeking, competitiveness, ambition and struggle that are not allowed precise expression in non-sporting life (although they exist in disguise) are stated precisely in sport. The whole business of human striving becomes a game. In 1950, Bertrand Russell said that Australia pointed the way to a happier destiny for man throughout the centuries to come; 'I leave your shores with more hope for mankind than I had when I came among you.' In 1886, J.A. Froude said of Australians: 'It is hard to quarrel with men who only wish to be innocently happy.' On an Australian beach on a hot summer day people doze in the sun or shoot the breakers like Hawaiian princes on pre-missionary Waikiki. The symbol is too far-fetched for Australian taste. The image of Australia is of a man in an open-necked shirt solemnly enjoying an ice cream. His kiddy is beside him.

Nation without a mind

Why write a book about such a happy country? One reason is that in some ways it is not so happy: one can learn something about happiness by examining Australia – its lingering puritanism, the frustrations and resentments of a triumphant mediocrity and the sheer dullness of life for many of its ordinary people. Another reason is that it is a matter of some general interest – of considerable practical interest to Australians – whether Australia will be able to maintain its happiness; have the conditions that led to so much success also weakened adaptability and slowed down the reflexes of survival?

Another reason is that – in a sense – Australia does not have a mind. Intellectual life exists but it is still fugitive. Emergent and uncomfortable, it has not established relation to practical life. The upper levels of society give an impression of mindlessness triumphant. Whatever intellectual excitement there may be down below, at the top the tone is so banal that to a sophisticated observer the flavour of democratic life in Australia might seem depraved, a victory of the anti-mind.

This is not a special plea for the comfort of intellectuals. And there will certainly be no argument against 'affluence', the satisfaction of ordinary appetites by ordinary people. I shall accept as *given* the attitudes to life of most Australians (although they are not my own preferences). One then asks: is it possible in a modern society to preserve all the prosperity and happiness of a nation that is so strongly inimical to ideas? There is another part of the question: is Australia really inimical to ideas? Or has there been something wrong with the ideas presented to it?

Even if the world were not to make demands on Australia – and Australians often seem to assume that since they leave the world alone it should do the same by them – the prosperity of the country might diminish compared to other countries. Throughout the world the basis of material prosperity in the future is likely to lie, for the first time in history, with clever, educated people. The need to build up a certain kind of cleverness will cause great social tensions in all industrialised countries; but especially in Australia, where cleverness can be considered un-Australian. Except in those few fields where it has a history of enterprise, Australia has not been a country of great innovation or originality. It has exploited the innovations and originality of others and much of its boasting is that of a parasite. As a transplanted society, it has had sufficient working similarities with the societies from which the innovations came to be able to exploit them with only a margin of inefficiency. But as the technological revolution passes into its new forms Australia may be left behind. It may not understand what is happening, or have the skills to implement new techniques. The present very great tendency for overseas firms to buy up Australian firms may accelerate. Australia could end up as an economically colonial country again – in manufacturing industry it is not far off it now – with foreigners managing its main economic affairs.

Australia faces an amazing number of other challenges. As Barbara Ward wrote in the *New York Times*, although each of these challenges is not in itself unique, no other 'Western' nation has had to face so wide a cross-section of the mid-century's typical dilemmas. One might add that, because of its history, Australia may also be uniquely unaware of the nature of challenge. To list these challenges – and they are another reason for writing this book – is to list most of the principal headings of the way the world talks now: the collapse of European colonial empires; the emergence of Communism in Asia; the lack of stability in the new states; the development of anti-racialism and of anti-colonialism; the pressures of underprivilege and of over-population; the surplus of temperate foodstuffs; the problems of maintaining growth in a sophisticated society; the problems of developing a physically 'have-not' country.

Australia merits sympathy for providing an encyclopaedic study of the main dilemmas of the mid-century. Until it has much greater strength – and ultimately that would seem to depend on a huge increase in population – there is nothing much it can do about some of its problems, except hope for the best. But it moves very slowly in doing anything about *any* of its problems. There are no great debates, there is little effective public discussion. The men in power do not seem able to excite first their own imaginations and then those of others into becoming familiar with these challenges. The government does not seem capable of getting a far from incompetent bureaucracy on the move. There are few 'new men' gathered together in the precincts of power to re-visualise the images of the nation so that change may become possible. The men at the top, the tribal leaders, are not in training for such a set of awkward situations. Their imagination seems exhausted by the country's achievements. Their own ideals – those of a more modest and earlier Australia – have been met and there are few people to whom they will listen to tell them that those ideals are now obsolete. Those who are now successful hold conventional wisdoms that belong to the first chapter of Australian history, a chapter that finished somewhere in the mid-twentieth century. There is no longer in Australia a generally accepted public sense of a future.

It is as if a whole generation has become exhausted by events, a provincial generation produced in a period when mindlessness was a virtue, the self-interest of pressure groups was paramount, cleverness had to be disguised, quick action was never necessary and what happened overseas was irrelevant. In some ways the study of contemporary Australia is a study of that generation. It was not a generation that allowed a place for the kind of extraordinary man who can see the new shapes of the future – or the present – and enjoy challenge, living life at a fuller pitch. There is little of the sophisticated political discourse that can refresh politicians; there are few channels for an intellectual breakthrough; in the universities (with exceptions) clever men nurse the wounds of public indifference; government officials are exiled in Canberra, away from the people they govern. A society whose predecessors pioneered a whole continent now appears to shun anything that is at all out of the ordinary. The trouble is that, by Australian standards, almost everything that is now important is out of the ordinary.

The Lucky Country

In a late draft D.H. changed the title of this, the final chapter of his book, to 'The Lucky Country' and the phrase resonated. After the publication of the book, D.H. continued to develop and prosecute his 'lucky country thesis' with its call for greater engagement with Asia, improvement in economic management and the development of a more independent national self-definition.

Living on our luck

AUSTRALIA IS A LUCKY COUNTRY RUN MAINLY BY second-rate people who share its luck. It lives on the other people's ideas, and, although its ordinary people are adaptable, most of its leaders (in all fields) so lack curiosity about the events that surround them that they are often taken by surprise. A nation more concerned with styles of life than with achievement has managed to achieve what may be the most evenly prosperous society in the world. It has done this in a social climate largely inimical to originality and the desire for excellence (except in sport) and in which there is less and less acclamation of hard work. According to the rules Australia has not deserved its good fortune.

The rules may be wrong. It is already becoming obvious that the belief in hard work may become one of the impediments to happiness in the future technological societies; some way will have to be found in which most people will work less without suffering comparative economic hardship. Australia has been one of the pioneer countries in cutting down hours of work and increasing holidays. In this sense Australians may be more progressive than the world thinks – in the very field about which they feel guilty. And however hard it is to imagine that a feeling for originality and excellence is not necessary for continuing prosperity, some people might say: if Australians can get away with it, good luck to them; after all, in a commercialist society, much of the originality and feeling for excellence is absorbed in matters of immense triviality – a new knob on a TV set, a new way of slicing beans.

Others raise the question that I have excluded from this book: what is the sense in there being an Australia at all? When it looked as if the Japanese might conquer Australia early in 1942 Vance Palmer wrote in *Meanjin*:

> The next few months may decide not only whether we are to survive as a nation, but whether we deserve to survive. As yet none of our achievements prove it, at any rate in the sight of the outer world ... we could vanish and leave singularly few signs, that, for some generations, there had lived a people who had made a homeland of this Australian earth ... There is very little to show the presence of a people with a common purpose or a rich sense of life.

Then Palmer gave his own answer to this question:

> If Australia had no more character than could be seen on its surface, it would be annihilated as surely and swiftly as those colonial outposts white men built for their commercial profit in the East – pretentious facades of stucco that looked imposing as long as the wind kept from blowing. But there is an Australia of the spirit, submerged and not very articulate, that is quite different from these bubbles of old-world imperialism ... sardonic,

idealist, tongue-tied perhaps, it is the Australia of all who truly belong here ... And it has something to contribute to the world. Not emphatically in the arts as yet, but in arenas of action, and in ideas for the creation of that egalitarian democracy that will have to be the basis for all civilised societies in the future. That is the Australia we are called upon to save.

This was an unusual outburst of rhetoric even in a wartime Australia that feared it might be destroyed. (And in which sardonic idealists in some of Sydney's water suburbs sold out cheap, afraid that their houses might be shelled by the Japanese.) However, the perils of war showed – on the whole – how, being laconic, Australians can take surprise in their stride. The very scepticism of Australians and their delight in improvisation have meant that so far Australia has scraped through. On the face of it Australia has had gamblers' luck. Even to use the phrase 'gamblers' luck' can be misleading; it suggests a knowledge of risk and insecurity, when it is a feature of Australian life not to take insecurities into account. The saving Australian characteristic – and this has some of the gambler's coolness about it – is the ability to change course quickly, even at the last moment, and seek a quick, easy way out. This can happen almost without discussion or dramatisation of the change. Australians have good nerves. They hate discussion and 'theory' but they can step quickly out of the way if events are about to smack them in the face.

Will the luck last?

However, there are two fields where reliance on luck and last-minute adjustment are not going to work; these are the fields of Australia's strategic environment and of reactions to the demands of technology. So far as the first is concerned, it is just remotely possible that events in Asia will pass Australia by, but it seems insane to trust to luck that they will do so. So far as the second is concerned, there does not seem to be even a remote possibility of luck coming to the rescue; Australia will not be able to maintain its prosperity in the new technological age without profoundly changing its life patterns. It is because these two demands cannot possibly be evaded that I suggested earlier that Australia has now completed the first chapter of its history. Things are going to change so deeply that some new kind of Australia is emerging; either that, or they will not change, and the present kind of Australia will go under anyway.

In the next few decades one can see such possible catastrophes in Asia that Australia might be overwhelmed whatever it does. There are all kinds of catastrophes less than total victory that could change the world for the worse for Australia. There are also several crises in South-East Asia, that, although not directly related to Communism, might also wreck things for Australia, if only, in the first place, in scaring off migrants and overseas capital. Australia can never have the strength to affect the results of the grand game; but it can play its part, and in some of the smaller games it could play an important part. The more its economic growth and population increase the greater that part can be. When the present ruling generations go, will the rigidities and obsolescence of Australian public life change quickly enough for Australia to accept its connection with events? It is easy to talk about increases in population, in economic development and in military strength and about making changes in attitudes to Asia. These may be necessary (although not sufficient) for Australia to survive, let alone to play a more important part in Asia (or actually play the part it has written for itself). But will they happen?

Will Australia be able to accept the wonderful opportunities for greater participation, and sometimes initiative, in the world in which it lives? Will it rid itself of the belief that it is a dull country, that nothing happens to it, that it is safe from the unpleasantness of history? Perhaps Australians are too modest, capable of more than they attempt, believing that as a nation they are not old enough or important enough for great events; too concerned with happiness to understand the possibilities of tragedy, projecting their illusions on to others.

The demands of technology will be less dramatic than the demands of Asia, but of immense economic and social importance. Australia is playing for a high stake: maintenance of a general level of prosperity higher than almost anywhere in the world. That is why the standards one applies to the people who run Australia's economic affairs must be high. There is no point in comparing them with the economic masters of some small country that is just struggling along. We're at the top. We must apply the standards of the top. The answer to the question, *Can we keep our standards of prosperity and our present way of life?* or to put it more bluntly, *Can the racket last?* Appears to be *NO*. That is to say, that if things go on as they are Australia will slip down the per capita national income scale. (It may be worth noting that since I wrote these words in the first edition of this book, according to one set of estimates, Australia dropped from fifth to tenth in the list of the world's prosperous countries – in one year.)

It has had its material success because its ordinary people were educated enough and adaptable enough to work in modern ways; because they were eager to buy enough consumer goods to keep the whole show going; and because their masters, although not usually of high calibre, were skilled enough, with government protection, to decode the instructions they received from overseas. Now something more than that is needed. It does not seem likely that in this new age material progress can continue at the highest rate unless society jumps into new life with higher standards of training, with an increasing proportion of scientists, technologists and technicians, with a greater emphasis on administrative and managerial capacity and an absorption of the technocratic approach into ways of thinking. All the industrialised nations are now reacting to this problem, but few of them are doing it as slowly as Australia and in few of them does it represent quite such a change in social pattern. In most industrialised countries cleverness and skill are part of the national ethos, even if they share it with contradictory elements. In Australia they play no part in it. Even if more and more of Australian enterprise is run directly by overseas firms, there must be enough Australians able to decode the new instructions and carry them out. It is unlikely that enough skilled migrants can be acquired to do the whole job for us. And given the present inadequate training programs it is likely that this crisis may become apparent at a time when it would take up to a decade to meet it.

When most Australians think of their economic growth they think that people should work harder. This leftover from puritanism may be the opposite of the truth. It may be desirable for the 'workers' to work *less*: what will be needed will be a great deal more thinking, training, organisation and cleverness. But we are now getting only about half the vocational results from our education system that we could be getting out of it and the position may become worse. It's easy to say that more money should be pumped into the infrastructure – and that talent should be sought out and given power and prestige. So it should. But it should be realised that to do this involves a social revolution, something that will change parts of Australian civilisation beyond recognition. It is such a social revolution that now becomes necessary in Australia if the standards of material prosperity are to remain the tests of policy.

That a revolutionary change in attitudes towards life is needed to further material progress does not mean that this change will necessarily be achieved. A politician, government official, union leader or company director who does not wish to change his beliefs and the habits that give life meaning for him will simply not change them; they are more important to him than the further material progress of the nation. Normally, people prefer their ways of life to material progress: it is one of the reasons why most nations are 'under-developed'. What is advocated is a radical overthrow and destruction of the prevailing attitudes of most of the nation's masters. If this does not happen there is likely to be a general demoralisation in Australia; the nation may become run-down, old-fashioned, puzzled and resentful.

One can go on advocating until one is black in the face but the concept of social revolution is nonsense if there are not the people to make it. The ordinary Australian people seem adaptable; it is a matter of the people on top. Here one can draw some confidence in the possibility of change (for better or worse) from detecting a difference between the generations. On top there is a stiff-necked carrying on of old ways based on enervated wisdoms. One has only to watch a top person on television to sense in the lowered eyes, in the inability to reach towards the camera and generalise, in the lack of excitement about the problems of the modern world, in the meticulous muddling around with trivia, that these are the symptoms of a lost generation. What Bagehot said of generations in politics is true of generations generally:

> Generally one generation … succeeds another almost silently; at every moment men of all ages between thirty and seventy have considerable influence; each year removes many old men, makes others older, brings in many new. But sometimes there is an abrupt change. In that case the affairs of the country are apt to alter much, for good or for evil; sometimes it is ruined,

sometimes it becomes more successful, but it hardly ever stays as it was.

Australians do not take easily to the concept of one generation taking over from another. There has been hardly any study of the process, and none of the journalistic labelling that goes on in most developed nations. Among writers this lack of interest may have come from the obsessive desire to define Australian characteristics in terms of the upsurge of the 1890s, instead of as a dynamic process or from the opposite desire (in rebellion against this one) not to find any Australian characteristics at all. There is a desire to maintain traditional standards of what 'Australian' should mean instead of finding out what it does mean. (To admit that generations can change would be to admit that a static concept of an 'Australian', based on the writings of the 1890s, is false.) And the continuing dominance of old ideas and ageing men has led to a lot of imitation or appearance of imitation in younger generations. Geoffrey Dutton said in *Nation* that there are probably more old men of thirty in Australia than in any other country in the world. Among some of the younger generations there is an obsession with 'maturity'. As Dutton says, 'A sure way of discrediting anyone whose opinion you disagree with is to tell him that it's time he grew up.'

However, beneath the pretence of sameness one can detect difference. One can make some guesses, at the same time qualifying generalisation by recognising that men are often born out of their generation. In general the remains of the Menzies–Calwell generation is antediluvian, nurtured in a backwater, strongly provincial. They are of the post-Federation generation, proud that the Australian states had federated; they developed their theories of the world in a context of British power. They can be more old-fashioned than men of the same generation in Britain because their imaginations have not been fundamentally stirred by any of the cataclysms of the last fifty years. The men who came of age between the two world wars see themselves as the innovators and men of iron will – the one-man shows who in their brilliant improvisations changed the face of Australia. Often the changes they made represent the dreams of the 1930s rather than the demands of the 1960s; though still believing supremely in themselves they have no trust in the men underneath them (often their problems of succession are their own fault); they trust in their own intuition (which is sometimes just luck), willpower and the handling of men. The wartime and immediate post-war generation understands the demands of the age better and sees life in more complicated terms than the men they are now beginning to replace. They understand the need for expertness and co-operation more. They are the New Generation, the men who see Australia in more sophisticated terms. Some of them have imitated the Men of Will. Others already seem tired. Some of the best may have been so long frustrated by the amateurishness of the Men of Will that they may have lost their punch. But they are Australia's immediate hope. The younger generation than this seems fresher, but it is still full of mystery, not defined. It is condemned as hedonistic and stupid. Yet some of its apparent stupidity may be indifference to the bogus view of life that is presented to it and some of its hedonism an expression of a strong Australian characteristic that is now less confused by puritanism. It may be a genuinely rebellious generation, developing its own style. It may be the generation that changes Australia.

Why is there no longer any sense of importance in Australia, no feeling that great events (except catastrophe) can still occur? Small nations usually have histories to sustain them or futures to enlighten them. Australia seems to have lost both its sense of a past and its sense of a future. In making appeals, in attempting to make policies 'rational' there is nothing to appeal to, no sense of purpose; yet people need some sense of definition to which they can relate their actions as an individual needs a sense of identity: a sense of having had a history, of having reached a particular point in it and of facing a certain kind of future. It may be that all this is because Australia sees itself as a dependent nation. It doesn't develop ideas; it looks overseas for support and recognition: it doesn't adopt policies because it has only a small area of decision. This is the way it may seem to the older successful men who are baffled about what they are supposed to do next. Among the more active younger people there is a feeling that Australia can resume its history, but in a different direction. They are fascinated by the idea of Asia. This fascination, combined with a greater concern for education and cleverness, could prove the creative, liberating element in Australia – if there is to be one.

Acceptance of the changes of technology, involvement with Asia, the shock (when it comes) of declaring Australia a republic: these possible events could set things moving again in Australia. Something else seems needed: accommodation on top to some of the values of ordinary Australians. It is among the younger Australians, less puritanical and less anxious to compare themselves with Europeans, that this may be developing: a greater acceptance of pleasure; an acceptance of the fact that all that one can see of the world is man and his environment; a concern for extreme ease in human relations; the ability to act without fundamental belief, to give it a go. Australians have for long both understood the inadequacies of action and at the same time enjoyed action. They know how to be heroes without a cause; to suffer ordeal sardonically; to accept rules in which they do not finally believe. Ken Inglis said in a paper to the ANZAS Conference that, in the commemoration of the dead in the Anzac monuments, the appeals are not to Christianity, but to the stoic view of life as an heroic ideal. In economic planning, for instance, this attitude could carry Australia along the way; a plan imposes morale and pattern; it leads to action; some of the action does not follow the plan; one improvises, changes the dogma; one then proceeds to further action with equal disbelief. One is both sardonic observer and cheerful participant. Nothing finally works but one proceeds with action as if it did. Such is life.

Everywhere one goes in Australia among sensitive, intelligent people of the middle generation – once the conversation reaches a certain depth – one meets a sense of desperation: what is going to happen next? In the younger generation it reaches a sense of outrage that public images of life should remain so freakishly irrelevant. Those who love their country, or (in the more restrained Australian idiom) are worried about the life their children will lead, or are simply wondering what is going to happen next – none of these can imagine the future. It is usually seen as a political problem: in the form of Menzies and Calwell the images of obsolescence stood there, improbable but apparently immovable; succession was seen simply as replacement by the same kind of thing. Among those who are frightened by this perpetual state of Stand Easy – and it is an emotion breaking through political party loyalties – there is a feeling of distrust for their own nation; a fear that responsible, clever people will just not be found; that there will be no breakthrough of new men; things will just go on; no one will do the job. This sense of hopelessness may prove to be an accurate forecast. The conventionalism of Australian elites may prove so strong that it breaks men who have new views of the possible; the desire to preserve certain beliefs and ways of going on may conquer all attempts to react to new demands or define reality anew. There are plenty of good people around but the conventions of the institutions by which power is reached stifle them or repel them. The nation that saw itself in terms of unique hope for a better way of life is becoming reactionary – or its masters are – addicted to the old, conformist.

All the same something is going to happen. The demands of the age will destroy the present conventions – sometime. As Bagehot said of a sudden change in generations, things are not going to stay as they are; the results may be good or evil, success or ruin. It is time in Australia not for consideration of minor change, but for broad, general views of change. These must be based on some sense of reality, but not merely on the practicalism of what is possible for the moment. Very little is possible for the moment. But the time might come when broad views of change that now seem impractical will seem sensible and to the point. A reformer must forget the present occupants of power; they are unteachable. In the irrelevance of the present, he has to look to the future, perhaps produce ideas that may prompt action at some later time. In this situation, to be impractical may be the only way of being practical.

One can hope that events will liberate what is good and progressive in Australians, not perpetuate what is bad; that the ideal of fraternalism will gradually extend to include the Asian races (as it appears to be doing among the young) so that ultimately – but perhaps not for some years – Australia's population problem will be solved in what may be the only way it can finally be solved – by large-scale Asian migration. Then, assuming huge advances in science that will make development possible where it now is not, Australia might really claim the name of continent, a continent in which for a second time, but more successfully than in the USA, a new nation will be created with values that have some relation to ordinary human aspiration.

For the present one sees only the impossible. But here again there are Australian qualities that can be liberated. The change in generations may meet some of the demands of technology and already there have been the beginnings of a breakthrough for the intellect and, more successfully, the arts. The talent in empiricism might add a new and practical dimension to economic planning, and save it from the doctrinaire. The laconicism and courage of Australians are waiting to be drawn on to face the world outside Australia: this reserve of Australian stoicism has not been summoned for many years but it still seems a feature of the existential young as it was of their fathers and grandfathers. The good qualities of Australians should be described and admired and brought into play. Their non-doctrinaire tolerance, their sense of pleasure, their sense of fair play, their interest in material things, their sense of family, their identity with nature and their sense of reserve, their adaptability when a way is shown, their fraternalism, their scepticism, their talent for improvisation, their courage and stoicism. These are great qualities that could constitute the beginnings of a great nation. This nation should be impelled to display its talents in a sense of reality. Many problems threaten the future of Australia. But we might have good luck. It's worth giving it a go.

FICTION

10

BUT WHAT IF THERE ARE NO PELICANS?

In this 1971 novel about the possibilities of politics, set in an imaginary afterworld, the narrator tries to make the best of things, despite not being entirely sure what is going on.

The last interrogation

THE COMPUTER SPOKE PEREMPTORILY. THE TIME for tests and fooling around had ended, it said. Nor was there time to waste on further general speculation. There had been some setback to the Prince's fortunes and although it was a matter that would no doubt end with the Prince's triumph, there was no time for complacent dawdling. I must make my report at once.

When I asked what I was going to report on, the computer said it had assumed that I had not gone on such an important mission for the Prince at such a critical stage of his glorious career without asking him why I was to go. Although the computer tried to bully me into some reply, I said nothing.

The computer now changed to a more leisurely, even coaxing manner. Surely, it said, there would be no harm in my offering something or other as an interim report? At worst I would simply appear stupid if well intentioned, but from the reprimands I would receive I would probably sense the kind of report I was in fact expected to give. In any case, even if my report was so urgently required, perhaps no one would read it. Perhaps a report was needed simply to make up a file. Even if someone did read it he might simply pick out of it a few sentences here and there and use them to a quite different purpose.

I said that existence was not like a book. There was not necessarily a message or a summing-up at the end, and even if there were, would it necessarily be better or more significant than what had occurred before? If I were to speak seriously I must re-examine the many reflections I had made in my fifty years on the beaches, in my three adventures, and on my return to Earth. I would need time to think. The computer said that I was not at this moment required to speak seriously, or to think: I was required to make a report.

In explaining why I could not do so, I said that the observations I had made on my mission had so far been limited to small parts of the worlds of my old comrade and my son. In these particular observations of mine there had been no evidence – at least none that I could for the moment remember – that goodness in any way existed; yet from such narrow experience I would not necessarily come to this as a general conclusion. Although I had found no goodness, perhaps if I thought about it longer I might do so: perhaps we expect too much of goodness: perhaps we take the humanity out of it: perhaps we look for it in the wrong way and cannot see what there is of it.

'You are being long-winded about the inadequacies of your observations,' said the computer, 'but fashionably so. Most reports now begin like this, so you might very well leave all of that in as a preface. We shall turn that into the first section of your report and put it on a different-coloured paper: the heading will discourage a man of action from wasting his time in reading it, but it will be there nevertheless, and if you are challenged in some of your findings you can always point to this opening section as a face-saver.' After a pause the computer said: 'I advise you now to dictate to me a quick, businesslike section with some positive recommendations. For instance, why not advise the Prince on the likely efficacy of some of his new slogans?'

Once again, I said, it would be ridiculous for me to reach any general conclusions on such slight evidence, but it had begun to occur to me that the idea of brotherhood – in some of its forms – could be overdone. It might have been misleading, for instance, for me to have made so much of the kind of brotherhood I had experienced with my fellow soldiers after we had stormed the wrong beach and then had to make the best of it. There had been nobility in our relations, but it was a nobility of desperation, perhaps akin to the sense of brotherhood of those who had believed that the world itself was about to end. It was not usual for such a clear sense of peril to exist, and although, as I had observed in the second of my adventures, it was often an act of statecraft to simulate or exaggerate danger so that men might act like brothers, it seemed wicked to do so, even if the result was sometimes good. Perhaps some of the violence of the rhetoric of brotherhood depended too much on a sense of catastrophe, making it seem possible that all goodness would disappear if some particular cause were not served. Some of the expectations of the Prince that we should have a universal pride in our species might depend too much on metaphor: at a time of peril, when some group we belong to is threatened, we might be able to take pride in a collective immortality transcending individual death, but a sense of immediate peril cannot be maintained indefinitely. In any case, it is hatred or fear of one section of the species for another that is usually most successful in engendering the sense of peril that inspires brotherhood: yet this kind of brotherhood is the most notable enemy of a universal faith in the whole species. Perhaps it was wrong to concern oneself at all with collective purposes rather than with the possibility of goodness as a relation between individuals, or as a quality within them. Otherwise we were left with the paradox that while the manifestations of brotherhood could inspire some of our most noble aspirations, these aspirations were most likely to be put into practice when, collectively, we acted at our meanest and most unbrotherly.

'That will be enough on brotherhood,' said the computer. 'We shall give it the sub-heading *(i) Brotherhood* and underline it. Now give us something to put under the sub-heading *(ii) Pride and Freedom.*'

I said that these ideas were not only the Prince's, they had also been my own; that this conjunction appeared to have been the cause of my present predicament. I would now like to make some quick qualification of them. I saw no reason to change my belief that action (or freedom) was impossible without the hope that came from pride (or faith); but in itself was this belief anything more than an outline of a therapeutic technique? Must we applaud action or freedom merely for its own sake as if we were automata of which the only test was that we should continuously twist and jump? If we must, then we should praise my old comrade, whose pride made him free to jump in directions of his choosing although the faith on which he acted was despicable.

'In what you say you have been to some extent critical of the Prince's slogan,' said the computer. 'Perhaps you do this out of stupidity or vanity. Perhaps you do it out of bravery. But it is also possible that you do it out of calculation. Perhaps you realise as I do – I have for so long been a receiver of reports that I know everything about them – that it is not necessarily prudent to deliver back to a great man what you can remember as having been his thoughts when you last saw him: in the meantime he may have changed his mind.'

I said that I had several things to add. In the first place I had not rejected the ideal of brotherhood; I had merely recognised the difficulties and dangers that came if its rhetoric took too much from that of war or other catastrophes. The brotherhood I now believed in was something more gentle – more like the idea of charity, and in this there was not only pride but also humility. We should not despise ourselves for not being what we cannot be; neither should we take too much pleasure in it; we should recognise in ourselves the humanity we saw in others; it might be bad; it might be good; but we should acknowledge our shared condition. I added that there was doubt as to whether we needed the concept of brotherhood if we had the concept of charity, just as there was doubt that if we thought long about faith and hope we needed the new concept of pride and freedom. Even with some scepticism and humility, faith could prompt action. In short, I concluded, I was no longer sure whether we needed these new words the Prince had given us.

'If that were so,' said the computer, 'what point would there be in the whole rebellion of the Prince? Why should we all be going to so much trouble?'

I replied that it was not unknown for a rebellion to occur for reasons other than those announced; in any case, to give new meaning to old words was often the principal substance of revolt.

'That is a good answer,' said the computer. 'I shall delete the first part of it, of course, but I shall place the second part of it up higher, as a cautionary paragraph introducing the whole section. If we left it as an end piece it might not be noticed, and that could be serious for you.'

When I said that something else was troubling me the computer replied that this suited its purpose: there should be several sections to a report and so far, apart from the preface, I had provided only one, even if it fell into three parts and was introduced by a cautionary sentence.

I said that I now saw, with something like agony, how little relation to the conduct of affairs there might be in what I had said, or the Prince had said, or anyone else had said, in the way of providing precepts for action. Were the workings of the human brain in any way related to our aspirations of how thought should go on? Or was there no relation at all between our aspirations towards thought and the jumpiness of the brain, its continuing, distracting bombardments, its feebleness, its turning on and off, its vindictive self-interest, its mirage-like qualities, and the distortions that came from the lying conventions of the senses that, second by second, mislead the brain like faithless courtiers? In the same way, was there any relation at all between our aspirations for the conduct of affairs and the actual practice of politics? Wasn't politics less a conflict between ideas than a conflict between men, and therefore day to day, and necessarily, little more – or nothing more – than a childlike shoving and pushing and seizing of advantages? It has been said that a great statesman must be a lion in boldness, a fox in cunning, and a pelican in selflessness and wisdom. But what if there are no pelicans, only lions and foxes – and eagles, vultures, snakes, mice, bears and rats?

The computer said that the heading he would give to this section of my report was 2. *GRAVE DOUBTS*. He asked if I had something more positive to say. I had raised possibilities, but what were my recommendations? If I could make any, they would provide a third section under the heading of 3. *PROPOSALS*.

There was little more I could say, except to put in my own terms some of what had already been said to me by the illusionist and the story-teller: that faith itself might be as much an illusion as the unreliable evidence of our senses, but that this was a risk we must simply bear; and that despite all the uncertainties of affairs we could at least seize on circumstances to set a good example, even if only in failure. There was perhaps something more. Even if, as the Prince had half-suggested, there was something in the condition of our political behaviour that necessarily turned even the wise and the good into fools and rogues, nevertheless faith demanded that this was a risk some must still take. Whether or not any good could come of it, we could believe that it might.

There was one more matter: hope was as good a guide to probability as fear; with hope and with a belief in goodness, even if of a modest and sceptical kind, it was possible to imagine that our species might slowly be improving itself. Perhaps none of our ideas would be realised in the forms in which we expressed them, but even if part of them could be realised in some other form, and even if this was largely by accident and in paradox, there seemed a chance of improvement: to be more positive, there seemed evidence that in many ways we had improved. Whether this was so or not, if all hope and all ideals were to be destroyed, what chance would there be that we should ever become better?

'I shall break that statement into four sections,' said the computer. '*(i) Confirmation of the hypothesis of the illusionist, (ii) Confirmation of the hypothesis of the story-teller, (iii) Confirmation of the hypothesis of the Prince, (iv) Personal conclusion.*' The computer paused. 'On second thoughts,' it said, 'I shall make the reference to the Prince the first section and renumber the others accordingly.'

When I said that the wording of these headings was more positive than the substance of what I had said – 'confirmation' was far too strong a word – the computer replied that it was the purpose of headings and sub-headings to attract or repel the attention of a busy man; the sub-headings it had suggested might be so attractive that no one would bother to read what was written under them; on the other hand, if the hypotheses referred to were no longer in fashion, I could always point to the highly qualified nature of the substance of my remarks as an indication of my dissatisfaction with the hypotheses. The computer then suggested that there could be one more section of the report: *4. SPECIAL PROBLEMS OF THE MODERN AGE.*

When I replied that it was even more ridiculous for me to comment on this matter than it was to have spoken of the other matters, the computer suggested that the heading should be altered to read: *4. A FEW TENTATIVE PRELIMINARY OBSERVATIONS ON THE PROBLEMS OF THE MODERN AGE.* 'It is not as good a heading as the first,' said the computer, 'but we must get on with this and finish it.'

I said that there was one special problem among the kind of people I had observed (and I could speak of no one else). This was not so much a lack of faith, or perhaps even of honour, but a certain dowdiness of belief. A faith in money as the calculus of good and a sense of honour in profit still seemed strong in them, yet this kind of avarice, perhaps understandable in the poverty of the past, no longer made complete sense in what seemed the prosperity of the present. There were in all ages jumpy, cunning creatures like my son, and bold brutes like my old comrade, but in ages with a sense of faith and honour that circumstances made convincing, their crimes could seem merely silly. What seemed to concern the Prince was that the present age needed a new rhetoric of honour. Times had changed and rhetoric should change with them. The faith of emulation and the honour of conflict could no longer really be believed in communities where there was enough prosperity for all to share and enough skill and intelligence for prosperity to continue to increase (its increase perhaps hampered mainly by those who struggled with each other in the name of prosperity). No doubt conflict would go on, whatever the rhetoric, but this was no reason for not changing the rhetoric; to do so might do good. It was obvious enough to me that there should be a return to some kind of rhetoric of love, although there was the danger, of course, that this could again excuse the violence it had previously aroused. If such a thing occurred, there might at least again be a relevant sense of the heroic, and although it was the heroism of martyrs that had previously best served this cause, there could also be a boldness in prudence. I recognised, however, that there would be political difficulties if the Prince raised the banner of love as his cause, even if the word were given a more careful and limited or even sceptical meaning that made it little more than, as it were, a practical extension of the sense of charity. At the same time it should be pointed out that it was not unknown in politics to put oneself forward as the true exponent of what one had previously opposed.

The computer said that I had provided enough for a report, too much in fact, and that if there had been no urgency it might have gone over what I had said and, for my own sake, suggested some deletions.

THE AUSTRALIA
DISCUSSION

11

THE AUSTRALIAN PEOPLE

Having written his 'snapshot' of how Australia seemed in the 1960s, The Lucky Country, D.H. had 'a go at the whole thing' in 1972. He wanted to write a history that might suggest some answers to the question: how did Australians become what they are? Here he looks at the 1940s.

The orphans of the Pacific

TROOPS IN AUSTRALIAN ARMY CAMPS WOKE ON 8 December 1941 to discover that Japanese aircraft had bombed the United States naval base at Pearl Harbor and blown up much of the US Pacific fleet. By nightfall many of the troops were moving to improvised battle stations here and there on the 19,000-kilometre coastline. At dawn they stood to, facing sand and sea. The Japanese invaded Malaya and the Philippines; after two days they sank the two warships Churchill had sent to defend the region and seized Guam; a fortnight later Hong Kong surrendered; five days more and the Americans evacuated Manila; another two weeks and Australian soldiers were fighting to defend the approaches to Singapore; a fortnight after that, they withdrew to the island of Singapore; a week later the Japanese attacked. A week

THE AUSTRALIA DISCUSSION

later Singapore fell, and into the smoke and flame of its quick destruction went the whole edifice of Empire defence. With a loss in prisoners of war proportionate to 100,000 British or 300,000 Americans, to Australians the disasters of Singapore could seem one of the greatest military defeats of the twentieth century. All the newspapers beat the drums that signalled, in effect, the failure of Empire: 'There have been few more serious miscalculations in all British history.' 'The results continue to be tragedy after tragedy, based on blunder after blunder.' The Prince of Wales had sworn in 1920 that as Australia stood by the Empire, so the Empire would stand by Australia. This had not proved to be true: there was talk of 'guilty men', and, among some, of British chicanery.

Surprise air raids on Darwin left blazing oil tanks, sunken ships, broken buildings: the Australian Chief of Staff warned that a Japanese invasion in the north might be expected early in April and an attack on the east coast in May. In Japan, General Tojo mocked Australia as 'the orphan of the Pacific, helplessly expecting Japan's attack'. Guerilla groups formed; there were suggestions for squads of blacktrackers and there was talk on both the Right and the Left of a 'people's army'. Some harbourside flats in Sydney emptied. Barbed wire and sandbags went up on its beaches. Signboards were pulled down, small boats impounded; 80,000 cattle were overlanded from the north to the south so that the Japanese couldn't eat them. There were plans for a scorched earth policy. Government departments moved their archives to safe places.

Two of the volunteer Divisions were brought back from the Middle East, and another 114,000 men were conscripted to add to the 132,000 already drafted into the militia, but there was a soreness about both the dispersal of forces home from Empire defence and the inadequate equipment and training of the home forces. The home army had only half the trucks and a sixth of the anti-aircraft guns it needed, only eighteen tanks, only six days' supply of anti-tank ammunition. Some of the men who went to battle stations in December had no weapon training. In theory the air forces had thirty-two squadrons, but their main equipment was trainers, and they were drastically under-crewed. It was decided that planes and men for sixty squadrons were needed.

Lines were drawn on maps. Not maps of France or the Middle East this time, but maps of Australia. The Newcastle–Sydney–Port Kembla area was to be held, and if possible, the 1600-kilometre stretch from Melbourne to Brisbane; there would be garrisons in Darwin, Port Moresby and a few other places. There was a certain amount of hope when General Douglas Macarthur arrived in March from the Philippines to be appointed Supreme Commander in April, and by June Australia had assembled, with varying degrees of equipment and training, almost half a million men in uniform, to which the United States added another 88,000. The Department of Information instructed the radio stations to play a new patriotic song, with the refrain, 'We're all together now, as we never were before; the Aussies and the Yanks, sure we're gonna win the war.' But by then Japanese submarines were sinking ships on the Australian east coast and had seized most of New Guinea. What was left of New Guinea was seen as the last stronghold from which to fight the battle for Australia.

Credibility was first given to the possibility that this battle might succeed when in the Coral Sea in May a United States naval force that had two Australian cruisers attached to it turned back a Japanese fleet moving to invade Port Moresby as part of a general plan to seize New Guinea, New Caledonia, Fiji and Samoa, isolate Australia and New Zealand from these bases, and attack key points in both countries to frighten them out of the war. The American repulse of this Japanese invasion force provided instant and enormous sustenance to Australians. They had lost Singapore, but gained the United States Navy.

In July, the Japanese seized Gona and Buna, pushed on to Kokoda, and threatened Port Moresby. In August, they attacked again, at Milne Bay, on New Guinea's extreme eastern tip, seeking its airstrips as a base for their endgame. They landed among Milne Bay's sago and mangrove swamps, but after a week's confused fighting in relentless rain, each side lacking maps and blundering into the other, the Australians won. It was the first land defeat the Japanese had known. Field Marshal William Slim was later to say, 'It was the Australian soldiers who first broke the spell of the invincibility of the Japanese army.'

On the newsreels the mud and rain of the Battle of the Owen Stanley Ranges now placed it alongside Tobruk as a continuing cinema story. Two small armies confronted each other, both weakened by malaria, strung out in the slush of tracks that cut a path through sweltering jungle. The Australians conquered the mountains and gorges, then the flat swampy country, then took their two bases back from the Japanese. It was 1943. Who would win the war still remained to be seen, but the feeling had begun that Australia was no longer in immediate danger. It was again part of something bigger. It no longer had to fight for itself, but for an ally.

*

Despite what had seemed a direct threat to Australia's survival, there had not been much appeal to national sentiment. Australians wanted to save themselves, but there was little speech-making about what they were supposed to be saving. In one of his first war speeches, staying with the prevailing fashion, John Curtin had said, 'We shall hold this country ... as a citadel for the British-speaking race,' as if Australians were holding their nation for King George. There was shock when he came out more realistically: 'Without any inhibition of any kind I make it quite clear that Australia looks to America, free of any pangs as to our traditional links or kinship with the United Kingdom.' The habit of wars being an occasion for imperial rhetoric was so strong that this speech (privately denounced by Churchill as 'flaunted round the world by our enemies') was treated as a stab in the back for Britain. The Archbishop of Brisbane said, 'The most audacious piece of Fifth Column activity hitherto seen in this country has been the effort to belittle Britain's part in the war.' Other changes, such as having more Australian commentators on Australian radio and attempts to make 'Advance Australia Fair' the national song, were seen as further blows to Australia's patriotism.

What summed up the laconic wartime faith of Australians was a sentence in a union newspaper: 'It is not in the Australian make-up to squib a fight.' But this was not the language of speech-making. Soldiers could still call each other 'mate' or 'Dig', as if they were their fathers, but this time within the army there was no sense of building a nation. The division between volunteers and conscripts caused much bitterness – there were two armies, not one – and there was not much pride in the despairing scramble to throw brigades into New Guinea, or in the lonely fear of fighting in some of the world's most difficult country, with malaria, dysentery and typhus greater killers than the enemy. As the war settled into shapes of possible victory, the Americans sailed north after prestige, leaving the Australians with the humble, debilitating, dangerous and strategically unnecessary role of mopping up leftover Japanese. The Australian war machine was now working so vigorously that it became overheated: soldiers began to be released from munition-making and fighting to maintain Australia as a supply base for the Americans; but the Australian Government wished to keep men fighting, so that Australia might have a voice at the Peace Conference. This time it was in the arena of world politics that the war and its aftermath gave intimations of nationhood. Dr H.V. ('Bert') Evatt, now returned to politics and become the External Affairs Minister, threw himself with a showman's enthusiasm into creating the drama of an independent Australian foreign policy. He issued a warning to the great powers that Australia might be small in the world but it was big in the Southwest Pacific: to make this sound real, Australia entered into its first independent treaty. All it could find was New Zealand, but Evatt discovered a bigger stage in the San Francisco Conference of 1945, called to settle the constitution of the United Nations. He appointed himself champion of the smaller powers, fought hard against big power domination, and achieved some reforms and a wide personal reputation.

With a rough-and-ready drive, and with the single-minded impatience of an ambitious entrepreneur, he threw up around him a bigger, if disordered, External Affairs Department to carry out his 'bustling diplomacy'. Australia now had fifteen diplomatic missions; it was one of the four nations of the Allied Commission in defeated Japan (where it represented Britain and India); an Australian commanded the British Commonwealth Occupation Forces; Evatt became chairman of the United Nations General Assembly. Menzies attacked 'the utter independence of Australian thought and action – which, for seven million people in a small island continent is more pretentious than sensible – as if no special British relation assisted at all', and Evatt's Australian style was derided as 'a sort of larrikin strain in Australian foreign policy, a disposition to throw stones at the street lights just because they are bright'. But Evatt was driven by the adventurous ambition of making Australia one of the consciences of humankind, determined on a fair go among nations, 'in the forefront of the councils of the world', with a policy on everything.

Although there were no Australian diplomatic missions in South-East Asia, there was a feeling of concern for an area where European colonialists, knocked over by the Japanese, were trying to put themselves back into place; there were attacks on 'outmoded, reactionary and feudal forms of government' and hopes for 'a harmonious association of democratic states in the Southeast Asian area'. When the Dutch began to try to put down the revolt of the Indonesian nationalists (describing it as a 'police action') Australia brought the conflict before the Security Council, and Indonesia appointed Australia as its representative on the three-man Committee of Good Offices. With the second 'police action' Australia moved on the UN for the expulsion of the Dutch, and when Indonesia entered the UN it chose Australia as one of its two sponsors, and saw Australia as one of its greatest friends.

But Australia did not feel big enough to face the future. 'Asian countries will undoubtedly be looking at us,' said Ben Chifley, who succeeded Curtin as Prime Minister, 'and there will be increasing pressure for an outlet for their populations.' Unless Australia quickly got more people these Asians might come and take its empty spaces. To fill them up, Australia could not be too fussy: for the first time in its history, it now had to buy immigrants who weren't British. At first there was a hope that 'for every foreign migrant there will be ten people from the United Kingdom'. But the British were harder to get than that. The Government turned to the International Refugee Organisation and contracted to give large numbers of 'displaced persons' free passages. As 170,000 Poles, 'Balts', Russians, Ukrainians, Hungarians and others from the refugee camps came to Australia, these 'DPs' began to outmatch the British immigrants. Immigration agreements were signed with other countries; assisted Italians, Germans and Dutch joined the DPs; the target of 70,000 a year for immigration went up to 150,000.

Many of the immigrants were tied for two years to working where they were sent, and this gave the Government a chance to send them to jobs Australians didn't want; but in a country which had always hated its immigrants there were fears of new outbursts of prejudice and hostility. The name 'New Australian' was invented to reassure Australians that even 'Balts' and Italians were fellow creatures, but for safety's sake the Immigration Department set up an Assimilation Branch in the hope that as quickly as possible these foreigners could be made to look like Australians. However, the immigrants' labour broke bottlenecks in steel production, housing, public works, transport. Things began to move again. There were again hopes that if it could be developed, Australia's potential would be unlimited.

*

This hope was nowhere stronger than among the businessmen who during the war had gone into the government departments and improvised an armaments industry. Because of the confident strength of the BHP and its associates, along with several other monopolies or near-monopolies, there had been enough engineering and management tradition for remarkable examples of wartime resourcefulness. The manufacture of the 4000 component parts of the first field gun was farmed out in two days, and the gun was being produced within seven months. The British had said it would take two years. Optical glass was manufactured against British warnings that the task was beyond Australia and against a boycott by the British manufacturers. An aircraft industry that produced 3500 aircraft of nine different types was thrown up. Destroyers, corvettes, frigates, merchant ships and 33,643 small craft came from Australia's shipyards. The BHP developed 140 specialist steels. Machine tools, not made on any scale before, were produced in great number and variety. Improvised technical training mass-produced tens of thousands of skilled tradesmen. There was not much of a science base to most of this, nor much technological invention – it was mainly a case of getting instructions and having a go – but there were inventive modifications.

With this further onrush of industrialisation and the broadening of experience in the production of capital equipment, an impressive number of buildings, skills and machines went off into private manufacturing when the war was finished; but an equally important product of the crash war program was the development, for the first time, of an influential class of manufacturers – emergent businessmen who saw themselves as 'the real life-savers that Australia always needed', and who had 'got into the habit of relying on their own resources on practically all occasions ... accustomed to making decisions all round'. They now saw themselves as the backbone of the long-delayed development of Australia as a manufacturing country: but Australia was still a country without industrial research, without management skills, and without a sophisticated banking community.

The improvisation of an Australian industrial effort had also made it a 'different war from last time' for women. In the first war, women had become, if anything, more marginalised, in the sense that, in relation to the great dramas of the age, they were being defined not in themselves, but merely in relation to the boys in uniform – as mothers, wives, sweethearts, sisters. This time, some women were themselves in uniform (although paid only two-thirds the male rate for equal work) and, at least over the time when it seemed possible that Australia might be invaded, women could also see themselves, potentially, in a frontline – instead of knitting socks they could dig air-raid trenches; with 'the American invasion', those who befriended United States servicemen were able to experience a sense of change available only to men in the first war. And this time a much greater number of women went to work in factories – a minority of them into men's work women had not been allowed to do before, where, although they were expected to go back home after the war, as a result of the interventions of a special Women's Employment Board set up by the Government, they were being paid up to 90 per cent of men's wages or, in some cases, as much as men (thereby building up a challenge for the future). However, those who went into traditional 'women's work' were paid scarcely more than half the male rate, a wage so low that a shortage developed, forcing the Government's significantly named 'Manpower Control' to draft women into factories, where they were made to work as cheap labour. (Finally, the Government overrode both the employers and the Arbitration Court and increased those women's wages – but only to 75 per cent of male rates.)

Although there were many humiliations for women in this, it was the first time in Australia's history when the State encouraged women to work in some field other than domestic service; it was a time of raised ambitions. But the *Australian Women's Weekly* and its advertisers worked to remind women of where their true ambitions should still lie – that whatever they were doing during the war it was still their first task to remain 'feminine'. 'She's doing a job of national importance,' said a Pond's Face Cream ad in the *Weekly*, 'but she doesn't forget the importance of looking lovely for *him*.'

The war had also given Australia its first complex national administration, parts of which also saw themselves as the backbone of national development. The number of departments had nearly doubled, the number of employees had trebled, and new powers had come to the Commonwealth: a virtual monopoly of income tax had been gained from a High Court decision and full powers over social services from a referendum. All except one civilian department gained new heads during the war – several in their thirties, one aged only thirty-two, others in their forties; the Public Service had become younger and much more ambitious in its sense of what it could do.

Some of the university-educated people who had pushed themselves into the departments stayed after the war and within them a smaller group, 'the planners', showed the same talents as the businessmen for hard work, devotion and improvisation, the same self-belief and resourcefulness, the same confidence that they could do anything without thinking about it very deeply. Attacked as 'long-hairs', they acquired special strength in the Post-War Reconstruction Department and as 'the Chifley men' – a group of advisers who surrounded Ben Chifley. At their most cohesive, this devoted group saw themselves as the agents of a social revolution based on the joint ideas of rationality and welfare; they represented another attempt to bring Australia into a state of Improvement through colonial governmentalism. With a stronger momentum and a more definitive sense of purpose than their Labor Party patrons, they became the principal initiators of policy. No field of endeavour seemed outside their talents: Government support for the arts, higher education, town and regional planning were on their list along with economic growth, full employment, immigration and social welfare. An Englishman was brought out to advise on the setting up of a national theatre.

When the bustle subsided, one of the significant changes that remained from the excitements of adventurous improvising carried out under the name of planning was that Australians regained some of the position in social welfare of which they had earlier been so unexpectedly deprived, although they were still to be behind most of the other prosperous countries. A comprehensive social security program emerged, based on 'non-contributory' methods. In a five-year battle, doctors sabotaged a proposed free medical scheme, but there were now widows' pensions, unemployment and sickness pensions, pharmaceutical, hospital and funeral benefits, an employment service, a housing scheme.

Colonial governmentalism produced bodies to control the stevedoring and coal industries and the marketing of farm products; it nationalised international telecommunications and the Australian overseas airline QANTAS, and it set up a government-owned internal airline, a shipping line, a whaling industry and an aluminium industry. The idea that humankind might be saved by public works and irrigation projects reached its apotheosis in the Snowy River Scheme, one of the largest engineering works in the world, declared by Chifley to be 'the greatest single project in our history. It is a plan for the whole nation.' It was more than an economic plan: it was a claim to Australian greatness. One of Chifley's most significant advisers said, 'In a very real sense public works contribute to a fullness in the national life by adding a sense of achievement and consciousness of growth to the life of the individual.'

It was now hoped, as had happened at the very beginning of New South Wales, that it might be the Government that controlled initiative in almost everything. The hopes of the planners reached their highest points in the last six months of 1944 when they were drafting a White Paper on full employment. A product of both the politicians' bitter memories of the Depression and the planners' ideals of rational conduct, the White Paper was to provide the theoretical basis for all future achievement. Its first draft was ready by December 1944; its seventh draft reached Cabinet in April 1945; by the time the politicians had finished with it, it had been rewritten enough for some planners to think about going back to their universities; but it was nevertheless seen as a 'unique and historic prospectus'. Chifley declared in the 1949 election, 'So far as it can humanly contrive, never again will dole queues be seen in this country.'

By then there had been defeat for an attempt by referendum to gain the Commonwealth all the powers it needed for controlling all the activities it wanted to control. Two more limited attempts were then also defeated, but the spirit of the White Paper remained: with initiatives coming from the Government, Australia would expand and develop through industrialisation and immigration so that there would be jobs for everyone and fair shares for all. The belief in economic growth was so great that Labor's plans were not really for a welfare state, but for a society of high economic growth: from this would come jobs, and jobs were the true basis of human happiness and prosperity.

'The planners' were part of a more general hope for an intellectual breakthrough. New painters in Melbourne wanted to apply to Australian complacency 'incessant waves of shock'. Some of them abandoned the naturalistic style for a version of the German expressionist movement around the time of World War I, in which what mattered was not that painters should 'convey' reality, but, by the way they painted, show their relation to existence. Painters in both Sydney and Melbourne had returned to the landscape as a symbol for Australia and the human spirit – but the landscapes they found were not the conventional hopeful grasslands of the sheep country but the red deserts of the arid interior. In the Adelaide-Melbourne magazine *Angry Penguins* there was a sense of literary and intellectual apocalypse; in the Brisbane-Melbourne magazine *Meanjin Papers* old democratic voices took new literary forms. As part of the revulsion against the savagery of the Depression, the drabness that followed it, and the near-disasters of the war, for a while the Labor Party had the aura of social change: it had won by such a landslide in the 1943 election that the already disintegrating UAP was smothered, and a new party, the Liberal Party, had to be formed out of its wreckage. New horizons seemed to break out; there were new senses of the possible. New men were seen as relevant for new occasions.

But things could also get back to seeming the same. 'I am a refugee from Australian culture,' said Albert Tucker, one of the new Melbourne painters, when he left Australia in 1947. Some of the planners did go back to the universities. Despite the noise, a dullness fell over focal points of political struggle. Chifley called for a 'golden age' but people could not find out which way he was looking. In a period of shortages and shoddiness, they wanted not distant goals of 'national development', for which austerely puritan sacrifices were said to be necessary, but something to go on with after the shortages and shoddiness of an economy debauched by war. (The economists derided this as 'the milk-bar economy'.) Political debate sank into trench warfare: from prepared positions increasingly intense barrages on both sides concealed a lack of movement. Newspapers engaged in 'constant propaganda to show that all politicians are knaves and fools, all Government enterprises hopelessly inefficient, all civil servants bumbling idiots tied up in their own red tape'. When Chifley abruptly decided to try to nationalise the banks he was cartooned alongside Hitler and Mussolini as one of the 'National Socialist leaders of the 20th Century'. From these crudities Chifley retreated to the over-simplifications of his planners. The businessmen who had shared much of the experience of the planners and had much the same improvising adventurous spirit began to retreat to the other side, joining the more conservative financial and professional interests who had been there all the time. In a situation in which there was on both sides an impatience with complexity and a brutalising of debate, and in which the Government seemed to be running out of ideas anyway, Labor was defeated by the new Liberal Party in the 1949 elections. But to many it seemed obvious that Labor would be out of office only long enough to fix itself up and come back fighting again. The 1940s had seemed Labor's decade and, as it had seemed before World War I, Labor could appear to be the natural ruling party.

12

MONEY MADE US

D.H.'s early writing had used some of the language of an economics primer. The world economic crisis of the 1970s caused him to modify his thinking. Money Made Us, *published in 1976, examined aspects of Australia's economic culture and is a seminal work in Australian cultural studies.*

The secular faith of growth

Faith in economic growth was perhaps the most widespread secular faith in the world after the Second World War, affecting communist and Third World countries as well as the capitalist industrialised countries. New methods of statistical measurement had produced new goals which were at first reflected in the phrase 'national income' and then in the phrase 'gross national product'. To those concerned with human welfare as much as those concerned with national strategic strength, estimates of gross national product, usually referred to in the abbreviated (and more sacred) form, G.N.P., seemed a simple test of failure or success. To students of the importance of a confident repetition of initials, G.N.P. might seem as significant in its time as S.P.Q.R. was to the Romans and A.M.D.G. to the Christians. To the magic of letters was added the magic of numbers: human activities that by G.N.P. statistical conventions could be given a number were what mattered in life; those that couldn't be measured (like housework) were not to be taken into account. They weren't part of the economy. Even among those who knew what the numbers meant, this limitation could be forgotten; laymen, whose use of the numbers could be largely incantatory, didn't always know about this limitation. There were many examples of a sense of Australian failure in the 1960s when a year's G.N.P. figures pointed in the wrong direction. I shall take my commemorative example from Arthur Calwell's book *Labor's Role in Modern Society* because it represents so many features of the Australian version of faith in economic growth:

> If one measures Australia's production performance against that of other countries with which we trade, our record is quite mediocre. Japan and Germany, both devastated by war, have doubled Australia's rate of growth ... Per capita income has grown no faster in Australia than in the United Kingdom – a country with a particularly stagnant economy. In the world growth-tables we are well down the list. Compared with such countries as Germany, France, Italy and Japan, our record in economic growth is not fast enough.

If Adam Smith was the ideologue of free enterprise, members of the new faith in a 'mixed economy' could look to the extremely lucid and convincing writings of J.M. Keynes; these made everything seem easy, for a generation and a half. In the economics course I took as a diplomatic cadet, we were run through this and that in the first year, then in second year when we sat down to Keynes's *General Theory of Employment, Interest and Money* we knew it was the main meal. Keynes's was a different rationality from Adam Smith's. It didn't find a natural rationality in events, to be discovered only if things were left alone; it looked instead for ways to impose a rationality that events might lack if left to themselves. What went on in an economy depended on what was spent by consumers, businesses and governments and it was up to governments to take the initiative and make both their own spending and that of the others more rational; to keep total spending up if consumers or businessmen cut down their spending, governments could spend more themselves and, in several different ways, encourage consumers or businesses to start spending again. It was 'the responsibility of Commonwealth and State Governments' said the White Paper of the 1940s, 'to provide the general framework of a full employment economy within which the operations of individuals and businesses can be carried on'. This approach pleased both old Labor hands with their belief that the panacea of cheap credit would relieve unemployment, and new university-educated men coming into government departments, who were looking for more sensible ways of running things. All it lacked was the depression it was designed for: as it turned out, by the late 1940s unemployment was down to 0.5 per cent, not 5 per cent.

Confidence grew that there wouldn't be another depression. Threat of a depression was one form of economic crisis that economists could always do something about. The tools were in the shed, waiting. Keynesian faith developed into the idea of 'fine tuning'. Economists could be imagined as being at the instruments console of an automated factory, watching indicators, making calculations, turning knobs. Taxation policy and banking policy could be moved around to meet whatever minor economic crisis turned up next. Sometimes there was a slightly uncomfortable jolt, especially when, by accident, a change of policy developed more force than was intended (like doctors, economists could cause a significant proportion of the total problems they purported to cure) but compared with the past, fine tuning appeared to work well; or at least it didn't seem to do much harm. Among what were thought of as 'comparable countries', only Germany was significantly lower than Australia in unemployment, and few of these countries had lower rates of inflation. There was a comfortable feeling when one thought of the world that the rules of the economy were known or were there for the knowing. If things went wrong in economic policy, in the form of 'stop-go' it would be seen simply as a mistake in diagnosis: the methods were there; the government's officials would do better next time. For the Labor Party of the late 1960s the economic problem almost seemed to disappear: it was a matter of 'achieving general welfare through full employment without inflation'. The shadow Treasurer, Frank Crean, read a number of books and did a bit of writing himself: he was getting ready for the job. Then when Labor was at the instruments console, with the 1974 inflation-unemployment crisis, things came apart in their hands.

By the end of the 1960s, when so many of the certainties of the rich, industrial countries began to be challenged, there had been reports in Australian newspapers of the phenomenon of 'stagflation', of inflation and slowness in economic growth happening together, a conjunction not allowed for in fine tuning. Briefly, this didn't seem to have much to do with Australia, but by 1971 Australia was quickly becoming like the rest of the rich industrial world and showed signs of 'slumpflation', of inflation and unemployment happening together. Among those who knew that Gough Whitlam had not caused the world economic crisis there began to grow an uncomfortable feeling, shared in all the other affluent countries that, after all, the rules of the economy were not known, or that there were some new rules but no one could find out what they were. Keynesian economics seemed busted. A substitute form of confidence had not arrived.

This was the real economic crisis that began to threaten the Whitlam government in 1974. What had happened was a crisis in faith: all over the world people seemed to be losing one economic faith without agreeing that they had found another; they didn't know what to believe next. When Whitlam realised that the old faith on which his program of steady amelioration depended was not working, he seemed to retreat into sulks: in fact what was happening was that he was recovering from culture-shock. He was changing from a concept of inflation being primarily caused by demand (too much money chasing too few goods) to a concept of inflation being primarily caused by the push of wages and prices, which somehow had got a momentum of their own. Snedden had learned some of the language of this distinction before Whitlam did. He spoke it during the 1974 election campaign but he was unable to talk about it as if he meant it or in a way that made people think they understood. Then for a while unemployment became the major scandal; briefly the crisis in faith seemed to ease – unemployment was a familiar problem; there were plenty of books on it, and Jim Cairns, then the Treasurer, had read them. But the crisis was still there. In 1975 there were new fashions, with great concentration on limiting the budget deficit to a sacred number and worrying about the money supply.

In the period of lost faith, I cannot believe that in terms of inflation and unemployment it made much difference whether the Labor Party or the Liberal and Country parties governed Australia. The Liberals may have taken a different direction from Labor's but they would probably have ended in a similar situation. If one looks at inflation from the traditional view, one can see it as being, in the first place, 'imported' into Australia, in the forms of higher export incomes and higher import prices. Liberal addiction to foreign money and Country Party dislike of upvaluing the Australian currency might have heightened inflation in 1973, as Labor policies did by other means. The Liberals might then have followed Treasury advice earlier than Labor and tried to deflate in the traditional manner, but this might have produced higher unemployment earlier, with no drop in inflation, and a panic attempt to increase employment, costing just as much money as Labor's, even if some would have gone to different people. The inflation rate would then have been pushed up. The unique magnifier of inflation in Australia may have been the arbitration system, and this would have produced much the same results whoever was governing.

But the real crisis was a conceptual crisis, a crisis of intellect and faith, accompanying a collapse in the economic order of the affluent age. The system wasn't working anymore. There was no longer an effective belief (one that seemed to get results) that certain kinds of events were the prime 'causes' of inflation and that therefore they were the events to change. The loss of faith was evident throughout the capitalist industrial nations. Each of these nations seemed able to produce its own causes for reaching a situation common to all of them. With the rules apparently gone, all policies ended in unexpected distortions. Everywhere there was inflation and unemployment. The optimism of the full employment era had gone. What was needed was some way of running things in which there could be both sustenance and honour in *not* working, or at least in not working at what was thought of as a 'job' in the Keynesian era. Instead, the phrase 'dole bludgers' was used in 1975 and 1976 to describe the unemployed, as if there were still jobs to have, and it was their fault they didn't have them.

Driving across the red-sand plain, some 900 kilometres west of Sydney, we saw a sign beside the road saying SUNSET STRIP. We drove off the highway along a sand track between recently planted trees and behind the trees we found a long street lined with a couple of hundred houses, tennis courts, gardens, speedboats. There was a lake for boating on one side, and a golf course on the other. Outside the recreation hut a noticeboard said SUNSET STRIP PROGRESS

ASSOCIATION. A man who proved to be the oldest inhabitant explained to us that Sunset Strip, which had started eight years before, was a retirement area. The economic significance of this oasis of suburban optimism in red-sand wilderness was that its only economic activity consisted of pension and superannuation payments and unemployment-relief schemes. In that sense, it represents what some people see as a spring of optimism for the future – the notion that the affluent societies, even if they have lost the trick of maintaining conventional full employment without hyper-inflation, will find new ways, quite different from our present techniques of job creation, to maintain welfare without destroying dignity. (Not all of them necessarily government handouts: new economic forms – collectives, co-operatives, communes – might also develop.) Left, right and centre political parties have tended to base employment and welfare policies on the expected growth of manufacturing. But it is the decline in the dynamics of manufacturing that is part of the present crisis. Perhaps we need a patriotism of not earning wages, or a new principle of sustenance such as a universal minimum income scheme. The search for a 'new Keynes', an economist who would light up some new path, may be a march in the wrong direction. It may not be economic policy we should be looking for, but changes in political policy and political idealism, and in social morality – and in the structure of social and economic power. It may simply have been an oddity of history that for a while we could make a prophet out of an economist.

The profit motive

When I think of the worship of money I think of the great principled sacrifice made in 1972 by Frank Packer. It would be quite wrong to say that money was all that mattered to Packer, but it would be true to say money was his god. He had many other diversions but as a serious man of principle with a view of personal values and social order, he spoke gravely of money, and of the greatness of profit. His perspective had profit as the great principle holding society together: men who made profits were the nation's benefactors. The atmosphere in his surroundings was heavy with money: there was a big steel safe sticking up in the middle of his office with money in it; stacks of papers with figures on them lay in neat batches on his desk; wherever his hand fell it was likely to be on figures; men came in and out with documents about money; people would sit around his desk and speak of profit and loss; in surprise raids he would call for the expense accounts, the petty cash vouchers, the contributors' claims, and with his felt pen scrawl out items, then wait and see who complained; in a crisis, records would be spread in front of him and he would look over the lists, point to names and order sackings; or he would order others to make economies, with the threat that if they did not do so he would make them arbitrarily; when he was holding court, dry martini in hand at one o'clock, whisky in hand at six o'clock, the conversation was likely to be about the goings and comings of money. But he did have indulgences in which money was used for other purposes. The most regularly extravagant of these was the morning newspaper he owned, the *Daily Telegraph*. He loved the *Daily Telegraph*. It lost money all the time; perhaps no one apart from Packer himself and a few of his court esteemed it; many derided it; by the kindest standards it was humdrum; but Packer loved it. It seemed like *power* to him; he would think of something and the next morning there it was in the paper. It appeared to give him political influence. It gave him interesting guests to invite for dinner, esteem when he was in London and New York, his knighthood. But I think he also loved it for itself – its racing news, the printing presses in the basement, the ledgers upstairs recording its failures, the comic strips, the newsagents' accounts, the sub-editors at their semi-circular desk, the attacks on the Labor Party, the teleprinters, the scruffy typography, the stereo department, the stock exchange reports, the letters to the editor, the lift-drivers (until he sacked them). Perhaps it also held for him reminders of promise – the excitements when he took it over in 1936, the improvisations and hopes of a younger man. Those who wanted the company to make bigger profits saw the *Telegraph* as their main enemy. There would be private meetings: for a while they would talk about improving the *Telegraph*'s sales; then they would stop; they knew they couldn't get their hands on it until Packer was dead. Sometimes they would dream that he might sell it. There had been offers, but nothing happened. Then in a couple of days of private excitement the *Daily Telegraph* and the *Sunday Telegraph* were sold to Rupert Murdoch, for $15 million. Packer didn't need the money; $15 million couldn't console him for the loss of the unique pleasures the *Telegraph* had given him; but he had sold it because he was a man of principle. Fifteen million dollars, even if he didn't need it, was too large to be refused by someone who saw profit as the prime mover of human affairs. He would have denied his own humanity if he had refused it. His reaction to this sacrifice was so great that people wondered if it might kill him. Several times he cried when he spoke of it; his face was pinched and his gaze distracted; he walked slowly like a wounded old man, his hand on a helpful shoulder; his words wandered; he spoke of the dead as if they were still alive and gave orders about men and machinery that it was no longer in his power to give. Those in his office who loved him spoke of the goodness of a man who could make such a sacrifice.

At times, in a country like Australia, the word 'profit' has been used as if the word itself contained the key to the mysteries of society; it can be seen as the dynamic that makes everything work either well, or lamentably. At times it has been even too sacred to be directly named. In a radio broadcast, for example, Menzies praised it without mention, except in the euphemism 'reward':

> If our material civilisation is to produce improved and improving standards it must have a dynamic quality. It must aim constantly at progress. And there can be no progress without enterprise; the encouragement of enterprise in the most direct human fashion, that is by the prospect of reward, seems to be fundamental.

On the other side, the Labor Party believed that control of profits, or even their abolition, would answer most human disappointments. It was natural that when Whitlam became Prime Minister he should want to set up a Prices Justification Tribunal to control profits and that for some Labor people the first, for some the only, remedy against the inflation of the time was to bring profits down. They brought profits down and when they found it hadn't worked, for a few of them that was the end of their policy. For their part, some of Labor's opponents, holding to the Packer principle that the profit-makers were the benefactors of the nation, seemed to think that the spirit of profit, if liberated in pure form, would drive away inflation. These differences on 'the profit motive' can for some people present the battle between the forces of light and the forces of darkness, the

Holy Spirit and the Evil Spirit, that in other civilisations is recognised more obviously as theological.

In what way profits are a decisive consideration is now harder to estimate than these opposite creeds suggest, as any reader of John Kenneth Galbraith would know. It is not only profit that makes a money civilisation; it is also income, property, price, the general emphasis on money-making as a basis of social order, the estimation of attitudes to money as measures of moral worth, the use of money as an exact language, as a confidence-creating abstraction, as a value-creator and as a grader of persons and objects.

The classic kinds of attitudes about maximising profits might apply to small businesses, or slightly more complicated businesses where people might still think they know what they are doing, or some (not many) larger businesses, such as Packer's company; although Packer's was a public company, it was made to appear in myth that he was 'the proprietor', and he, like other newspaper proprietors – but to an extraordinary degree – had the knack of seeming to run the company as if it were a corner store. But the difference is easy to see in large, abstract business bureaucracies with no sense of personalised ownership. Such formations are so complicated, and the conditions in the outside world about which they must make guesses are so complex, that they have much more serious matters than just maximising profits to worry about. To stay in business, to keep their shareholders or their overseas controllers quiet, and to increase their own salaries and benefits, the persons who run them have to produce regular increases in annual earnings and they have tried to do this by getting bigger rather than by running their firms more efficiently. In this context 'profit' means making enough money to stay in business and to satisfy the nominal owners (the mysterious shareholders) or the overseas controllers: what is critically important is to continue to get funds to finance continuing expansion. In this context 'profit', with all of its rich associations with free enterprise as the basis of social order, may be most important simply as a legitimising idea, as a sacred word that should be present in all serious discussion, just as in other situations there is a use of words like 'democracy', or 'the people'.

A 'government-controlled' enterprise (a government-owned enterprise run by a bureaucracy but 'answerable' in unpredictable ways to some parts of the government) can sometimes get funds for expansion without showing profits. So can a foreign-controlled enterprise (an enterprise run by a bureaucracy that is a colony of a bureaucratic business-world empire in which the top of the hierarchy is located in a foreign city); if its world controllers develop a fancy for it, an Australian branch can expand although showing regular losses, usually because this is part of an operation against a world rival; from a profit viewpoint this may not make much sense but such seasons of indulgence can last for some time – at least until things get too tough back home. Funds for expansion are not so easily raised by 'shareholder-controlled' Australian enterprises (enterprises run by bureaucracies, but answerable, in that unless they produce a certain level of dividend the shareholders may accept another company's takeover offer). A company will get funds to expand despite losses if it is part of a larger Australian company whose controllers for some reason or other feel like expansion and have some spare money. But in the top company it is hard for them to go on raising money for expansion without overall profits or at least the promise that at some time there will be profits. (Occasionally this is done by cheating.) Continuing to get extra funds is a condition of continuing to expand business. It is expansion – growth – that is the dynamic, not profit-making. Profit-making is one of the ways that make possible continuing funding of continuing expansion.

Why is there this obsession that companies should go on getting bigger? At its most elemental, company growth feeds the esteem of those who preside over it. A great explosion of importance can come with the increase in the mass of their wealth and property. Imagine the self-esteem at his commercial height of Ben Boyd, the 1840s stockbroker turned Australian colonial speculator, one of the 'haughty, gentlemanly selfish class', 'always devising some plan of pleasure or business', controller of two townships, a bank, a whaling station, a whaling fleet, coastal steamers, wool stores and more than 2 million hectares of sheep runs before he went broke, unsuccessfully tried his luck in the Californian goldfields and then disappeared on an expedition to the Solomon Islands where he was reportedly concerned with establishing a 'Papuan Republic or Confederation'; presumably he was killed, perhaps eaten. Packer, more like Ben Boyd than like a modern company executive, had a similar sense of personal expansion through activity; as his business grew, he grew. His money, and the machines, buildings, staffs, furniture, newspapers, magazines, books, television programs about which he could make decisions, were part of his personal substance: they gave him bulk. To these he added his horse-racing, his expensive America's Cup challenges, his knighthood, his generosities, his ruggedness, by these means giving his bulk glamour.

By people looking for easy answers to the problems of human misunderstanding he was seen as desiring power over people's minds and over governments, but I don't think that from day to day this meant much to him. Others may have tried to use him for these purposes, but when he went in for them himself he wasn't much good at it. The power he wanted was the power of size and achievement. It was for the sense of infinite expansion that he bullied old machines, fought for market shares and strove for baubles and trophies. And usually, when he used his *Daily Telegraph* in the opinion business, the power of expressing his own opinions excited him more than the prospect of influencing others: just as he wanted to control big companies and win big cups, he wanted to make a big noise and say what he thought was right. To try to influence people would have been demeaning.

For Ben Boyd and Frank Packer there was a sense of personal ownership. This was partly untrue in Packer's case in that he was using shareholders' money as well as his own, and, as it turned out, altogether untrue in Boyd's case because all his enterprises simply rose on a bubble and burst: but they both saw themselves as proprietors and had their sense of importance extended by the size of what they were seen to own. Most modern executives don't own as much. Nevertheless, most modern executives can feel they are increasing their bulk and glamour by extending the number of digits magnetised in their companies' names in the memory banks of the computers.

However, something more than satisfaction of size pushes executives into a craving for external growth. What also pushes them is, simply, fear. In the mysterious shiftings of the anonymous 'market', who can be sure he knows the secrets of how to survive? For those who are competitive, continuing compulsive anxiety about their share of the market produces continuing novelty, new marketing plans, new production techniques, new advertising styles, new office systems, above all, new brands or continuing revisions of existing brands. If a company is not ever-active, ever-growing, there is a fear that competitors will reduce its 'market share'. Firms startle themselves by buying other firms or lurching into quite new lines of business, hoping that somehow, if they keep moving, the whole show won't collapse. Even monopolies keep moving, diversifying into new kinds of ventures, spreading out, afraid their luck won't last. For some this anxiety is also pleasurable: they are gamblers whose delight in growth is partly found in its uncertainty. Others are afraid of risk; they dread the excitement of new policy; but they can't avoid it. Others believe in prediction, research, programming; they move confidently and methodically into the unknown. But whatever their reaction they see growth as essential to survival. Packer, for whom the excitements of risk and the lust for achievement may have been even more compelling than the delights of bigness, was nevertheless also afraid. He could look at his properties and see how each could quickly die. Only ceaseless activity would save them. At other times even that belief went and he was left only with the stoicism of the gambler. I remember one Saturday night being uncharacteristically caught in a drinking session with him and some others in his boardroom; as everyone drank more we all agreed that life was a game of cards.

In the money civilisation as well as the accuracy and abstractness of money, its carefulness and respectability, there are the gamblers and desperadoes – not only the larrikins, but many of the 'monied people' themselves. Respectability earned great victories in the Australian colonies when wage earners invested in savings banks and building societies, 'owned their own homes', and joined friendly societies; but throughout the nineteenth century a large proportion of the rich were not respectable and prudent, but lucky gamblers, traders, squatters, gold-mine promoters, land sharks. Stock exchanges developed most vigorously out of speculation in gold shares. The 1960s and early 1970s stock exchange gambling on minerals came from a long Australian tradition of risk, greed, carelessness and crookedness.

The stock exchanges display the ambiguities of money. On one side they are temples of moral and social significance, of intelligence and efficiency: carefully articulated by electronic equipment, they can be seen as the backbone of private enterprise, itself the basis of social order. They represent growth, production, investment, expansion, progress, *capital*. The other side is pure recklessness: the yappings of voices at the time of a boom, the quick scribblings on boards, the telephone calls, the conning of trusting clients, the fiddles, the muddles. When the minerals boom collapsed and there was not much business in the brokers' offices, some of those who had done best out of the boom had to spend months finding out where everything was, clearing up the mess.

The shareholder has been seen as the archetype of capitalism. Yet one can say a great deal about Australia's buying and selling without talking about shareholders. In effect, big businesses now are bureaucracies concerned with the anonymous and mysterious idea of 'the shareholder' only as a threat in a takeover campaign. Even the few freaks – some media companies, some retail chains, a few others – that still look like old family concerns can do so only because shareholders are kept in their place. People from certain rich families remain company directors in big companies that are not foreign-owned, but this is less because they have financial control through their shareholdings than because they are part of a self-perpetuating social oligarchy of rich office-holders. The major shareholders in most companies are other companies, and much of the investment money of firms is raised not by selling shares on the stock exchange but by borrowing money. The bureaucracies interlock.

It might not be profit or shareholding that is essential to the way things have been running in Australia, but the ability of governments to produce economic policies which are consistent with growth, or which encourage it, or offset its unsettling effects. (That I don't know which word to use – 'consistent with'? 'encourage'? 'offset'? – is an example of our present predicament.) Growth has been the dynamic, not profit, although profit may have been necessary to growth. If growth no longer worked we'd be in for a new period in history.

13

DEATH OF THE LUCKY COUNTRY

This book, mainly about the sacking of the Whitlam government, took its name from its last chapter, which looked at Whitlam's legacy and the effect of the changing world economy. It was seen as a kind of 'cultural betrayal' by many of D.H.'s conservative friends, but it otherwise struck a chord, selling 50,000 copies in its first four weeks.

Landscape of disaster

BY THE TIME I GOT OUT OF THE BUS AT MARTIN Place, on Wednesday, the third day of the 1975 election campaign, it was obvious that the retina was buckling at the back of my right eye: there was a grey patch in the vision of the inner corner. I bought a copy of the *Bulletin* at a newsstand and began reading the piece I had written – 'Why I wouldn't vote for Malcolm Fraser'. Then I looked for the Morgan Gallup Poll. I had heard about it the Friday before at Tony's Bon Gout, a restaurant associated with the Whitlam years, at which I had said that if Whitlam won the election I would cry in front of the television set. In victory one should cry, because of the perils of success; one should laugh in defeat. A friend said I'd better start laughing: next week's Gallup Poll was going to show that after the Governor-General dismissed the Whitlam government the swing had gone strongly to the Liberals. The Whitlam government had been sacked by an official it had itself appointed who showed his difference from other people by the number of times he wore striped trousers and top hat, and the voters – or a significant margin of them – had accepted his action. Now in the doctor's waiting room I read the detailed poll figures. It was true. The hour of glory had not arrived. The people had not responded. I shut my left eye and with my right looked at the page: the grey blindness had spread half across the eye. Now the figures were obscured. That was better.

I was to have the night at home resting before they admitted me to the Eye Hospital the next morning. I would then spend twenty-four hours with both eyes blindfolded, then they would operate and try to put the retina back where it belonged. My wife and I went through the list of things-to-do I had scribbled out on the back of the *Bulletin* while I was at the doctor's surgery. There was only a sliver of vision in the far right of the eye now. When we finished with the list I shut my eyes and imagined what it might mean if the poll figures accurately represented a significant mood. Humiliatingly, the suggestions they made at Tony's Bon Gout might be right: there were enough authority-respecting Australians for them to change sides when a Governor-General had spoken. Australia was still colonial enough for the will of Government House to prevail. Alternatively there was the pragmatists' theory of the hip-pocket nerve: when the Senate was using the blocking of the supply money to force the government into an election, support had swung to Labor because people felt their incomes threatened. Now that there was to be an election the hard heads had swung back to the Liberals, thinking there was money in it for them. (Which would show them to be as stupid as hard heads often are.) Perhaps, because of this marginal shift, the Australian people were about to betray what might have been their destiny: positively affirming themselves a nation self-confident in its democratic forms. Two nights later, delirious as I recovered from the anaesthetic, I struggled with the nurses and my wife, on and on, for a couple of hours. I knew they had me in a cage. Downstairs were the documents that would prove the Morgan Gallup Poll was wrong. They wouldn't let me go down and clear the name of the Australian people. Later, at midnight, when I had reorientated myself as a hospital patient, and one who had to accept the Morgan Gallup Poll, the nursing sister wrote on the post-operative report that the patient was 'conscious, co-operative, vague'.

In the tunnel of darkness in which I lived for eleven days, as well as cassette music of Handel, Haydn and other positive thinkers, I heard all the radio news, listening for more opinion polls. I rang my wife after breakfast each morning: was there any good news yet in the polls? I had a new theory: the Liberals' concentration on the economy as the main issue of the election would bounce back on them. During the campaign a significant margin of the hard heads would detect the fraudulence of the idea that the economic crisis was simply due to either Labor's 'bad management' or its 'socialism' and that once the Liberals took over, the crisis would go away and 'prosperity would be restored'. On the day before the election I came out of hospital into the glare of a heat wave. A band of dock workers, banners calling for Labor for Australia, marched along the road on their way to a rally. A policeman was with them, to stop the traffic at intersections. We bought an afternoon paper. The opinion polls were as bad as ever.

While I was in hospital I decided that if the frauds did work, if there was to be success for the most sustained and corrupting campaign to destroy a government in our national history, with outrages committed against the decencies of our political life, a huge campaign of political misrepresentation and a vendetta journalism so virulent that it makes me ashamed to have been a journalist, then I should write a book giving meaning to these events and suggesting some of the puzzles that have been cast into the future.

The day Whitlam was sacked he said to the crowd on the steps of Parliament House: 'Maintain your rage.' If you felt rage at the time this book is intended to help justify it; and, if you did not feel rage then, to understand and now perhaps join with those who did.

The book is addressed in part to that coalition of Labor supporters and concerned people who were deeply motivated during the December 13 election campaign. But it is also addressed to those other Australians who may have taken another side at the time, but who share similar principles and priorities. Those who voted Labor may see more clearly how they were robbed. Those who voted Liberal may begin to understand how they were misled. For both, the book may help crystallise common feeling and a new consciousness of politics in Australia.

The book is not intended to be wholly or mainly polemical, although there should be no shame in writing spiritedly. It is intended to throw up the shapes of what have been dark and sometimes unexamined aspects of Australian political life, and to look into matters that might previously not have seemed worth investigating. After the sense of atrocity suffered by so many Australians, we have to learn to see our politics in a new way.

What happened?

This: The Governor-General secretly made a decision, the effect of which was to support the political plans of the Liberal and National Country parties.

Against all contemporary practice he did not discuss that decision with the government that was then in power. But having contemplated the decision privately he secretly got for it the support of the Chief Justice, a person of no more constitutional significance in this matter than you or me, but one whose respected office could seem to give extra authority to what the Governor-General had decided. The Governor-General then mounted a time-tabled operation, for which the phrase 'constitutional *coup d'etat*' seems a useful description. It was an operation which had the general effect of leaving the Prime Minister with a false sense of security, then, without discussing any alternatives, kicking him out of office, installing the minority leader as Prime Minister, then dissolving Parliament. It all happened so quickly that no preventive action could be taken.

What were the political effects of this action?

It got the Liberal and National Country parties a chance to fight an election at a time that suited them, and under circumstances that favoured them quite extraordinarily. After the constitutional *coup d'etat* the quick plebiscitary election was conducted in unparalleled circumstances in which Labor could seem a guilty party dismissed by rightful authority. This impression could have been strengthened by a continuing campaign of 'revelations' none of which was to be substantiated. An unfair electoral system magnified the swing. In the House of Representatives, with 43.3 per cent of the preferred votes, Labor won only 28 per cent of the seats while the coalition parties, with 56.6 per cent of the preferred votes, gained 72 per cent of the seats. In the Senate the coalition parties gained such a majority that even if Labor wins the next election it cannot control the Senate; in such an event the coalition parties could use their Senate majority to prevent reform of unjust electoral boundaries and then at a favourable moment sack another Labor government and start all over again.

Yet if the Governor-General had taken the advice the Prime Minister had intended to give him – Whitlam's advice to hold a half-Senate election was demonstrably constitutional – a different kind of election would have been fought, under different circumstances. The Labor Party might have won it. If a general election had been held at some other time, the Labor Party might have won it, or even if the coalition parties had gained a narrow majority in the House of Representatives they may have lacked control of the Senate.

In pointing out that the Governor-General's action gave the Opposition parties the election that best suited their interests and that was most likely to destroy the Labor Party I am not discussing whether the Governor-General had thought about the effects of his actions. Perhaps he did. Perhaps he didn't. I am not suggesting that he intended to give the coalition parties an extraordinary political advantage. Nor can I suggest he didn't, since the motives of a Governor-General are not easily examinable. What one can say is that, whatever his intentions, never before has an Australian Governor-General intervened in a way that so much favoured one party and so threatened another.

Consider some of the ways in which the Governor-General's action had the effect of favouring Labor's political opponents.

One of the most important was that the Whitlam government was going through a change in character that might have kept it in office if the next election had been held at the normal time, at the end of 1976 or in the first half of 1977. It was in the coalition parties' interests to bring Labor down before this change could be demonstrated. In three years Labor had produced many great achievements; it had also produced many blunders, as might have been expected of a party that had been out of office for twenty-three years; but ironically, just as the follies of its petrodollar dealings with Khemlani received their greatest publicity, the government looked to have a new pragmatism and efficiency. It had become seasoned. It had been a reform government that was patchy in general administration; now it was a reform government that might seem more competent in administration than its rivals, who also had their own follies and blunders.

Labor had blundered in economic management (as the Liberals had in 1971 and 1972) but by 1974 there was a world economic crisis of a new, puzzling kind in which there were no more certainties and the consequences of mistakes were unusually magnified. If things went wrong, they went wrong on a grander scale. If they had won the 1972 or the 1974 elections the Liberals would also have suffered from this magnifying effect. But by the second half of 1975, the Labor government was adjusting itself to these new circumstances. A few months free of political crisis and Labor's economic ministers might have been seen by a significant margin of voters as economic managers who were sounder (as well as more humane) than the Opposition was likely to be. For the Liberals it was vital that Labor should not have time to do this. Some Liberals had developed such belief in the strategies of Labor's Treasurer Bill Hayden that they wanted to win an election to gain the benefit of these strategies.

The Governor-General's action got Malcolm Fraser off the hook. Fraser's tactic had been to use his political majority in the Senate to cut off the government's money supply and so force an election. This tactic seemed to be failing. It had aroused public antipathy – the opinion polls showed a swing to Labor – and it was being attacked inside his own party. If the game of parliamentary bluff and counter-bluff had been played out, Fraser might have surrendered. Whatever the Governor-General's intention, his intervention saved Fraser from a reckless failure that could have led his party to sack him as leader.

For authority-respecting, innocent-minded voters the drama of dismissing Whitlam and putting Fraser in as Prime Minister could seem an act of punishment for a government that had done wrong. Such voters might see the election as under vice-regal patronage. In itself that may directly have influenced votes. The drama of dismissal certainly pushed Whitlam fatally off his stride. He was pulled away from most of the team he was used to working with, and pushed into sudden improvisations, many of which didn't come off. The Labor team was fractured: it broke into disconnected parts; in some cases they were seriously distracted by the caretaker government's reducing their staff and even by such banalities as attempts to remove office equipment.

The incoherence of the crisis meant that voters barely noticed that Fraser was opening and shutting his mouth without saying anything much. He evaded the questions of media interviewers, slipping off into the magic words of the campaign: 'extravagance', 'international safaris', 'jobs for the boys', 'dole bludgers', 'private sector'; and all the newspaper managers seemed determined to give him an easy run home. The election came and went without voters realising they had put Fraser in power without knowing anything much about him or his plans. The sensationalism of this extraordinary election made it, in policies and programs, remarkably brainless, but remarkably suited to a party that, not wanting its credibility tested, had a vested interest in brainlessness.

Perhaps the greatest scandal was that Labor supporters and those who, more generally, saw themselves as supporters of reform, could see the political set-up stripped of its legitimacy. It could seem as if reformers were not accepted by the Australian political system. They might be tolerated for a while; but they were easily outlawed. For some this was reduced to the simple conspiracy of a CIA coup, as in Chile. For others there was the diffused shock of an affronted trust in which they felt that the democratic decencies were not for Australia. The political system seemed to have powerful devices available only to the opponents of reform. In a showdown the reformers could see the system as stacked against them.

In a community like Australia people usually accept political defeat as legitimate because they imagine that some other time they might win. During the twenty-three years of Liberal rule Labor people still saw themselves as part of the set-up. The media was usually against Labor. The electoral system favoured the Liberals. (Labor won an outright majority of votes in the 1954 election, and a majority of preferred votes in the 1961 and 1969 elections, although they didn't get a House of Representatives majority.) But Labor people could still see how they might win.

Under Menzies certain people despised Australia because Menzies was its leader; under Whitlam other people, like White Russians, felt dispossessed. But in either case there could still be a feeling that their time would come again: their own lot would get back in. The campaign to destroy the Whitlam government went on for so long, involved so many powerful institutions, and had such an infamous victory that many people who believed in reform believed it possible that their time would not come again. There was too much power on the other side. They could never win.

To the Labor government supporters, or to those who came to its support because the destruction of the government affronted them, the sacking of Whitlam had the shock of an assassination. It was followed by a dream-like period of physical disorientation: when the words 'prime minister' came over transistors or television sets people still saw the face of Gough Whitlam. They would wake up in the mornings and for a moment imagine it hadn't happened. As the election caravans moved across the landscape of disaster the media put up such a brutal clatter that the sense of shock became sharper. Has there ever been such a crying on an Australian election night? It was not only the Labor Party that was being destroyed, but the sense of trust of hundreds of thousands of Australians.

14

IDEAS FOR A NATION

D.H. wrote this book in the wake of the excitement surrounding the 1988 Bicentennial celebrations.

Australia is ordinary

Most books about Australia look for the extraordinary. (Perhaps that was partly why late nineteenth-century Australian writers gave the bush such a good run. If you wanted to make some money writing about Australia, the bush made a good story – just as in the United States at about the same time money was to be made by writing about cowboys.) Australia has been seen as exceptional in the oddities of its plants and animals. Exceptional in the bravery of its men in battle and the overall excellence of Australians in sport. Exceptional in democracy, in envy of tall poppies, in contempt for democracy. Exceptionally egalitarian, exceptionally class conscious, exceptionally classless. Exceptionally racist, exceptionally hedonist, exceptionally puritan, exceptionally male-dominated. Exceptionally progressive, exceptionally reactionary. Exceptionally prosperous, exceptionally slothful. Exceptionally improvising, exceptionally derivative. Exceptionally rural, exceptionally suburban. Exceptionally lively, exceptionally boring.

But, whatever the exceptions, if you look at Australia from the basis of modern industrialism, it is an ordinary modern-industrial society, although of colonial origin. It is from Australia's similarities with the other three or four dozen modern-industrial societies that one can start to examine this country.

*

The beginning of modern Australia can be seen as part of Europe's view that the rest of the world was there to be plundered for the benefit of Europe, a process that was to be explained as the spread of civilisation, in the form of Christianity and, later, in the form of material progress. Countries outside Europe could seem mere *sources of supply* as if the rest of the world were Europe's, with pantries, gardens, wells, heaps of fuel, storehouses to provide raw materials to keep Europe going. Even the people in these other countries could see their own societies in this limited and subordinate way, as places you got something out of, either by trade (Singapore's image of itself), or by exporting what had been produced in the hinterland, as was the case with Sydney. Minerals, fuels, foods, fibres – the sense of importance and success was related to the size and value of what could be sent to Europe. It was as if, finally, it was only trade and exports that mattered: shake life free of its accessories and trade and exports were the reason for everything else. Just as Singaporeans could define themselves in terms of entrepot trade – that was why Singapore was *there* – Australians could define themselves as an exporting country. That was why *they* were there.

The habit of seeing Australia in this way became so important that it is worth several paragraphs to put it into context. In the sixteenth century the changes began that would soon allow the whole world to be seen as a storehouse for Europe. The East Indies provided the Portuguese, and then the Dutch, with spices. Mexico and Peru provided gold and silver for Spain. Brazil supplied diamonds and gold for Portugal. Russian fur traders went across Siberia and into Alaska, French fur traders spread out from the Great Lakes, and the British moved along the west coast of North America – all of them seeing the place where they happened to be as important because from there they could send pelts to Europe. At about the time Australia was being possessed by the British the southern oceans were being hunted over for whales whose blubber could be boiled down to make soup or lamp oil for Europeans, and whose bones could be used as stiffening in umbrellas and corsets or used to make buggy whips and fishing rods. Africa was to supply human beings to be sold to the plantation owners of the West Indies and eastern America. The function of the West Indies was to grow sugar, tobacco, rice, indigo and cotton for Europe.

During the industrial revolution, sheep were moved into virgin pastures in Australia, New Zealand, southern Africa, North America and Argentina because Europe's textile and carpet factories needed wool. Europe's purposes could also be served by mining and exporting copper, nitrates, nickel and tin, or by setting up plantations of tea plants, rubber or cacao trees or coconut palms. European planters would look over a new region, clear its vegetation, arrange plants in straight rows, build houses, set up labour lines and turn it into an engine for producing exports. With the growth of railways, new wheat farms spread across Siberia, across the centre and west of North America, across the South American pampas, across Australia and southern Africa, transfiguring landscapes and producing new towns, new political pressures, new social types. When refrigeration was invented, some of the acquired lands were used to turn grass into exportable beef and mutton. With the invention of the internal combustion engine the 'oil producers' were created, territories whose main, or only, interest lay in their pipes and derricks and docks. They were noted for what went out of them, not for what they were. The very words 'raw materials' suggested simplicity, prime importance.

This is part of the story of the colonial background of Australia. An even wider development ensued from the general aura of the word 'economic': reality was seen as economic and material, just as in earlier societies it had been religious and supernatural. In some of the settler societies, where the Europeans had simply taken over, supplanting and sometimes destroying 'the natives', the supremacy of the economic as a human value became established even more quickly than in the parent societies. As Louis Hartz pointed out in *The Founding of New Societies*, there was less opposition to this tendency: there was no aristocracy, for example, or peasantry, or state church. Since such institutions were fragments more of late feudal Europe than of modern Europe, this supremacy of the economic was least likely to happen in the Latin American settler societies. It manifested itself most strongly in the English-speaking settler societies, because they were similar to Britain, the initiator of the industrial revolution. Indeed the United States quickly became the most uninhibitedly capitalist society in the world. Modern Australia, formed at the beginning of the industrial revolution and part of it, was, in this sense, 'born modern'. It became a materialist, capitalist and developmentalist society without there even being much discussion about it. The truth of the principle of utility could seem self-evident. The test of an action was: *Is it useful?* And in turn the best test of that was: *Will it make money?* By the end of the nineteenth century, Australia was being reckoned, by conventional standards of measurement, as one of the world's most prosperous communities.

Two of the basic changes given to the meaning of existence by modern industrialism were, in Foucault's words in *Discipline and Punish*, the 'accumulation of capital' and 'the accumulation of men' (which might be better translated as 'the accumulation of labour'). The Australian colonies were slow in the development of manufacturing but in these two broader senses they were 'industrial' early on. The accumulation and investment of capital were an article of faith in national development. Without this, material progress seemed impossible. Equally important was the need for the belief in work – not as productive enterprise but as paid labour. And since the colonies were so strongly urbanised it also became self-evident that one of the essentials of a society became the provision and maintenance of an organised 'work force'.

What also defined most of the colonial societies was the belief that, as well as the investment of local capital, there was always the capital of industrialising European countries, the British, in particular, to rely on. The British were spreading their capital surpluses not only through the empire but wherever in the world there was money to be made. British investment was essential to the early industrialisation of the United States, and, at the height of British power, Brazil and Argentina, the two largest Latin American nations, were economically part of the British empire; the oligarchies who controlled them were keen to keep in with the British.

In Argentina, British money pushed railway tracks across the pampas, throwing up small, bleak railway villages, changing Buenos Aires into a considerable railway centre and port. The result was the extermination of the pampas Indians, the lavish enrichment of the *estancerios*, the creation of the new class of impoverished *peons*, and a deluge of European immigrants. In a couple of decades, Argentina was rearranged. It had become an effective raw material supplier. Its purpose in life was to send wheat to British flour mills, mutton and beef to British wholesalers, wool to French and Belgian carpet factories.

In Australia the national development programs were partly programs for borrowing British money – but we should understand that in its affection for foreign investment Australia was merely one among many.

In Europe itself, new supplies of bulk labour came from the villages, many of whose inhabitants found even the horrors of the new industrial towns more attractive than the poverty of village life. In the colonial world, if 'the natives' could be induced into labour, they came cheap. But if they could not be made to suit this purpose, or if there weren't enough of them, extra labour was imported. These supplies came in four main forms, three of which were used in Australia. Unlike the West Indies and eastern America, Australia did not resort to importing slaves: but, like Siberia, some of the British colonies in North America and Singapore, and some of the French colonies, a cheap and productive labour force was found in convicts; as in South America, Africa, South-East Asia and the Pacific Islands, indentured labour was used, for a season, in Queensland; but, principally, the building up of a 'labour force' in Australia derived from the great planned movement of peoples that began with the immigration drives of the nineteenth century. Europeans were packaged off to North America, or Siberia, or Argentina – just as they were to Australia – ticketed as producer fodder.

*

When Manning Clark published the first volume of his *A History of Australia* in 1962 it was a time when historians were inclined to take a hard-nosed view of Australia. Economics, some politics: that was Australia. Clark challenged this materialist vista by describing in the opening three chapters of his book the arrival of Europeans in

South-East Asia and the South Pacific in terms of the three great European faiths they brought with them – Catholicism, with the Spanish and Portuguese; Protestantism, with the Dutch and the British; and the Enlightenment, with the Dutch, the British and the French.

Christianity came to Australia in the four main forms that had emerged out of the eruptions of earlier disturbances within the British Isles and in Europe's wars – three Protestant, one Catholic. Divisions between Anglicans, Presbyterians and independent Protestants (and, for a while, between the Presbyterians themselves) were transported, along with the differences of nationality and of class that had become integral to these sects. There was no parallel in Australia to the nineteenth-century revivalist movements in the United States which produced distinctive religious enthusiasms. (Given the nature of religious fundamentalism there, this was no loss to Australia.) For a time there was an attempt to set up in Australia an imitative model of Protestant religious life as it was lived in the United Kingdom, to be reinforced by bringing out English and Scottish clergymen.

Catholicism, suppressed at the beginning, was run by the Irish, with considerable obedience to Rome and with the imported hatreds that made British Australia, for most of its existence, a dourly divided society. In his famous essay 'Faith', Manning Clark sees another imported division: the Irish, when they brought their religion, also brought the perception that the person who had compassion was to be preferred to the person who had gained the whole world. The Irish view that 'the saint and the larrikin lived in one man' was an affront to the British Protestant view of righteousness. What brought Catholics and Protestants together however was the dominant theme in religious observance of limiting the possibilities for human enjoyment: Australians did not invent 'wowserism', they just gave a new name to British puritanism and evangelicalism and Irish Jansenism.

The third imported faith of Australians, which Clark sees in terms of the Enlightenment (and which I see as one of the best things Australia has going for it), began to develop in the seventeenth century, the golden century of the Dutch. There was the confidence of the new merchants and traders, the assurance of French and English philosophers and scientists in the rationality of the universe, and the new belief, cogently expressed by the Amsterdam Jew Baruch Spinoza, that there should be freedom of conscience in religion and that the liberty of the individual should be the basis of the state. In the eighteenth century, French and Scottish writers – and Thomas Jefferson in the Declaration of Independence – articulated a rational optimism based on science and reason in which, as Sidney Pollard puts it in *The Idea of Progress*, 'firm convictions had been expressed about the inevitability of progress in wealth, in civilisation, in social organisation, in art and literature, even in human nature and biological make-up'. In the nineteenth century, such beliefs took on highly articulated forms in Darwinism and Marxism, but for Australia the most convincing imported idea was the English notion of Improvement. As Asa Briggs chronicles in *The Age of Improvement (1783 to 1867)*, this could lead Englishmen in the 1780s to boast how the 'discoveries and improvements' of their own generation seemed to 'diffuse a glory over this country unobtainable by conquest or domination'; forty years on even the traditionalist Walter Scott could write of 'the improvement of national taste and delicacy'; twenty years after that the statistician G.R. Porter reported that 'all the elements of improvement are working with incessant and increasing energy'; the Great Exhibition of 1851 was a monumental parade of achievement; Macaulay's *History of England*, the century's most influential English history book, opened with the announcement that 'the history of our country during the last hundred and sixty years is eminently the history of physical, of moral, and of intellectual improvement'.

The material achievements of the Australian colonists did not come from the novelties of a new land. They came because the colonists were British and they brought with them to that new land the Improving belief that things could be made better – that merino wool could be made crinklier than it was in Europe, that blades of wheat could be grown where none grew before, that if roads were being macadamised in Britain they could be macadamised in Australia, that if steam engines worked flour mills in London then they would work them in Sydney. This was why Charles Darwin said, when he visited Sydney on the *Beagle* in 1836, after his research in South America, 'Here, in a less promising country, scores of years have done many times more than an equal number of centuries have effected in South America.'

As part of the spirit of Improvement in the manufacturing towns of Britain, ordinary people were beginning to imagine that they might better their own conditions. Some of the colonists also brought with them the belief in the possibility of 'mutuality' in collective action that was to lead to the formation of friendly societies, temperance societies and the 'trade societies' that were the precursors of unionism. In bringing the new, 'methodical' habits that made a labour force possible, they also brought that working-class urge towards respectability that exerted such influence in Australia. As Janet McCalman describes it in *Struggletown*, the wisdom of respectability was that only through habits of cleanliness, sobriety, extra-marital chastity, thrift, punctuality and 'manly independence' could workers provide a perception of themselves that would give them some control over their own lives.

As a child of the Improvement, Australia was also a child of modern European secularism. When the Spaniards and the Portuguese made their conquests, the Church was, as it were, part of the task force. What later appeared were not only nations but Catholic nations. In contrast, there was only one chaplain to provide a spiritual basis for the colony of New South Wales. He had to wait five years for a church and when he was able to build one it was wattle-and-daub with a thatched roof. Five years later the convicts burned it down because of a new regulation commanding church attendance. Beginning existence as a secular state was another of the ways in which Australia was born modern. Christian churches found themselves in competition with systems of knowledge and ways of seeing the world as comprehensive as the old systems of religious belief. Roughly speaking, that's where Australia fits in. But Australia is not a society where anti-religious movements have had much of a public run. Instead there has been (and, again, this provides an extensive potential) a pervasive Australian humanism, albeit, as George Shaw suggests in an essay in *1988 and All That*, 'a sentimental humanism' and a 'humanism without doctrines'.

In political life Australia can also be looked at in the light of what was happening in the industrialising world. The people who were doing well out of the colonies in the early period wanted to transfer to Australia 'true British freedoms' such as trial by jury, freedom of the press, and parliamentary checks on government, even if, as also occurred in Britain, they wanted these freedoms not for everyone, but for themselves. When the British Chartist movement, the first European working-class movement, began demanding that all men (although not, at that state, any women) should have equal civil and political rights, the Australian colonies moved faster in instituting democratic reforms than almost anywhere else in the modernising world. British liberals and radicals came to Australia and set up, as closely as they could, a replica of the British parliamentary system of government. 'Having imported their whole constitution and law books holus bolus from England,' wrote R.E.N. Twopenny in *Town Life in Australia*, 'the legislative equipment of the young Australian corresponds pretty nearly to the tall hats and patent leather boots which fond mothers provided for the Australian colonists.' But by imitating aspirations that were still only hopes in Britain the colonists had also made their parliamentary arrangements more democratic than those they were imitating.

For a few years (years of considerable reform) Australia seemed behind the rest of the modernising world in only one respect of its political life: no system of political parties had formed. It was significant then that the first party to be founded was a labour party. Yet in the development of a labour movement, Australia was also open to outside influences – from the United States, as well as from Britain, with little influence from continental socialism. The union movement had struggles of a kind that were greater than the struggles for political democracy, and in founding the Labor Party it developed a stronger political arm than the union movements of most other industrialising societies. This was reflected in the early successes of the Labor Party which were seen as a lesson in achievement and were discussed in some of the European socialist parties. It was a puzzling victory because, as reported by Albert Métin, a French socialist who had visited in 1899, Australia was practising a 'socialism without doctrine'.

In the theorising about government intervention there were some Australian novelties but they were marginal variations within the general fields of European (and United States) discourse. To take several examples: Pope Leo XIII's encyclical *Rerum Novarum* helped articulate Australian Catholic views on social justice; Herbert Spencer's doctrine of 'survival of the fittest' was used to legitimate anything from trade union strikes, to the destruction of Aboriginal society, to free trade, to hanging the Kaiser; Tocqueville's and Bryce's views on United States democracy influenced views on class and equality in Australia; and for a while there was a Bergsonian current in some intellectual attitudes.

There was a rapid spread to Australia of European concepts of what we now think of as the welfare state, first developed in the nineteenth century partly as a way of handling the problem of 'the useless' (the young, the sick, the old, the poor) so that society would stay together, but also presented in terms of human rights. In fact, for a season, Australia appeared a pioneer in social reform. There was fairly easy acceptance of the practice of 'the mixed economy' (since that was what Australians had been practising anyway) and of the approach of J.M. Keynes, in which government intervention was seen as essential to prosperity as the activities of private business. When governments turned to 'de-regulation' during the economic crisis that followed the long post-war boom they were also taking up a new overseas fashion.

The standards and practices of international 'mass culture' spread very easily across Australia – newspapers, theatre chains, magazines, the movies, the gramophone, the talkies, the wireless, hit tunes ... As a new society, whose public cultural standards were, in any case, soundly based on good, solid, English middle-class philistinism, Australia lacked the resistances that could come from remnants of the old ruling-class cultures and the folk cultures of Europe; and as the newest of the new societies it established less resilient regional cultures than those of the new societies of the Americas.

In one form of mass culture, Australia was among the pioneers. It was an early developer in the democratisation of playing games – if more for men than for women. One of the colonial boasts became that in Australia 'there is no class too poor to play, as at Home'. ('Home' being Britain.) Australia was also an opener in the standardisation of spectator sport as a principal form of leisure (the idea of leisure itself also being a novelty) and invented Australian Rules Football. The reduction in working hours, the building of large playing areas, the use of mass transport, the formation of codes and the establishment of associations and clubs occurred, in due course, in all of the industrial societies. In Australia, they occurred earlier – so that Australia could be seen as 'the most sporting of countries'.

Competitive sport, as W. Mandle suggested in *Sport in Australia*, may have been the earliest effective nation-definer in nineteenth-century Australia. But, even in this, Australia was not alone: the Spaniards defined themselves in the bull ring; the Norwegians on the ski run; the Finnish victories in the Olympic Games in 1912 helped stimulate Finnish nationalism; for a period, one of the ways of being a typical American was to be a baseball star.

Insofar as Australians went in for defining themselves, the forms in which this expressed itself were much the same as those used by other peoples over this period. Throughout Europe nationality was defined in landscape paintings: the same techniques were used in the bush landscapes of Australia. Throughout Europe the true national virtues were found in rural types: so, also, in Australia. Social bandits, to use E.J. Hobsbawm's phrase, could signify the worth of a people; Australians glorified Ned Kelly (whose armour-clad image provides the end papers for Hobsbawm's book on mythic outlaws). The wild fringe men of colonial exploitation – the Cossack, the *gaucho*, the frontiersman, the *bandiera*, were seen as expressions of national character; so was Australia's swagman, still commemorated in 'Waltzing Matilda', which remains the unofficial national song.

And where Australian creations of nationality differed from those in the newly created nations of Europe, whether in Belgium or Bulgaria, Ireland or Iceland, they may have differed from them in the same ways as did the other colonial societies. In a section of *The Founding of New Societies*, called 'New nations out of old', Louis Hartz suggests that it became intolerable for the citizens of the United States to continue to define themselves in English ways, so they invented the idea of 'the true American', although in effect 'the true American' was a development of the true spirit of the English petty bourgeois. If this approach were applied to Australia it might be found that the character of 'the true Australian' came from a mixture of nineteenth-century English and Irish working-class manners, disguised, and that 'mateship', seen as a specifically Australian form of comradeship, was, in effect, a version of European working-class fraternalism.

Australia's distinction (which it shares only with Canada, New Zealand, and a few others) has been to fail to bring the processes of nation-defining to a conclusion. This derives from the fact that the real jingoism in Australia was never nationalism, but imperialism. But, in this imperial mode, Australia was certainly part of the world.

15

A STORY OF WHAT MIGHT HAVE BEEN

From the 1986 William McKell Lecture. D.H. speculates that there is no inevitability about how the events that make up history unfold; within certain guidelines things can be different. History might be there for the making.

BY 1900, AUSTRALIA WAS ALREADY ESTABLISHED AS a 'social laboratory'. It was fulfilling, to a large extent, many of the liberal aspirations of the old world. One must recognise, of course, that Australia was also as racist and sexist as the worst of them, and that there were other aspirations of the late twentieth century that were not met by late-nineteenth century Australia. But by the standards of the late nineteenth century, Australia was one of the world's most progressive societies. The purpose of this address is to prompt a bit of speculation about what went wrong after that.

To try to get a bit of discussion going on these subjects, I am going to tell you a story.

Before storytelling time begins, let us first look at the situation at the turn of the century. Initially, South Australia had led the way. By 1893, the year of financial collapse in Melbourne, a new South Australian government, uniting both liberal and radical elements,

A STORY OF WHAT MIGHT HAVE BEEN

was to institute, among other measures, women's franchise, a State bank, factory inspection, land taxes, progressive income tax and death duties. By the beginning of the new century there were many other changes. By then, overall, Australia's labour laws were seen as 'not matched elsewhere in their number, boldness and stringency'. Compulsory arbitration in industrial disputes was unique. Factory Acts had become more extensive. There was early closing in shops. Colonies were adopting workers' compensation legislation. New South Wales and New Zealand were two of the first places in the world to set up government employment bureaus. Wage boards were concerned with maintaining minimum living standards. Graduated income and land taxes and death duties introduced a mild redistribution of income. When New South Wales imitated New Zealand and legislated for old age pensions in 1901, the only other place with a non-contributory scheme was Denmark. When New South Wales introduced a non-contributory invalid pensions scheme in 1908, it was the first place in the world to do so. The divorce laws of New South Wales, Victoria and New Zealand were among the world's most advanced. Payment of Members of Parliament and women's suffrage were introduced ahead of most other places. Governments were the main landlords, with intricate rules for land administration, land reform and subsidising of farmers. Many saw the tariff as the basis of human progress. Governments owned the railways, controlled central education systems, pursued active policies of immigration and ran homes for neglected children and the aged and infirm.

'Australia,' said a trade union newspaper, 'has ever been an exemplar of the old lands ... it has steadily forged ahead, initiating and perfecting, experimenting and legislating on new lines.' Social scientists from other countries came to Australia and New Zealand to write books about these two paradigms of progress.

The driving impulse of the time was liberalism – not the 'big L' liberalism of today, but a liberalism somewhat similar to what still goes by that name in the United States. Much of it became the policy of Alfred Deakin, the leader of a progressive party, who became the first national figure to successfully articulate Australian political aims for Australians. Deakin believed in government intervention as a method of 'employing the machinery of the State to cope with the very great injustices which at present beset our social system'. Even George Reid, leader of a more conservative party, spoke much of the language of this liberalism, as when he said: 'Even in the field of social economics, Australia can win victories and set examples which will teach the rest of the world.' But it was Deakin who remained master of a rhetoric in which (to use some of his favourite words) there were to be 'economic justice', 'equal laws and opportunities for all', 'healthy lives', 'honest toil', 'fair wages', 'fair hours', 'fair prices', 'fair conditions of employment' and 'State mediation to end social conflict'.

It was Deakin's sponsorship of a policy of 'New Protection', in which manufacturers would be protected from foreign competition only if they offered 'fair and reasonable' wages and working conditions, that became the most ambitious statement of this Australian liberalism. As orator of the New Protection, Deakin offered Australians (to quote from the language of the time) 'civilised growth through a well-planned manufacturing industry', fostered by a 'scientific, carefully adjusted program of protection' and based on the 'indisputable knowledge of capable independent experts' who, as well as aiding manufacturing growth, would assist the further development of agriculture and 'even throw light on the mysteries of unemployment'. Along with these distinctively Australian political aspirations, for some, went a belief in a people's army, on the model of the Swiss militia, 'a citizen soldiery inspired by patriotism'.

A STORY OF WHAT MIGHT HAVE BEEN

Well, so far all I have said is true. By the standards of the age, Australia was a paradigm of progress. What happened? What went wrong? Why, in particular, did Australia fall so behind in the 1920s and 1930s? Why was it to Sweden and to other nations that people began to go for their models of an efficient, progressive society, rather than to Australia?

To some of us, this can seem one of the most useful problems in Australian history, connected as it is with examining the present mobilisation of power in Australia, and in particular that form of power that lies in people's habits and opinions and forms the 'common sense' (as Antonio Gramsci used the word) of a large part of the society, making it seem perfectly 'natural' that some things should be thought and done and that the doing or thinking of other kinds of things should seem 'deviant'.

And connected with this (this is one of the reasons why I am raising this significant historical puzzle today) is a related question: why is it that general Labor attitudes and ways of behaving are often *not* seen as natural? Why, in fact, have they frequently been seen as deviant? And also the question: how is it that while a larger proportion of Australians have regularly voted for a Labor Party than in most other nations on Earth, Labor governments, at least nationally, have been so infrequent? As Francis Castles records in his stimulating book *The Working Class and Welfare* (a study of the development of the Welfare State in Australia), over the thirty years, 1950 to 1980, Labor's average vote was 45.6 per cent and over the same period the Swedish Social Democratic Party's vote was 45.7 per cent, yet while Labor was in power in Australia for only three of those thirty years, the Swedish Social Democrats were in power for twenty-six years out of thirty.

Obviously, I'm not going to answer those questions. Partly because there isn't time, but mainly because such questions can never exactly be answered. Nevertheless, to raise them is highly important, because it is one way of thinking about the present. As I have already warned you, the way I shall raise those questions today is to tell you a little story. It will be the story of what might have been if the Australian colonies had federated later, if Labor had come to power later, if it had lost elections at the right times, instead of winning them at the wrong times, if it had adopted different electoral laws and if, in some ways, Labor had been a marginally different party.

The story begins

To play this game, let's go back a little. You will remember how I was giving evidence for seeing Australia as one of the most liberal societies – by the standards of the time – on Earth. Let us now imagine that the story went on something like this:

Given their remarkable talent for progress, it can seem all the more remarkable that the Australian colonies did not federate until 1912. Despite his national leadership in a political rhetoric, Deakin was Premier only of Victoria. However, it may have been significant that it was in this period of late liberal hegemony that the Australian Constitution was framed and that it was also in this period that the Labor Party was beginning to strengthen. As will be recalled, in the late 1890s the Constitutional Conventions had failed to agree on the terms of federation and had settled merely on the compromise of setting up a Federal Council to co-ordinate defence and a few other matters. At this time, the infant Labor movement had quite prudently opposed federation. As W.M. Hughes, then the great anti-federation orator, had put it, the Senate as it was proposed was 'a mousetrap – once in, never get out, an Upper House not to conserve State rights, but to retard social reform'. Hughes's slogan at the time had been 'an Australian Constitution to suit Australian needs' and

A STORY OF WHAT MIGHT HAVE BEEN

when the federation movement was revived in 1910, both Deakin and Hughes – the two principal speakers at the Constitutional Conventions – spoke in the spirit of this slogan.

By now they were preaching to the converted, since the Convention was dominated by delegates of progressive liberal persuasion and delegates from the Labor parties. There was another factor. In England, it was a time of parliamentary crisis and the crisis had ended only when there was taken away from the House of Lords the power to block supply, or to veto bills. This had an electrifying effect on the 1911 Constitutional Convention in Australia. That Convention confirmed the Senate would be merely a house of review. (It is difficult to imagine the opposite: how could one imagine an Australia that would remain governable if the Senate could veto legislation and block supply?) But there was also that great wave of amendments to the draft constitution that made the Australian Constitution the most liberal and democratic on Earth.

In the 1912 elections for the first Commonwealth Parliament, the Labor Party had another stroke of luck: it lost the election. Although his success at the Convention was based on solid Labor support, Deakin had become the hero of the hour (it is not for nothing that we still commemorate him as 'the father of Federation') and he easily became the first Prime Minister of Australia (although, as it was later to develop, Prime Minister of a government with enormous strains between its liberal and its conservative elements). Think of the disaster that would undoubtedly have overtaken the Labor Party if this had not been so and Labor had been the government in August 1914. How could one possibly imagine a Labor Government fighting an imperialist war? The strains of such a contradiction would undoubtedly have smashed the party.

It was also a stroke of luck that the Labor Party lost the 1915 election, a result partly of the euphoria of an election campaign cynically called by the government to exploit post-Anzac patriotism and partly of the confusion with which Andrew Fisher had led the party, uncertain as he was about how to approach the war.

Fisher's replacement after Labor's defeat by W.M. Hughes was one of those masterstrokes by which the party has shown its genius for sometimes sacrificing present popularity for future principle. Hughes at once swung into a campaign in which he showed the Labor Party as fighting (to use his own language) 'for the working class against the greed of the war profiteers'. At the same time, with that penchant for showing the capitalists how to manage the economy that has been such a successful feature of Labor governments, Hughes campaigned for a more efficient conduct of the Australian war effort by greater and more efficient government economic intervention. In this campaign he scored his most remarkable success when, although merely Leader of the Opposition, he goaded the government into breaking up the base metals combine and reorganising it under Australian ownership – the first of Hughes's many key moves in the development of Australian manufacturing industry.

It was, however, for his opposition to conscription that Hughes's wartime career is most justly remembered. The extraordinary verve and courage with which Hughes threw himself into the two NO campaigns (joined, of course, by Archbishop Mannix) has provided one of the heroic legends of Australian politics. The pamphlet Hughes wrote after his brief gaoling still survives as one of the most moving examples of the aspirations of the Labor movement in Australia.

Was Hughes impelled partly by political opportunism in these campaigns? The suggestion that, if he had been on the other side, he might have campaigned equally ably for a YES vote for conscription seems to be pushing political cynicism too far. [*As a biographer of Billy Hughes, D.H. was well placed to assess the potential of his political opportunism.*] But it is certainly the case, as recent documentary evidence has clearly established, that Hughes was conscious of maintaining that wisdom that has been so essential to Labor's long success: *We must stand by our own people.* His single-minded determination during the NO campaigns united the Labor movement in ways that have never really been weakened. (And this unity seemed to be directly related to the formation in 1917 of a strong Australian Council of Trade Unions, so that the Australian union movement has not been weakened by the debilitating factionalism of some other countries.) Furthermore, Labor provided an attractive alternative when, inevitably, the government began to crumble in 1918 and then, as soon as the war had ended, split into two parties – a moderate and enlightened Liberal Party and a Conservative Party, a division that has remained with the anti-Labor forces ever since and has been one of the reasons for Labor's long success.

The great Labor victory of early 1919 opened a miraculous decade in which the Australian Labor movement was seen as 'the most advanced in the world'. The Labor Party controlled the national government and was the decisive power in most of the states, although the Deakinite Liberals were still dominant in Victoria. In several other states, in what has been described as 'the long struggle for the middle road', it was the Liberals who provided a more significant opposition to Labor than the Conservative Party and the newly formed Country Party (recognising, of course, that in Victoria the Country Party seemed at times to be the most radical of all the parties). In the states, both the Labor and Liberal parties combined in reforms such as abolishing Upper Houses, in giving greater power to the people through referendums and in instituting proportional representation, a reform then extended to elections to the Commonwealth Parliament.

As was to happen later in Sweden (a country for which Australia was to set so many examples), it was probably to the institution of proportional representation that the Labor Party owed much of its political success. This system of voting meant that Labor votes were not wasted in key areas, but it also perpetuated a split among its opponents that had two highly significant effects. One of these was that it allowed the survival of strongly progressive Liberal parties in most of the states and in national politics and the presence of these parties had an invigorating effect on the Labor Party itself through their power to force coalitions (on which, in some cases, Labor had to rely) and it also had an enlightening effect on the more conservative parties. The other significant effect was that because there was not one strong conservative party in Australia, it was not a country in which the capitalist image of society dominated the public culture: it was a public culture of the centre, both liberal and social-democratic. Another significant effect was that proportional representation allowed the formation of the Australian Democratic Socialist Party, a small party to Labor's left – thereby aiding the continued unity of the Labor Party itself, but also at times providing stimulation to the party. Since then, of course, Australia has remained a pioneer in electoral reform, continuing to show much of the rest of the world how to go about its voting – as it had begun to do in the nineteenth century.

In economic affairs, State Labor Governments set up many important industrial enterprises, but it was the National Government that was pre-eminent, first under the Prime Ministership of W.M. Hughes and then, after Hughes became the first Australian Governor-General, under the Prime Ministership of J.T. Lang. Hughes led the great modernisation of the Australian economy that was to make Australia such a successful modern industrial nation. He took over from Deakin, and then greatly expanded the concept that in Australia business was too serious a matter to be left to businessmen – that it was the role of the State to help businessmen make their profits, but it was also the role of the State to make businessmen more efficient – and also to ensure that there were wider social benefits from economic growth. Hughes was especially far-sighted in understanding the need for a science base to industry. When he founded the Council for Scientific and Industrial Research in 1919, Hughes insisted that, while its research would be even more essential to farming than marketing schemes, it must also provide a basis for metallurgical research. Then, with the great iron ore discoveries in Western Australia in 1920, Australian skills in advanced metallurgy soon made Australia the world's most significant producer of specialist steels. It was then that Hughes engaged in the most remarkable of all his programs. With the élan with which earlier he had established the Commonwealth Shipping Line, which has been so important to our prosperity (imagine exporting our specialist steels to Japan in Japanese ships!), Hughes brought scientists from all over the world to provide the research on which were soon to be based the great Australian specialist manufacturing industries on whose world leadership so much of our present prosperity still rests and whose success at this time of world economic crisis has made our economic record so remarkable.

However, it was J.T. Lang, during his Prime Ministership, who built the other basis of our national prosperity – with a creative use of protection policies that proved as successful as in the United States, Western Europe and Japan; with an institution of sophisticated government banking systems of all categories, a task beyond the imagination of the private banks as they then existed; and with a tight regulation of international financial relations. But it was in the field of welfare that Lang was most noted. It was under Hughes that the party first initiated its emphasis on welfare, but it was with Lang that plans reached maturity. The beginning had come with the great Labor conference of 1921, with its 'social justice objective', a conference at which it was argued that socialism was not achievable in a few easy moves, but that it was possible to introduce a 'Welfare State' – a phrase, it will be recalled, that was given to the world by Australia after Lang had introduced his three great programs of welfare reform.

Then the Labor Party had another of its strokes of luck: it lost the 1929 election. In the political crisis that followed the replacement, in 1929, of Hughes by Lang as Governor-General, the government lost its support from the minor groups and, forced into a premature election, the new and somewhat ineffectual Prime Minister, J.H. Scullin, lost to a coalition of all the non-Labor parties who then, under the Prime Ministership of F.W. Eggleston, had the ill fortune to take office only a few weeks before the Wall Street crash and the onset of the Great Depression.

Given its internal contradictions and the stresses of the times, it was remarkable that the Eggleston government lasted for two years before it split into its three constituent parts, to be replaced, in the greatest landslide in Australian electoral history, by the extraordinary successful government of E.G. Theodore, whose plan for expanding credit as a way of fighting the Depression produced Australia's famous 'economic miracle'. It is, of course, believed, as every schoolchild knows, that it was E.G. Theodore, rather than F.D. Roosevelt, who should be seen as the most imaginative leader during the Depression.

The Australian workers did not forget that it was the Labor Party that had protected their interests during the Depression and they showed a firm loyalty to the party thereafter. This loyalty was made even more secure when Theodore introduced the trades unions into many of the consultative processes of the State, by the famous agreement that became known simply as 'The Accord'. After the Great Accord of 1936, there began that process in which trades unions are seen as a normal and necessary part of the nation's wellbeing. It is a measure of the success of the Great Accord of 1936 and its aftermath of industrial democracy that even now, fifty years later, all the public opinion polls still show the trades union movement as the most respected institution in Australia.

It was in the 1930s that Theodore, with extraordinary foresight, helped strengthen an Australian intellectual class. The scientists and technologists had grown rapidly in numbers and esteem since the early 1920s: now they were joined by many others. Theodore had been at first impeded in some of his plans by the weakness of economists in Australia. He gave universities extra facilities so that there could develop that distinctively Australian style of economic thinking that is still with us, so that the myths of the classical model of economics still have no currency in Australia, even at a time when strange forces calling themselves 'the New Right' have been manifest in societies less politically developed than Australia. (How could one imagine a New Right in Australia itself?) But Theodore passed beyond cultivating an interest in economics to the cultivation of a distinctive Australian sociology, then to the development of Australian studies generally, and then he moved into that significant general expansion in universities and other forms of higher education that has both enlivened Australian life and provided a vigorous, adaptable basis for national policy and national prosperity. His establishment of the Australia Council in 1937 was later imitated in many other countries.

The rest of the story is well known: the party split in 1938, when its right wing, supporting the Franco side in the Spanish Civil War, defected from the party and formed the Democratic Labor Party; it was narrowly defeated in the 1939 election, but by 1941 the party was again in power and, although sometimes being refreshed by spells in opposition, it has continued to dominate the scene.

Especially memorable, of course, was the great Whitlam ministry of 1961 to 1974. Australia still remains 'an exemplar to the old lands'.

Well, I hope you enjoyed that fable. Perhaps the remarkable thing about it is that so much of it might almost have been true.

Certainly, some of it was beyond probability. Unlike Labor parties in some other parts of the world, the Australian Labor Party was not basic to the struggle for political democracy in Australia and perhaps for this reason it has had a tendency, with exceptions, such as the Wran government, to see constitutional reform as peripheral. It is also beyond probability that the party would have understood in the 1930s the great contribution the earlier development of an intellectual class might have made to Australia. (It is equally improbable that any other party might have done so.) And the party has never had the local community penetration that has marked the most successful of the world's Labor parties; if anything, the Labor Party's connection with local government may have taken forms that have done the party more harm than good. But most of the other reforms I mentioned were there in potential – in Hughes, in Theodore, in Whitlam and perhaps even in Lang, if he had been a big fella in a bigger and more supportive field. And what is demonstrable is that the party did have bad luck – bad luck in winning the 1914 and 1929 elections – and, for that matter, in winning the 1972 rather than the 1969 election.

But I don't want to make too much of all this in detail. This kind of thing is better left with some of the mystery attached to it – the mystery of why a country once so innovative became, in many fields, so sluggish.

16

THE IMPORTANCE OF SYMBOLISM: AUSTRALIA SHOULD BECOME A REPUBLIC

In 1992 D.H. and others produced The Coming Republic, *a collection of essays and interviews addressing an issue that he had been raising for nearly thirty years.*

How we see Australia is not just a theoretical or a symbolic matter, but a *practical* matter, affecting our actions – because if we see the world, or our nation, as a certain kind of place, then we act as if it *is* that kind of place. To take just one example: the long dominance of 'the bush' as the true Australia had overwhelming effects on how we behaved in policies and priorities. It concealed from Australians that they were largely an urban people, and this did damage to cultural awareness and social policy and enormous damage to manufacturing. And in the entertainment, tourist and advertising industries it still goes on. There was a sense of moral outrage from many when Paul Keating said, in June 1991, that there was more to Australia than Paul Hogan's 'shrimp on the barbie' ads might suggest. Well – isn't there?

In the era of the quick fix the 'pragmatists' were particularly contemptuous of anything other than what they saw as hard facts. Yet at the very beginning of the end of that era, it was the visit of Queen Elizabeth herself in 1992 that accidentally produced a superb example of what I have meant in saying that we must have a constitutional and symbolic declaration that we are an independent and distinctive society.

At the parliamentary reception the Prime Minister read a speech that was intended to make it sound as if Australia was an independent nation – a matter about which there is no practical doubt, but about which symbolic statements can do some good. After congratulating the Queen on the fortieth anniversary of her accession, the Prime Minister said that the relations between Britain and Australia had changed and that Australia's outlook was necessarily independent. What is there that is republican about that? Absolutely nothing – unless you assume that Australians are expected to be loyal not only to Queen Elizabeth, but to Great Britain. The attacks that Mr Keating's speech produced demonstrated quite clearly that to some of the people who attended the parliamentary reception this is exactly what 'loyalty' is expected to mean.

This shows how the continuing failure of Australians to have their own head of state can go along with postcolonial mindsets, not of confidence and national interest, but of infantile dependence, and 'loyalty'. If we are going to be 'loyal', why cannot we be loyal to our own concepts of Australia?

This is not just a matter of form. It is a matter of substance. The symbolic structure at the centre of a nation can be the expression of its common sense. It can be one of the most important ways in which a nation 'sees' itself. The way in which, officially, *we* 'see' ourselves is as a place that cannot even provide its own head of state and in which its distant head of state represents loyalty not only to her own person (whatever *that* might mean) but to Great Britain.

In the days of Empire, the symbolic structure of the monarchy made sense: it was an accurate representation of Australia's colonial status. Now, it is ridiculous. Scarcely any Australians are still mad enough to see an economic or strategic priority in our relations with Great Britain and most of them no longer see a cultural priority, but apparently many of them may still see a mystic connection. This means that as a symbolic structure the monarchy has ceased to work. What has happened now in Australia is that we have a symbolic system that is defunct – or, if it still has meaning, it maintains illusions of some inexpressible kind about our relationship with Great Britain. And, if these still contain latent traces of 'Anglo-Saxon' chauvinism they become an endemic disease of a nationally debilitating kind.

As we contemplate the future of our country as it moves, alone, into the twenty-first century, we don't know what dangers – or what opportunities – lie ahead. All we can be certain of is uncertainty. How important it is, therefore, that we should be, at least in external appearance, one independent nation, speaking in our own name and with some confidence in the right to independent judgement. For reasons that are cultural, social, economic, political and strategic, we must entirely rid ourselves of a dependent mindset and of a symbolic centre of nothingness.

Consider the changes that have occurred inside this country since Australia was founded on January 1, 1901. Consider the changes that have occurred in the world outside Australia since January 1901. Shouldn't we now recognise our own *Australian* distinctiveness in a way that recognises once and for all that this is no longer January 1901?

Shouldn't we, by some symbolic kickstarting, learn again how to take a long-term view of ourselves and of our nation? Australians were once idealistic. We must learn to be idealistic again – but with a new idealism, a practical idealism that is related to the potentials of our own country in the twenty-first century. By doing this we can become not a lucky country, but a *better* country, and a country with a new and safer future. And in that process one of the essentials is a democratic definition of our capacity for independence and self-reliance.

IT'S ALL ABOUT THE CULTURE

17

THE INTELLIGENT TOURIST

In The Great Museum, *published in 1984, D.H. examined what museums and monuments said about a society;* The Intelligent Tourist *in 1992 consolidated some of his thinking. D.H. had a large bookcase full of travel books: each one pored over, written on and bookmarked as he planned his next trip.*

How to be real

Rituals of the camera

The appetite for 'authenticity' in tourism is itself part of a wider modern craving – the infatuation with the 'real' and a sense of actuality. There is no better example than the camera – because a photograph can be more real than real, which is what Walter Lippmann had in mind when he told the story in his book *Public Opinion* of a mother who listens to praise of her baby and then says: 'But wait till you see his photograph.' This belief in the transcendent reality of the photograph has been as important to tourism as the transport revolution that started the railways. How can we imagine tourism without it? The camera authenticates our journey. It proves we were there.

And while some of the early tourist emblems – the Pyramids and the Alps – were conceptualised in lithographs and engravings, it was the camera that invented most of the sights we were expected to see. In *100 Years in Yosemite*, Carl P. Russell describes the process of 'framing' the Yosemite Valley. In 1855 the first lithograph was published, followed by four engravings in an article in *California Magazine*, then twenty glass plate negatives, providing evidence that Yosemite was the world's greatest single Wonder of Nature. Yosemite was declared a public park in 1864, and railroad and shipping companies promoted it as the West Coast's answer to Niagara Falls; trails were built, camping grounds were laid out, hotels went up. A tourist wonder had been created by the camera.

When George Eastman invented the Kodak with its roll of flexible film, photography became an art form for anyone with the price of a camera. ('You press the button; we do the rest.') In the industrialising societies, professional photographers were already authenticating events (a wedding wasn't a wedding without a photograph) and solemnising persons, with studio portraits. Now, with easy amateur photography, the family photo album became one of the symbolic bonds of family life. And among the family photographs there began to appear holiday snaps. By the 1920s, Kodak was advertising that 'A holiday without a Kodak is a holiday wasted'. Unless you photographed a view or a famous site you might as well not have been there.

On my first visit to the Ryoan-ji rock garden in Kyoto, I saw a group of Japanese tourists participate in a characteristic modern ritual. In turn, each approached their guide and, standing on exactly the same spot, positioned a camera. The guide's lips moved. The camera clicked. I asked my interpreter what the phrase was that the guide was repeating. She said, 'What the guide is saying is "F-stop 2.8, shutter speed 250".' One of the rituals of tourism is 'doing' the particular sights already defined by professional photographers, and then, like the Japanese tourists in the Ryoan-ji garden, photographing these sights in the same way as they have already been photographed in the travel literature, preferably with your companions in front of them.

Making sure reality is still there

This concern with 'reality' goes beyond framing existence into convenient stereotypes. When the supernatural stopped being the main way of explaining what was going on in the world, a voracious appetite developed for other kinds of reassurances that there really was a reality out there. The camera offered the extraordinary assurance that it could not lie (even though, of course, it 'lies' all the time – in the sense that there is inevitably selection in *what* is photographed and *how* it is photographed and what is *not* photographed). Tourism, especially in its concern with authenticity, became part of this fear that unless the world was constantly made 'real', it might go away.

One should see this in context. It was science that made the world 'real' – with its emphasis on the materiality of existence, on empiricism and on the certainties of proof. The most obvious extension of this certitude into tourism was museums. Except for art museums, modern museums were founded on the rock of a solid, definable, objective materialism. All the objects in a museum could be taken to represent reality accurately and scientifically. In a museum the very idea of reality as something to theorise about could seem absurd. There they were, the objects themselves, behind glass, classified and labelled. They were *proof*. There was a reality out there and these objects were representations of that reality.

However, the forms of presentation in museums and historic sites were also related to what was happening in the arts, especially in the thirst to be 'realistic' (a word that did not exist until the nineteenth century). The concern of tourism with reality can be compared with the nineteenth-century obsessions with naturalistic presentations in painting, literature and drama. They offered more reassurances of the materiality of existence than had ever before been necessary.

Novels created the appearance and the feel of the nineteenth century in expansive passages of detailed physical description. New types of painting, both in style and content, caused scandal by their concern with 'showing things as they are'. In the fine arts these naturalistic styles were abandoned in the twentieth century, but by then for most people what mattered visually was the camera, and the camera offered and still offers illusions of reality unimaginable in any earlier art form. In the theatre, the desire for realism put ordinary language into the mouths of actors and it crammed stages with hoards of real things. This obsession was to disappear, but in the world of drama it was the camera that mattered for most people: movies and television can bring illusions of actuality over the full twenty-four hours of the day.

And 'travel books' continue the descriptive traditions of nineteenth-century fiction. Ordinary travel books, even those grumpy ones that are concerned with the discomforts and disappointments of travel (such as Paul Theroux's), are exercises in refined sensibility. They provide sensations of acuteness of observation that none of us (including the authors themselves) are ever likely to experience when actually on the trail. A travel book can be a reality not available to our experience. Travel writing might be seen as the pornography of tourism: it offers satisfactions that are obtainable only by reading travel writing.

The particular trick of realistic travel writing is to make things seem actual; to make you feel you are *there* by the use of material detail. Travel writing uses techniques of fiction writing to project illusions of travel, but travel writers are not usually crooks. In this they are different from travel journalists, almost all of whom are corrupted by free trips and the need to attract advertising. They sell clichés in ways that can make the travel supplements one of the more dishonest parts of a newspaper.

An equivalent in the traditional natural history museums were the 'habitat groups', in which stuffed animals were placed in 'real' settings – producing real stereotypes: the gorilla forever pounding his chest ... the bear with paws forever raised ... the deer forever poised, its delicate nostrils picking up a scent ... the predatory jaguar forever surveying the scene for prey. (You don't see animals in such conveniently photographable poses on, say, a game drive in Victoria Falls.)

This search for authentic things could reach the heroic in a museum such as New York's American Museum of Natural History. The process would start with a field trip to a location. Drawings and paintings were made. Photographs were taken. Samples of plants, soils, rocks and barks were packed and labelled. Sometimes a whole tree was taken back to New York. In the laboratory some of this stuff was preserved with chemicals and painted to make it look real. Some of it was reproduced in wax or cellulose acetate. The original soil and small rocks were used. For the larger boulders, casts were made and reproduced in plaster and then treated to look exactly like the real thing.

Smelling like real

At least the habitat groups were made up of real things or imitations of real things, even if assembled stereotypically, and you could look at them in your own way and at your own pace. Now there are attempts in some museums to turn your visit into a total illusion of reality of the kind you get from a movie. (In some places, of course, they just put on a movie.) Such attempts try to leave nothing to the imagination. For a start, there isn't much time for imagination. You can't look at things at your own pace and in your own way. You can't feel your way around an object. You are taken through, with no choices. And, as attempted representations of reality, the more detailed they become the sillier they are.

One example – one of the silliest serious museum presentations in the world – despoils the reputation of the city of York, in the north of England. York has a famous cathedral – Britain's largest Gothic church. It has city walls, and streets of largely medieval buildings, as well as attractive Georgian facades and one of Europe's most elegant railway stations. But that is not why the streets of York are now awash with tourists. A profitable hysteria came from a new marketing hype: York has a cult tourism trap – the Jorvik Viking Centre, which tuned the enticements of realism to a new pitch by offering authentic Viking sounds, authentic Viking sights – and authentic Viking *smells*. It might have been the extra appeal to reality offered by the authentic Viking smells that made Jorvik Britain's top-rated new tourist show of the 1980s. One of the sights of York is the faithful queue outside the Viking Centre, spaced with notices telling people how long they will have to wait before they can experience a Viking smell. The sales pitch worked so well that 'the traditional celebration of Jolabcot' has been invented to bring life to the deadest part of the winter season. For the three weeks of this pseudo-event 'the ancient streets of York ring to the sounds of Viking cries' with Viking feasts, longship races, traditional processions of Vikings and Anglo-Saxons, and fortunes told in Old Norse.

Come with me to the Jorvik Viking Centre. Stand in the queue for half an hour, or even an hour; then, having bought your ticket, shuffle forward under flickering lights through a semi-darkness of black and red, hearing simulated sounds of distant thunder and reading portentous messages about the arrival of the Vikings (as if this were the biggest thing before the Second Coming). Then find yourself loaded into a time-car which, when full, moves backwards – passing in reverse chronological order through centuries of York civilisation, represented by dummies, which don't represent much because you are moving too quickly. The time-car's personalised soundtrack announces that you are about to enter the ancient city of Jorvik. It is a typical market day, late one October afternoon in the year 948 A.D.

The personalised soundtrack tells us to listen (hear the children squabbling in ancient Scandinavian tongues), to look (now we pass Svein's leather shop and the shop of Snarri the jeweller), and to smell (the stench of the pigsty and the salty tang of a boat that comes in from the sea). What we are passing through is a lifesize mock-up consisting of dummies and simulated houses, shops and lanes, passed so rapidly and in such confusion that all I could coherently remember was a dummy of a man in deep meditation inside what seemed to be a large basket. (When I bought a guidebook to find out what I had seen, I discovered he was using a latrine.) Our time-cars then take us to the site of the excavations that had prompted the guesswork for this confused dream, but all the rotted wood and old fish bones and other relics have been so thoroughly conserved, before being put back where they were found, that this seems just as phony and unmemorable as what we have already passed. When the personalised soundtrack tells us our time-car journey is over we walk through a simulated archaeologist's laboratory, so furnished with lifelike dummies of archaeologists in front of high-tech equipment that it is not possible to also look at the specimens. The vertigo of simulated reality diminishes only when we reach the Jorvik Gift Shop.

It wasn't even the simulated reality of the habitat groups in the natural history museums. Tawdry invention seems a better description – an appeal to commercialised fantasy rather than to the imagination. Because one is hurried through, with no control over pace or perspective, what becomes remarkable is not what is seen: what matters is the working of the contrivance.

IT'S ALL ABOUT THE CULTURE

I looked back from this nonsense to remember the sense of wonder and illumination that came, years ago, when we visited the Viking displays at Bygdöy, near Oslo, and Roskilde, near Copenhagen. In Oslo, the ships were venerated in a cruciform building the size of a cathedral. Each of the three ships, of old blackened oak dug out of burial grounds and in differing states of wholeness, was displayed in its own 'chapel' of rounded white walls and stone floor. You could spend the whole day looking if you wanted to. One was probably a ceremonial ship, restored, with elegantly carved serpents' heads and intertwined beasts; one, also restored, was sturdily useful; one had partly rotted away, but that meant you could see how it was made. In the fourth chapel were goods found in the burial sites, including a chariot, and in the Historical Museum, iron ingots and smithies' tools presented the Vikings as a kind of early industrial society.

At Roskilde, the Danes chose a relaxed rather than reverential presentation (in Norway, the Viking finds and the construction of the museum had helped expressions of national pride in a glorious past). At Roskilde, the display hall was like a small shipbuilding yard, not a cathedral, and it was set beside the fjord where the conservators had gathered the thousands of pieces of oak, pine, lime and birch that were slowly being turned back into five ships – most of the work being done in front of visitors to the museum, with tools left around when no one was working. As each ship was put together, they did not replace the missing bits; they just sketched out with thin struts what the rest of the ship might have looked like. Back-up models gave an idea of the vast trading operations of the Vikings: one ship was presented as a transatlantic cargo carrier, another as a coastal merchant vessel. The Vikings were shown as farmers and as a merchant society. Among the models of casks and chests were little Viking figures, wrapped soberly in long cloaks, as grave-faced as nineteenth-century exporters and importers.

I compared and contrasted the two styles of museum presentation, the one reverential, the other open, and thought about how both museums allowed for the speculative element in museum display. I read up on the Vikings and even thought for a while of planning a trip concerned with the tourism of relics of the Viking Age, as one of the first periods when Europeans could see the world as theirs by navigational right. (This trip would have taken us from the Caspian and the Black Sea to the Eastern Mediterranean, England and Ireland, and then west to Iceland and Greenland.) What I am saying is that going to those two museums was a big experience.

At about the same time as the Jorvik Centre was opened (note the pseudo-scholarly phoniness of the word 'Centre'), the Yorkshire Museum re-staged its presentation of antiquities, telling a story of Roman, then Anglo-Saxon, then Viking life in York. If any of the fragments from the past appeal to your imagination, you have time to look, and register your own impressions. Models, graphics and words are also there, telling a story. It is quite clear what is authentic and what is reconstructed. There is no attempt to fabricate 'reality'. If you want to reconstruct the past you have to use your imagination.

People should understand that, along with 'real things', some imaginative devices may be needed to release a visitor's imagination. But reconstructions should contain visual hints within them: dummies can be faceless; a reconstruction of a dwelling place can be incomplete; audio-animatronic dummies can show some of what is going on under the vinyl skin. Museums simulating naturalism should admit the uncertainties of what they are doing in the display itself. If that is done, they cease to deceive. They help the presentation of the hypothetical nature of reality. And they are of more moral and intellectual use to us than fantasy-reality, the fast food of the imagination.

18

THE PUBLIC CULTURE

The ideas in The Public Culture, *first published in 1986 and revised in 1994, were a development of some of the themes DH started to explore in* The Great Museum.

A national mirage

In a 1976 bestseller, *The Russians*, the United States journalist Hedrick Smith found that the people of the Soviet Union were 'the world's most passionate patriots'. They could still be bonded by recalling 'the shared ordeals and triumphs' of 'the Great Patriotic War' of 1941–1945 and, from exploits in space to victories in sport, they shared a 'pride in the power and accomplishments of the Soviet Union'. He spoke of the people's 'moral chauvinism', their addiction to patriotic songs, their 'basic unquestioning confidence in their own way of life', their simple faith that 'ours is best'. Then he spoke of their 'Victorian pride in national power and empire and a conviction of moral superiority that echoes America's earlier age of innocence'.

Fifteen years later, the Soviet Union had gone. And with it had gone not only a perceived Soviet élan but the total program for changing the nature of things, that was expressed in the redeemer

THE PUBLIC CULTURE

cult of Lenin. Every material reminder of Lenin was revered as a holy relic, with his every famous saying carved into the walls of tens of thousands of buildings. His life was divided into exemplary tales, each of which, like a saint's, had its own mode of representation in painting (with tens of thousands of reproductions of the most famous paintings), and with tens of thousands of statues, from granite colossi to small plaster casts, that were almost as stylised as those of Buddha. His face appeared on vases, in tapestry, in glass, in ceramics. His name honoured hundreds of towns and city districts, hundreds of industrial enterprises and recreation centres and thousands of squares and streets. There was a Lenin Straits, a Lenin Mountain, a Lenin Atomic Icebreaker. There were hundreds of Lenin museums and memorials. (It is in these that the schoolchildren 'Pioneers' stood in their red caps and scarves, flowers in their hands, and dedicated themselves to the ideals of Lenin.) The party leaders explained each change in the party line as one in which they were being faithful to 'the correct Leninist path'. The great slogans proclaimed Lenin's supreme virtue: 'Lenin is with us', 'Lenin lived. Lenin lives. Lenin will live', 'Lenin's name and Lenin's case will live forever'. His body, on display for the pilgrims, sanctified the world.

And along with the Lenin cult were the cults of sacrifice, enormous parades, endless ceremonies, with constant banners and slogans in the streets and the peculiar language that was expected to mark all public discourse. And yet when all this went – as, earlier, with the collapse of Nazism – it was almost as if it had never been. Most people were able to shrug it off. In fact it was *laughed off* with a witticism of Yeltsin's in the confrontation with Gorbachev in the Russian parliament (live on television) after the farcical coup failed in August 1991 and the old Soviet regime was summarily signed out of existence. New political parties formed with slogans such as

'Freedom, Property and Legality' and 'Family, Property, Motherland'. Stalin had caused the deaths of so many innocents in vain.

Hedrick Smith's book was written in 1976, when its author thought that the age of innocence of 'America' had gone – as it seemed to have done in the Nixon–Carter years. But times changed, and soon, for the United States it was the Great Patriotic Year of 1984, when the United States won all those gold medals in the Olympic Games ('Number One!') and Ronald Reagan achieved re-election after a campaign in which both sides tried to outdo each other in waving the stars and stripes and invoking 'America' (with that casualness with which United States citizens appropriate to the United States the name normally given to two continents). It was generally agreed that 1984 was 'America's' year, yet this also proved to be a mirage as Ronald Reagan, the genial cowboy, rode back into the West.

*

Modern-industrial nation-states can seem to have a 'national mirage'. The existing social order in modern-industrial states is maintained – or is given the appearance of being maintained – not only by coercion but by the dominance of certain assumed truths. This raises questions of privilege: questions of how these truths that dominate the public scene may favour one economic class over others, one sex over another, one ethnic group over others, one racial type over others, one region over others. It also raises questions about strategies for change, of how creating new self-evident truths can sometimes help change a social order.

In some ways the processes of a 'national mirage' are as old as myths and legends, images and words. But, more often than not, they are now carried out in new ways, in which most people in a nation-state have limited or no apparent participation but in which all the people are likely to be reached. And, while some of the elements of a mirage are older than the formation of modern-industrial nation-states, some are uniquely related to modernity, industrialism and nationality. In fact, the development of a complex 'national mirage' is an essential part of a modern-industrial nation-state. Most earlier societies got by with very much less. In *Discipline and Punish* Michel Foucault suggests that in premodern societies the rulers displayed their power irregularly, through demarcations, signs, levies, ceremonies – among them the ceremonial theatre of punishment with its exemplary torturings and killings, conducted irregularly, in periods of intense terror.

This could be sufficient for ruling: it could reach its apex in the great courtly displays, or in the suppression of a peasants' revolt when the bodies of peasant leaders were likely to be dismembered in ceremonies of some complexity and the pieces sent throughout a kingdom with considerable solemnity as a lesson to others. It was a time, as Herbert Gans puts it, in *Popular Culture and High Culture*:

> when European societies were divided culturally into high culture and folk culture. The latter was sparse, homemade, and, because peasants lived in isolated villages, largely invisible. The former was supported by the city-dwelling elites – the court, the nobility, the priesthood and merchants – who had the time, education and resources for entertainment and art ... Because of the low social status and geographical isolation of folk culture, they also had a virtual monopoly on public and visible culture.

There was not much concern with how the peasants lived or with what they thought – except from the church, and then often only in a desultory way, although sometimes with a brutal intensity. Thinking was not the business of peasants. Their role was to contribute to levies, whether of kind, or of labour, or in military service, and, for some of them, to provide raw material in exemplary ceremonies such as nose slittings, floggings, bone breakings, evisceration, beheadings, hangings and burnings.

We now live in a time when there is a demand for what at least appears to be a shared 'public and visible culture', in which both rulers and ruled can appear to be common, if differentiated, participants in a shared national life, sharing a national vision of the certainties of existence. How could this not be so? As they began to develop, the modern-industrial nation-states were too complex for people to understand. Without a simple mirage of public life a modern state could not have existed. People had to receive their 'instructions', as it were, about how to be modern and industrial and national; they had to have some ideas of what was going on; and, since these states are industrial states, they had to be trained in how to react to change. One example: among the declared principles of modern societies, whether capitalist, communist or fascist, has been the principle of 'work' as a true means to human dignity and welfare. In capitalist societies there have been, of course, the unemployed, but the very name given to them – 'the unemployed' – is a declaration of the importance of work. Most of the communist prisons were *labour* camps. The great slogan above the entrances of the Nazi concentration camps was 'Work makes you free'.

With a few exceptions the privileged do not justify their importance any longer by vast displays of frivolity and enjoyment, but by displays of hard work. The mark of authority is not now the throne, but the desk. One of the most prestigious of all the photographs of the United States presidents is a photograph of a president, the Stars and Stripes beside him, in the Oval Office working at his desk. One of the ways in which the Watergate tapes profaned political decency was that such things were being said in *this* place, and being recorded by a tape recorder concealed in the leg well of *this* desk. Some of the most

THE PUBLIC CULTURE

revered of the relics in the V.I. Lenin museums when they were a light to the world were the actual desks, or replicas of the actual desks, at which Lenin worked so hard for humankind. Under Mussolini, in the Palazzo Venezia some of the rooms were likely to be a blaze of light until late in the night: passers-by could look up and know that the Duce was there, working for Italy behind his colossal desk.

The phrase 'national mirage' suggests that the whole thing is a hoax, whereas many individual elements of a 'national mirage' are true. (Even if many other truths are missing.) The phrase 'public culture' is more useful. But there is no preliminary assumption that a whole culture has been organised as a conspiracy, even if a great deal of it can be contrived, nor that a public culture is necessarily dominated by the self-evident truths (whether in thinking or in acting) of one group. And no assumptions are made, one way or the other, about how widely the values and prescriptions to action of a public culture play a part in the lives of most people. Those things need to be worked out. But there should seem little doubt that a public culture exists. What its effects are is harder to talk about. But to see it, all you have to do is open your eyes and look.

*

Where does one look for a public culture? (I am assuming that 'culture' means a repertoire of habits of thinking and acting that gives particular meanings to existence.) To be worth doing, it must be done in ways that will allow comparisons between different kinds of modern-industrial states, whether capitalist or communist, fascist or theocratic, militarist or cronyist. That means that in all of them we might look in much the same places. Obviously, one looks to the great public face of the state – in the ceremonies of civil religion, in the rituals of voting, in the declarations made in the state's monuments, public buildings and open spaces, in the speeches and other ceremonies of official political life (including, in liberal-democratic societies, the 'official' opposition movements) and in the public manifestations of the state's monopoly of violence (judiciary, police and military). One also looks to the public face of the great bureaucracies – in all cases, the bureaucracies of government, the financial, industrial and commercial organisations (whether owned by shareholders or the state) and the labour organisations (whether self-managed or not). In some societies there would also be the great political bureaucracies. One also looks to the view of the world, of the nation, and of the past projected within the educational and religious institutions, in bookshops, museums, theatres, concert halls and galleries. In addition, sport, shopping and 'leisure' all project values – and tourism becomes a celebration of the nation and a definer of the national past. And in all societies there are certain legendary personalities, 'celebrities' and 'public figures' who are expected to catch the imagination and who are exemplars of various values. In all societies there are certain characteristic forms of expression, some of which are favoured over others.

Rough lists of the elements in the repertoire of a public culture are relatively easy to work out provided one accepts a certain level of abstraction (it is lists of collective habits we are talking about), and provided one jettisons all ambition for performing acts of measurement, and provided one abandons, at least at this listing stage, an instant concern with 'effects'. Examples of 'meaning'-maintenance can be found in a coach tour of the battlefields of Verdun or on a 'Tourmobile' visit to the sights of Washington; in the days of the Cold War it could be found in the similarities between a spy drama about the KGB on United States television and a spy drama about the CIA on Soviet television; it can be found in the way the annual Melbourne Cup race has become, in Australia, a national day, or in the way that under the communist regime the Easter Mass in Sofia's

Alexander Nevsky cathedral became an annual fashionable event with national meanings. The Christmas shopping festival in Tokyo can tell us something. So can the skyline of a Stockholm community housing settlement, or the expensive reconstruction of old Warsaw. So can the bookshop in the British Houses of Parliament, with its emphasis on royalty rather than democracy, or a Fiat showroom in Turin, or the way a restaurant queue behaves in Budapest. Meanings can be found in the annual report of the board of directors of a Swiss manufacturing company and compared with the meanings in the annual report of a Singapore manufacturing company.

In looking for examples we can be as concerned as much with what is done as with what is said, because doing things can at times be an even more important form of meaning-maintenance than speech. For example, in most of these societies voting is an essential ritual, yet if you consider how all this voting proclaims meanings that are refuted by an examination of the actual operations of power you discover that voting *says* more than it *does*. Another example is work punctuality. By turning up to work on time, automatically, without questioning it, we make one of the fundamental declarations that distinguish industrial from other societies. Given this, one can again see how sometimes what is not said can be more important than what is said: it can show that something has become so ingrained as a bodily habit that it is taken for granted. It is not in the societies where there continue to be exhortations to arrive at work punctually that one can assume the work ethic to be most flourishing, but in those societies in which punctuality is so taken for granted that there is no longer any need for exhortation. In a communion of saints there would be no exhortations against sinning.

A declaration of 'cultural rights'

D.H. was also a strong advocate for 'cultural rights' and the arts more generally when he was chairman of the Australia Council.

Just as we have learned to speak of political, social and economic rights, we must now learn to think about cultural rights. Just as governments must at times intervene to maintain an economic market, so it is with the market of ideas. A public culture overall might be thought of as an oligopolistic market, and it is even easier to think of the mass culture industries in that way – so strengthening a market of ideas requires intervention. In ideal terms, it should seem as natural in a liberal-democratic society that in all levels of public life there should be a concern about 'the cultural factor' as there is about the health factor. Yet it is a feature of modern-industrial societies that, unlike members of folk and tribal societies, so far as participation is concerned, most of their citizens can be seen, in varying degrees, as culturally unemployed. The idea of imagining ordinary people being encouraged to speculate and to use their imaginations, to go beyond consuming to producing, could seem impertinent. Indeed a great deal of art and intellectual speculation is presented in a way that goes *against* our fellow citizens.

Yet a high public concern about cultural life can be argued for on liberal grounds because it is essential to a liberal society that there should be a marketplace of values, knowledge and ideas, providing diverse opportunities for opening out human potential, both for individuals and for groups; and on democratic grounds, because it is essential to a democratic society for its citizens to be knowledgeable and reactive to change and that society should be open to cultural engagement by its citizens. Concern with cultural life can also be argued for on grounds of tolerance, to gain understanding of the enormous cultural resources provided by diversity; on economic grounds, because imagination, creativity, capability and knowledge are essential to a productive culture; and simply because people need an active and independent cultural life to be able to take an intelligent interest in their own society and the world around them, to have theories about who they are and where they stand, and to have confidence in their right to enjoy a distinctive culture.

We need to make a declaration of cultural rights – so what rights should we declare?

It is possible to imagine them in three groups (although the groups are linked): rights of engaging with the human cultural heritage; rights of engaging with new intellectual and artistic production; rights of engaging in their own forms of intellectual and art production.

Rights of engaging with the human cultural heritage

Relics of the human heritage are what have survived of the old tribal cultures, ruling-class cultures and folk cultures, along with what has already been preserved from modern 'high culture' and mass entertainment culture. It is all constantly reinterpreted in new terms – in theatres and concert halls, or in universities, in conserved monuments, or in museums and libraries. Frequently – perhaps usually – it can be interpreted in ways that can make it seem alien, even threatening, to the mass of people.

There can be enormous mounds of rubbish within the storehouses of cultural heritages, some providing some of the prime anti-intellectuality of the age. There can also be much that is corrupting in the practices of the custodians: brutal snobberies, arrogant mystifications, obsessive suppressions, inane time servings, moribund talmudisms, manic avant-gardisms. Some of its products and its practitioners can be turned to the advantage of prevailing social classes and prevailing social repressions.

But merely because the Bolshoi in Moscow and the Metropolitan Opera Company in New York become, sometimes, display areas for the privileged does not make ballet and opera themselves ineradicable ruling-class art forms. Works of the imagination are reinterpretable: the greatness of 'great' works of art or of the intellect may lie, partly, in the varied richness of their reinterpretability. Both art forms and intellectual forms – the artefacts of 'high culture' – are there for us to use for our own ends in making our own views of existence and, if we care to use this facility, no one can prevent us. If one imagines the intellectual mode as a special, and self-conscious, concern with being a serious critic of existence, seeking meanings, then it is usually within the 'high culture' that this activity is pursued at any length. High culture might be thought of as a battleground for the interpretation of the human heritage.

Human liberation is not won simply by fleeing from this battleground, and assuming that somehow Madonna is the same as Mozart, and soap operas the same as Shakespeare. Yet that has been claimed by intellectuals who have built careers on the idea that all that distinguishes 'high culture' from 'popular culture' is the esteem in which it is held and its scarcity value. (The phrase 'popular culture' suggests a voluntary, participatory activity – but this is not the case. It is better to use two phrases: 'popular culture' can be thought of as a repertoire of activities that do originate among a group of people; 'mass culture' can describe the mass standardisation of cultural products and services, with centralised control, almost universal reach, and low levels of participation.) We should remember that many participants in the activities of high culture don't just parade their high culture around us as status signs. They have enlarged their lives by using access to whole ranges of knowledge about the human potential and what our physical environment might be, and they have used access to various techniques – abstract thought, critical analysis, and so on. Most people don't have these resources. This means that a small proportion of people can use the repertoires of both high culture and mass culture, but most people have access only to mass culture, and much of it highly commercialised mass culture. The thing is to ponder how to encourage people who are alarmed by the mysteries of high culture to acquire some facilities in engaging with a little of what it is offering so that they can use it for their own purposes.

Rights of engaging with new intellectual and artistic production

As to new intellectual speculation and new art, the 'experimentalism' of modernism, throughout the century, alienated great masses of people, rulers as well as ruled, just as the 'universitisation' of intellectual life alienated them with a new talmudism. (There was a difference: although it later became a market fad, the style of experimentalism in art at least began with a great human predicament – the crisis in reality construction that became a characteristic of societies as they modernised and industrialised, but the expansion of scholarly talmudism came more from an arid division of labour increasingly related to the administrative manipulation of universities into specialist disciplines with career paths measured in citations.)

But even if some new intellectual and artistic production can, at first, be seen as simply for the few, one might regard support for even arcane new art or difficult intellectual speculation as the R&D program for the whole entertainment, arts, culture and information industries. Such an R&D program develops new perspectives and styles that even if they do not reach the mass of people directly, can reach them indirectly, by influencing people who can popularise them, and touch them with meaning.

But that's only the beginning. People also have to be reached directly, as they always have been, in images, dance, song, instrumental music, drama, verse, narrative and lore and in this there must be some responsibility for providing a diversity of material in broadcasting, film, publishing and performance spaces. New and varied intellectual, entertainment and artistic production can provide a diversity of ways of organising new experience, new perspectives, and new perceptions of the world and of human vision. Without them, even the reinterpretability of all the old stuff would cease.

Rights of engaging in their own forms of intellectual and art production

One enlivening feature of a liberal-democratic society can be its 'parallel education system' – the world of community centres of all kinds, of libraries, clubs, museums, community history movements, adult education services, community radio, regional art galleries, theatres and concert halls, community arts movements, folklore societies, fringe networks and newspapers, open learning programs, community performing groups, community museums, heritage bodies, and a number of other community activities in trades unions, churches, ethnic groups – and in its public intellectual life, at the point where popularisation is not a dirty word. It is in places like these that citizens can become culturally engaged. They are all there. But do they only represent the end of nineteenth-century aspirations toward universal edification?

A fuller community cultural participation would be a restoration of art and the intellect to life. A fully performing society – which is the aim of cultural participation policies – would be the end of 'industrial man'. (That doesn't mean people would stop working for a living but that they would have greater chances not to live for work, and this understanding would be part of a public culture.) It would also be the end of 'art' and 'the intellect', since if all people became, in one way or the other, 'creative', we would no longer need such specialist words. (This does not mean sinking into mediocrity: on the contrary, a performing society can show more discriminating judgement of performance and a higher regard for the greatest performers – of a kind now often restricted to sport in modern-industrial societies.) I understood this when I visited the Neighborhood Cultural Center in San Francisco's Western Addition. A black American with a high reputation for mural paintings was at work on a side wall of the Center. The surface had been treated, the scaffolding was up; the outline had been sketched for a mural on black entertainers. His apprentices were with him, learning their craft. Members of the community were around him, saying what they thought. That night I wrote down in my journal that the scene was medieval: but that was understating it. This is the kind of way in which we can imagine the very beginnings of art.

19

THE POLITICS OF THE AUSTRALIAN TRIBE: A CONFIDENTIAL REPORT BY AN ANTHROPOLOGIST FROM OUTER SPACE

From The Abundant Culture: Meaning and Significance in Everyday Australia. *D.H. contributed to this 1994 book, so named as a sign of how far Australia had moved from the old 'cultural cringe', a journey in which he had been a key figure.*

LIKE ANY OTHER TRIBE, THE AUSTRALIANS HAD A number of festivals. The Melbourne Cup festival of the god of luck celebrated Australians as a people who understood the chancy nature of existence and the need not to take yourself too seriously. The Father's Day festival, the Mother's Day festival and the Easter Bunny festival celebrated the values that money could buy – although the latter was also related to the legend of the death of a god in the Christian cult. There was the arcane festival of Australia Day, celebrated so secretly that its meaning was not obvious to the observer. Agricultural Show festivals celebrated rural virtue; and the Queen's Birthday and Labour Day festivals celebrated the unimportance, respectively, of the distant monarchy and of trades unions. Some of the greatest festivals were those of sport, solemnising the universal themes of loyalty, achievement, competitiveness and the differences between the sexes: in the most ambitious of these sporting spectacles there were displayed some of the 'logos' of 'the sponsors' – the great icons of the forces of the market among the Australians that played such an important part in the development of the tribal imagination.

However, it was the Christmas festival that was seen as the greatest festival of the year. This festival was related to legends of the birth of the founder of the Christian cult; it later also acquired the significant function of honouring the family; but its most important function, seen as central to the prosperity of many Australians, was to glorify the institution of shopping as a carnival of choices. Regular 'figures' would be announced during the Christmas festival recording attendance at the shopping temples, and the offerings left there, and comparing them with previous figures. During the festival, which ran over most of the month of December, the cities and towns were decorated and appropriate chants and entertainments were provided for the black boxes of the 'television sets' through which most of the tribe's messages were received, but the people themselves – especially the women folk, who had been described as 'goddesses of the gift' – were, by custom, expected to be the main celebrants. It was their special task to go to the shopping temples and proclaim the importance of choice by cash transaction and the declaration of love and friendship by purchase. Some of them devoted weeks to this service to social stability.

But the most remarkable of these festivals, that of 'the election', was of a different order. It was seen as what determined the affairs of the whole tribe. As with the Easter Bunny festival, its date was indeterminate. There were documents that gave guidance to the measures that should be used for deciding the date of this festival, but the 'calling' (as it was known) of an election was also a subject of much divination. In each of the meeting houses, called 'parliaments', there was a powerful body of diviners, called 'the press gallery' (because they sat, like owls, or perched, like roosters and hens, on a ledge under the roof) and one of their main functions was to make predictions as to when the next election would be 'called' and who would win it.

To understand this, it is essential to understand that the principal functions of the tribal bard and the tribal soothsayer were operated by a tribal institution, directed by mysterious forces of its own, called 'the media'. It was the media who addressed the tribe through the black boxes; and it was also the media who whispered into the ears of the tribe through 'the radio' and who held up words and images for the gaze of the people in 'the press'. The media cast up images of what life was expected to be about. Instead of tribal fires, the people would sit around the black boxes every night and see performed for them 'corroborees' that would reiterate the values of the tribe. Important in this process was the legend-telling of what was described as 'the news'. The news was a series of anecdotes purporting to tell all that mattered over some time period, ranging from an hour to a day; this meant that the principal story-telling and legend-making of the tribe was carried out, not by reinforcing old values by repeating old stories, but by telling new stories each day, some of which reinforced old values and some of which spoke of change.

Among the most important stories were the cabalistic signs called 'the figures'. Although the meaning of these was far from clear (if they had any meaning at all) they were used as auspices in divining whether the gods favoured Australia – in the form of indexes, surveys and other 'statistics' that were taken to be the only appropriate method of explaining the mysteries of existence and the judgement of the gods. It was the figures that provided a principal source for the divinations of the gallery about when an election might be called and who would win it. The power of the figures could be so great that one of the perched fowls of the gallery (they were sometimes also spoken of as vultures) might glance at the figures of, say, how many people were not being paid to work or, even more mysteriously, of what 'the economic growth' was, and at once divine from this when the next election would be held and who would win it: this could be done with such zest that little sympathy was spent on those who were not being paid to work. And no sooner would an election festival be concluded than the gallery would begin a new cycle of predictions about the calling of the next election, and what it would be about.

However, it was not within the power of the gallery to actually call an election, even if they spent so much time calling *for* an election. Calling elections was the prerogative of a head person called the 'premier' or the 'prime minister' (although on two occasions elections were called by a different kind of head person, the governor or the governor-general who represented the real presence in Australia of the mystic body of the Crown, whose source was worshipped in London by hordes of patient pilgrims).

One of the remarkable features of the election festival that distinguished it from other festivals was that it was not only a festival. It also concluded in a ritual called 'polling day' when it was the duty of all the people to move their bodies to the 'polling booths' where they were to make secret signs on pieces of paper as to who the tribal elders would be who would, for a limited time, sit in the parliaments and perform the rituals, ceremonies and propitiations associated with governing the land (the actual governing occurred somewhere else). The principal elders were grouped into 'parties' and, although anyone could present their names to the people, it was usually only those whose names were offered by the parties who received most of the secret signs. Yet such is the power of faith and ritual that many of the people believed that by making the secret signs they were 'choosing the government' and deciding how the land should be governed. As to the elders, when the secret signs were all examined, those whom the secret signs had most favoured would then proclaim that they now embodied the spirit and the will of the people and could take actions in their name – although in this they could be limited by an important part of the lore of the tribe called 'the Constitution'.

Much of the lore was stored in huge repositories called libraries and was little known among the people although there could be instruction in this lore to some, who would go through an initiation rite called 'the examination', and then forget much of what they had learned once the initiation rite was concluded. The Constitution was the most sacred part of this lore, and, as such, was never seen among the people, although its sacred name could be evoked among them when they were called upon 'to defend the Constitution', a document about which they knew nothing. Within the Constitution there was contained the inner mystery of government – that the prime ministers and premiers and the parties did not exist. Those who were governing the land were the governors and governors-general, who embodied the mystic person not of the People, but of the Crown, far away in London, and adored by the hundreds of thousands of pilgrim-tourists. However, exactly what the Constitution meant was decided from time to time by 'the High Court', a temple where the high priests of law divined the meaning of the Constitution – and received honour or blame according to their divinations.

Another remarkable feature of the election festival was that, while a festival normally defines certain common values, the election festival defined important differences between the tribes. It became a method of promoting division rather than unity. Not that all the people participated in this process. Some (who took as their symbol the donkey) chose the secret signs at random; others (who took as their symbol the swing) saw themselves as outside the parties. But many were enthusiasts of the cult of the parties and at election times they would divide themselves off (a process also noted in the festivals of sport) as if nothing could ever unite them again. Iconic images of the principal elder in each party would be displayed as messages of hope and love to some, and of fear or hate to others; certain simple phrases would be chanted, as in a mantra, as a sacred formula; and on the magic box some of the tribe's most spiritual icons would be displayed – the dollar bill, the picket fence, the happy child – as important spiritual devices.

Yet, along with this promotion of division, there was also, among the icons and mantric phrases, a certain unity in myths of what mattered in life. One was the myth of the majority – that the voice of the people, as determined by the secret signs, was the voice of the gods. Another was the myth of the clink of coin – that the profit motive was the driving force in the tribe. The myth of progress was still strong – although it was often seen as something that depended on the correct economic plan – and so was the myth of work – that the only true way to dignity and welfare was through working for money. However, at the time these observations were taken, the strongest myth was the principle of economic growth – that what mattered most in life were the figures about the economy, especially those that came together as the Gross Domestic Product – given sacred form by the revered initials 'GDP'. It was the GDP that became the principal test of the tribe's failure or success, combining, as it did, both the magic of figures and the magic of numbers; changes in the GDP were compared with the GDP of other tribes, and there was great shame and some panic if the comparisons seemed bad. Graphs appeared almost every night on the black boxes, telling Australians about their latest performance in some particular field of the economy.

For, along with a belief in the figures went an even wider belief that what the Australians belonged to was not really a tribe. It was the Economy – seen as a machine, or as tables of figures and graphs, an abstraction beyond ordinary human understanding, but an abstraction that was to be served faithfully by the people, even if the Economy did not always serve *them*.

The Australians had many festivals and rituals, but they did not have many ceremonies honouring the whole tribe. They had the pilgrimages of tourism, with their tribal celebrations of Nature (in particular, the solemn photographing and reverent ascent of Uluru in the Dead Heart) in which it was not the goodness of the tribe but the land itself that was celebrated, and of Culture (in particular, paying devotion to the facade of the Sydney Opera House by walking around it), but the only ceremony that seemed to go to the heart of the tribe were the Anzac ceremonies and they had the peculiar characteristic of defining the tribe in a way which excluded most members of it.

The mystic body of the distant Crown had provided a certain amount of glamour to many ceremonies at a time when belief in the Crown was strong, but, at the time when these observations were being made, even the visitation of a Royal Person was ceasing to work its magic. For these reasons the ceremony that marked the conclusion of the election festival, the Opening of Parliament, was seen as of little further significance, since its meaning relied on belief in the mystic body of the Crown – in that all the elders were required to make a great oath of allegiance not to the tribe, not even to the Economy, but to the Crown in which most of them no longer believed.

However, after this mechanical ceremony, the parliaments (of which there were nine) played several important symbolic roles as places of significant ritual. (Of these assembly places, the most significant was partly buried in a hill in the sacred plain of Canberra –

made sacred by the presence of the Australian War Memorial.)

According to the lore of the tribe the function of parliament was to make laws and govern the people. It is not known whether Australians actually believed that this was happening, but in any of the palaces housing the parliamentary assembly places there were many other rooms – secret rooms in which the parties met and discussed what they would do next, other secret rooms in which the principal elders discussed what *they* would do, sometimes with each other, sometimes with the notables from other great buildings called 'the departments', and there were other secret rooms in which the entourage of each of the principal elders discussed what *they* would do, and those in which the bards of the gallery would decide what simple little tales they would make of all of this in that day's legend-telling.

In fact, for most of the year the palaces of the meeting houses were inhabited only by these kinds of people. But on the comparatively few weeks when all of the members of parliament did meet they would perform their grand ceremonial function, by engaging in a great antiphonal chant, called a 'debate', in which they arranged themselves into two main choruses: the first of these choruses would proclaim that everything it did was right and everything the other chorus did was wrong; the second chorus would proclaim that everything the other chorus did was wrong and everything it did was right.

Usually the great antiphonal chorus of the debates would be preceded by a prologue called 'question time' in which the elders would dance up and down and cry out to each other in a litany of invocations and responses, which would be watched eagerly by the hens and roosters of the gallery for signs of who, among the elders, seemed most favoured by the gods on that particular day.

But the most important function in the assembly place was to consecrate the laws.

IT'S ALL ABOUT THE CULTURE

This was done in a highly esteemed ritual of transubstantiation in which sheets of paper were transformed into the will of the people, stage by stage, in a complex liturgical process.

This revered process began with the presentation in the assembly place of unconsecrated paper. The paper was introduced in what was known as 'the first reading'. As might be gathered from this phrase, in this first reading no actual reading occurred. A few words were spoken, then the unconsecrated paper was 'tabled' (viz. placed on the altar of parliament). The ceremony was brief and usually conducted as if no one knew what was happening. Maintaining this impression was not difficult.

The next, and lengthiest stage, was called 'the second reading'. Unconsecrated paper was again placed on the altar, but this time it was written all over with words, which had been 'drafted', a process that usually meant that no ordinary person could understand it. It was at this stage that the antiphonies of debate would begin, with each chorus chanting in turn its prayers and curses, in an essential part of the process of hallowing the paper in the name of the people. Then occurred the most moving part of the whole ceremony. (Each time the parliament was to reach a decision, one of the elders would say 'I move'.) The parliament declared itself to be 'in committee'. The principal celebrant then sat down lower, at the altar, with a greater sense of community and with less formality and presented the words of the paper, piece by piece, while the antiphonies proceeded, with occasional cries of 'aye' and 'no' and, climactically, in what were known as 'divisions', the ringing of the bells and ritual movings and groupings. When this part of the liturgy was over, the throne was again ascended and after a final chanting of 'ayes' and 'noes' the paper was pronounced to have passed its second reading. In a small, almost private, ceremony the still unconsecrated paper was read a third time (which is to say that it was not read at all, but merely lay on the altar while a few prayers were muttered over it).

The unconsecrated paper was then taken to another assembly place in the meeting house – called 'the upper house' because it was on the same level as the first assembly place. Here the same processes of sacralisation occurred. On some occasions, however, there might be a louder crying of 'noes' than of 'ayes'. If this happened, the paper might be sent back whence it came, unhallowed, or altogether abandoned.

If, however, the process of sacralisation proceeded unimpeded the piece of paper was taken in a special ceremony to the person who embodied the spirit of the Crown, who would then breathe life into it, as he signed it. By this act of faith in the Crown the paper would then become the will of the people.

And the owls and the hens and the roosters of the gallery would then examine the paper and explain to the tribe what the true meaning of the paper was and whether the paper helped divine who would win the next election.

20

IT'S THE CULTURE, STUPID

D.H. looked at the potentially catastrophic effects of being culturally unaware in his last book, Dying: A Memoir, *published in 2007.*

THE WORD CULTURE IS NOW USED ALL OVER THE place, well beyond its older meaning of great art and intellectual attainment. When police superintendents, for instance, started to say, 'We have to change our culture,' it meant that the word was now being widely used in the anthropological sense of habits and customs. Habits and customs are enormously important to the conduct of human affairs, and policy makers run great risks if they don't take culture, and its manifestations in different ways in pluralist societies, into proper account.

The ways in which people do things and say things, and their beliefs, very largely determine who they are, and the idea of pluralism, of a number of communities within a society with different habits and customs, is one of the most important ideas there could be.

When you think pluralism, think of people of different ages, genders, sexuality and education. Living in different locations, with a variety of institutional loyalties, or few loyalties at all. People living in all kinds of families, or not in any family. People of many faiths, both secular and religious. People of many ethnic backgrounds.

People with many different conventional wisdoms and with many different ways of making sense of their lives and filling their time.

Change in such societies should take all this into account. For instance, the failure of the Americans to allow for the pluralism of Iraq is a tragic story whose complexities, horrors and absurdities will continue to cloud the historical record for many years.

How can one country say to another, 'We're going to change your regime and make you democratic'? Devastated political landscapes, such as Japan after the Second World War, may flourish with benevolent victors. But functioning nations, however tyrannical and cruel, have their own local customs and habits, and even if outside assistance and ideas are welcomed by a viable opposition, they should be allowed to work out their own brand of democracy, if they are capable of it.

There are, of course, limits to respecting habits and cultures. Cultures aren't always cosy. Some are disastrous, and we have to draw boundaries. The Nazi SS had a mature and confident culture, one based on a binding community spirit and an impelling sense of history. Its monument is to be found in Auschwitz. There are also the cultures of criminal gangs, and the cultures of wife-bashers, paedophiles, and playground and workplace bullying.

Societies with a single culture are unusual today, and most people, especially in modern cities, are affected by a series of different cultural traditions and habits, which they may come across several times a day. The days of widespread – if only on the surface – acceptance of a single orthodoxy are long gone.

THE THOUGHTS OF OLD DONALD

21

INTO THE OPEN

Approaching his ninth decade in 2000, D.H. looked back on his public life, in this memoir. Here he describes the time when he assumed the editorship of the Bulletin.

Knocking down a national edifice

ON SUNDAY, 16 OCTOBER 1960, I WAS AT HOME sitting in the recess of the bay window in our sitting room drafting a memo when Myfanwy said Frank Packer was on the phone – calling, for some reason, from a public telephone box. In a soft, almost whispering, but somewhat comradely voice as if, after all, we had quite a lot in common, he said that Rupert Murdoch was likely to put in an offer for the *Australian Woman's Mirror*, so he had just bought it: that would stop Murdoch getting his hands on it. Now I want you to take over the *Mirror*, he said. Put in an extra sixteen pages. Make up a dummy showing what you'd do with it. He then explained that the *Mirror* people owned the *Bulletin*, too, so he had had to buy the *Bulletin* as well, and he also had to buy the building: 'The point is: do we kill the *Bulletin* or do we kill the *Observer*?' I said that if something was to be killed I suppose it would have to be the *Observer*.

It was not to be taken over until early December but, like someone looking down from a high hill onto a city about to be liberated, I examined copies of the *Bulletin* in what I knew would now be its last weeks of decay as the 'Old Bully'. The 'famous pink' of the cover, seen as being as Australian as the gum tree or the kangaroo, and going back to the 1880s, was still there, but, with its flimsy, inferior paper, it seemed a clumsy souvenir of long ago. On turning over the pages one could see a few ill-printed photos – a racehorse, a farm, some trees, a frilled lizard – but the tone and period were set by the headings on the regular features. These showed the man's world of the early twentieth century. A professor (mortar board and gown) and a barrister (wig and gown) were laughing away beside the heading of the 'SOCIETY' page, so that was the city; an 'Abo' in a top hat squatted down and grilled a goanna beside the heading on the 'ABORIGINALITIES' page, so that was the bush; a hearty bloke was barracking for his team, so that was 'SPORTING NOTIONS'; a farmer was pushing wool into a sack beside a shorn sheep, so that was 'THE MAN ON THE LAND'. 'SUNDRY SHOWS', the only modern heading, done in 1930s art deco, promised, among other things, reviews of 'the talkies'. (At the *Bulletin* they liked to hang on to old words that were once smart: to express their contempt for papers like Packer's *Daily Telegraph* they still deployed the phrase 'the flapper press', using a word coined during the Great War as an expression of contempt for silly young women who challenged some of the conventions.) Of the dozen and a half jokes in each issue, apart from stock stuff on desert islands or modern art, there was always an 'Abo' joke, and often a reffo joke, although the reffos no longer had Yid noses, but the largest single category was jokes about the daftness of old women and the bodily curves of young women. I kept in my mind the gag line in a girlie joke, showing a dentist contemplating his patient, a young woman with 'uplift': DENTIST: *When I said 'What lovely falsies' I was only referring to your teeth.* There were two pages of 'PERSONAL ITEMS' about men, reading like the in-house journal of a small, modest club and two pages of 'WOMEN'S LETTERS' recording who wore a little black dress and who wore a mist-blue ensemble.

In its heyday, most of the regular sections had been contributed by its readers, mainly in short pars, a technique also used by *Titbits* and *Answers* in England, but these had now come down to items that might very well have been found in a Christmas cracker. From 'SOCIETY':

> Mrs D.E. Shakespeare, lately arrived from England at Mayfield (N.S.W.) migrant centre with her husband and six children, says her marriage is of 'quite literary interest'. Her maiden name was Bacon.

There was an arcane, ineffable style about some of them as if they were to be fully understood only by faithful readers. I learned later that so few readers were still contributing pars that the staff were writing some of them, earning threepence to fivepence a line to supplement their low pay.

The political stuff often read as rewrites (sometime rewrites from 1920s papers) and the small foreign affairs section ('UNCABLED ADDITIONS') consisted almost entirely of extracts from London newspapers. Except for book and arts reviews, analysis of women's frocks at society 'do's', write-ups of agricultural shows and a section splendidly entitled 'BUSINESS, ROBBERY, ETC', a relic of the *Bulletin*'s radical days, the whole thing read as if most of the people producing it hadn't been out of the office for forty years, shooing off the present with short, cocky, resentful pars.

I knew that the *Bulletin*'s democratic radicalism and republicanism had vaporised half a century before, at about the same time as its nationalism was replaced by nostalgia for the bush and enthusiasm for the British Empire. But not having opened a copy of it for years I hadn't known that with former colonies being 'shuffled into the British Commonwealth in a curious kind of legerdemain' even imperialism had declined into a quiet, stubborn belief in continuing loyalty to things British and that immigration was 'weakening our British ties' as the country was flooded with immigrants from 'places like Cyprus, Poland and the depressed toe of Italy', living in 'national enclaves, each sticking to its racist and religious habits', where even the offspring 'might not become Australians in the true sense'. It was an example of this challenge to 'the fibre of Australians' that 'occasionally some Continental lashes out into a crowd with an axe or wipes out a family', committing 'horrifying crimes unknown to Australians'. Meanwhile now that 'the flapper press' was 'making pets of Colombo Asian students' serious persons should return to the old question: can we keep Australia racially in one piece? Of the centrality of that question the *Bulletin* had no doubt. Its slogan had remained embedded under the masthead of its leader page:

THE BULLETIN
'AUSTRALIA FOR THE WHITE MAN'

Weekend was still my main job, but I needed to decide how to increase the *Bulletin*'s sales – which, I found, were down to about 27,000. Since what we were concerned with, I wrote to myself in a manifesto, was 'the introduction of weekly quality journalism' into Australia surely we could lift sales to 50,000 to 70,000 copies a week? ('Many Australians are educated to this kind of taste by their experience abroad or by reading overseas publications.') I went on in my manifesto to describe to myself the new sections I would create in the *Bulletin*, giving 'an informed picture of the life we lead in this country and its extraordinary diversity'. In section after section, I sold myself great ideas, unaccompanied by the budget to carry them out, then ended up affirming that when the newsprint was of the right quality, there would be people in advertising agencies who would see the prospect for the 'smart' kinds of ads one saw in overseas magazines; we could be a new medium in Australia for sophisticated minority markets – well-educated bottles of whisky, knowledgeable aeroplanes, intelligent motor cars.

I didn't place sixty sheets of paper on the living room floor and spend a weekend working it all up into a dummy of the *Bulletin*. That was an error. But even if I had produced a dummy, I couldn't have shown it to anyone in The Firm. There was no one who believed the *Bulletin* could be changed as completely or as quickly as I intended.

In my secret manifesto I also announced to myself that people felt the *Bulletin* was a national institution, but it was not a national institution that belonged to *them*. The contributors and the staff were writing for each other, not to readers. (I later found out that even this wasn't true: they didn't read each other's pieces.) It had a reputation for 'an arid kind of diehard reactionaryism, even among conservatives'. It should be *for* things, as well as against them, and if it was going to attack, it should be ready to attack established institutions, etc. It should spring surprises. I knew I had to get a move on.

On the day before the takeover Packer arrived at the *Bulletin* building and climbed the stairs with great gravitas to the mezzanine, wheezing a bit, since he had been in hospital, and, in dark glasses (he had been in hospital for his eyes). When he addressed the inmates of this occupied territory from the gallery as they stood below, he said the *Bulletin* had 'a life of its own'. But I wasn't sure how steadfast he would stand when the complaints came in. I had to knock down what was left of this nasty national edifice, so that they would never be able to put it together again.

On the day of the takeover I told Ken Prior, the former owner and managing director, that I would remove the slogan 'AUSTRALIA FOR THE WHITE MAN'. Surely you can't do that, he said. It has been the *Bulletin*'s slogan from time immemorial. No it hasn't, I said. Earlier it was 'AUSTRALIA FOR THE WHITE MAN AND CHINA FOR THE CHOW'. When I went down to the composing room, there it was, face up, in metal type, in a page forme, on the printer's stone: 'AUSTRALIA FOR THE WHITE MAN'. The compositor pulled that line out with tweezers, held it up like an extracted tooth, and then threw it onto the waste metal box for remelting. Well, he said, that should have been done years ago.

22

LOOKING FOR LEADERSHIP: AUSTRALIA IN THE HOWARD YEARS

D.H. and John Howard obtained their Leaving Certificates from the same Sydney high school, Canterbury, but they disagreed on some of the issues of the day.

Putting on a show: leadership in a liberal-democratic society

The good leader

Political life is necessarily a muddle. Politicians naturally try to stay in power, or to push themselves into power. Events can override all their plans. And, because of the contrasts between the high public aspirations of political life and the low comedy of much of what goes on privately, politics can easily fall into farce. Nevertheless a political leader has to be a *leader*. It's part of the job description.

Being a leader doesn't necessarily mean being a seer or a priest or a Führer, but as a minimum it does mean competence in public performance – speaking clearly and persuasively and, at times, touching the imagination. That can sometimes require good preparation, and even rehearsal. It's no good just standing and yakking away: like any other performer, a good leader should try to engage with the audience, try to *reach* the audience by enlisting whatever skills are needed. In the Howard era Kim Beazley showed a fairly steady basic competence, but with low imaginative skills. Howard showed less flair in holding sympathetic interest than almost any of the prime ministers we have had over the last sixty years, talking and talking as if he were making a minor point at the kind of Young Liberal subcommittees through which he talked his way into politics. With a set-piece speech, Keating could be magnificent in a patchy, offhand way – at least for those who liked him. Hawke, at his best, was a polished vernacular speaker. (John Gorton was also a vernacular speaker, often faltering, but when he threw his notes away he could come through like someone who meant what he said. And, in a lifesaver's cap, he could engage in the rhetoric of action, as when he rowed out with a surf-boat crew from Bondi Beach.) Fraser was dry, but his firm, patrician and ordered presentation could suggest that he had thought it out and meant business. Whitlam, like Alfred Deakin, the founding father of Commonwealth oratory, was a brilliant conceptualiser. Even Harold Holt, who just blathered on, blathered as if he were in a good mood, almost always with the permanent smile of an old-style tap dancer. And even Gorton's successor, Bill McMahon, perhaps the silliest prime minister we have ever had, projected an elfin charm, as confident as one of the lesser characters in *Snow White*.

A minimum to be expected from a political leader is the ability to make a few memorable remarks that seem to sum up what leader and party stand for, and the kind of meaning we might find in existence. Two exceptional examples since the Second World War are passages from Bob Menzies, usually a high performer, urbane, clear and sometimes amusing, and from Ben Chifley, often somewhat faltering, but with sincerity and simplicity. (I think they go well in free verse.)

CHIFLEY:
I try to think of the labour movement
not as putting an extra sixpence into somebody's pocket,
or making somebody prime minister or premier,
but as a movement bringing something better to the people,
better standards of living,
greater happiness to the mass of the people.
We have a great objective –
the Light on the Hill –
which we aim to reach by working for the betterment of mankind,
not only here,
but anywhere we may give a helping hand.

MENZIES:
I speak for the forgotten people,
those people
who are constantly in danger
of being ground between the upper and nether millstone
    of a false class war;
the kind of people who,
properly regarded,
represent the backbone of this country.

Theodore Roosevelt, one of the great revitalising presidents of the United States, said the US presidency was a 'bully pulpit', from which a great deal could be done by talk alone. There are times when a prime minister can have more important things to do than running the country. (Not that a prime minister *does* run the country. That's just a silly phrase that has been picked up by pundits.) A political leader should take time to try to affect events by talking about them.

A political leader can show sympathy. In the period of the economy turning upside down, no leader showed credible sympathy for the people who, through no fault of their own, had suffered pain from economic change. A good leader should at least have shown that we, their fellow citizens, knew who these losers were and what they were putting up with – and from this a good leader might have gathered political support for action. There were votes to be gathered, too: to a large extent Hansonism as a movement came from people who felt that the rest of their fellow citizens didn't know they were there.

A good leader can praise strategically (as Keating did with artists) so that citizens can consider that excellence comes not only with sporting success. A good leader can talk of change and the future, to set people thinking – even doing it honestly, by talking difficulties and alternatives. A good leader can try to make present events sound interesting, to wake people up and feel part of things, or pick up good ideas from outside the political loop and amplify them. (With his 'blood, sweat and tears' speech Churchill gave everyone in wartime Britain something to think about.) A good leader should be expecting the unexpected and when it happens recognise what's happening out there and, in new problems, look for new opportunities to produce new policies. A good leader can seek the good in people and articulate it, making it stronger. There were plenty of normalisers around over the periods of immigration reform but good leaders could have made a special thing out of praising the Australian people for their tolerance and adaptability. Once a week, say. A good leader could have ensured that if there was also race hatred in some Australians' hearts no political action encouraged it to grow larger.

Thinking up new things at times of change

At times of change we need great articulators to help make new action possible, and, if they are prime ministers, you don't just look at how their governments governed, you look at their conceptual influence. In the long run, even after their governments are forgotten, this influence can live on.

The most contentious example is Gough Whitlam, but what people are most likely to argue about over Whitlam is not what he articulated, but how his government governed. I happen to think that, despite the clownishness of some of his ministers, on a point score his government did much more than it is often given credit for, and it was blamed for more than it deserved (the world economic crisis, for one thing). Six examples: it set up Medibank and, in general, Australia's first comprehensive healthcare program. It began tariff reform. It put the outer-city suburbs onto the policy agenda. It formally ended the White Australia immigration policy. It took measures against discrimination against women. It abolished appeals to the Privy Council.

But for a moment forget what you think about Whitlam's governing. Consider two other things. One, the way he shoved the Labor Party back into politics, in a tough, intricate mixture of bringing the boys into line (in which he had strong former enemies as ruthless associates), and in talking policy, page after page, week after week, hundreds of pages, month after month, year after year, for five years – and in this he was the only front performer, if with advisers and speech writers behind him. (And what a contrast with the amiable dilly-dallying of Kim Beazley with his faction chiefs, who spent most of his first five years not producing one real policy that anyone can remember.) Also consider how, at the time Whitlam was making his run, Australia's political life was, to put it very mildly indeed, behind the times. Changes were going on, but in a conceptual desert. Whitlam made sense of what others were doing as well as what he proposed to do himself. His 'It's Time' campaign in 1972 (a song as well as a speech!) even inspired people who had previously voted against him to confirm their view that government needed a different style and, as we say these days, a new agenda.

With so much not done in the '60s, Whitlam could seem an heroic figure, bringing Australia back into the world. The test of his success is that most of what he brought into government stayed there. Malcolm Fraser showed who was boss by doing some retaliatory slicing and bludgeoning when he took over, but Whitlam had, in effect, modernised the Liberal Party for Fraser. Fraser carried on much of the Whitlam government's agenda. In several cases – multiculturalism, Asian immigration, Indigenous land rights, family allowance – he out-Whitlamed Whitlam. (Although he did not follow Whitlam's economic rationalism in making a 25 per cent tariff cut.)

Menzies? Menzies was a confident orator, able to reach into many householders' hearts and to present to them the world as they saw it better than they could themselves. Quick-witted, eloquent, urbane, ironic (with a reassuring touch of the avuncular and an incisive brutality with interjectors), he was a poet of the ordinary. But in the last years of his prime ministership the future had fogged out in the mind of the country boy who had gone to school before the Great War. Change was all around him but he had nothing to say about it. He was not concerned with new action and thereby he began to create more problems than there were. In the non-Labor parties the greatest future-looker and conceptualiser was the mellifluous Alfred Deakin.

Deakin preached an Australian liberalism, a translation into Australian of the theories of T.H. Green, an Oxford don. Green wanted to soften liberal individualism with a social liberalism in which the social 'obligations' of the state were set against individual rights. In supporting the idea, Deakin developed a rhetoric of 'New Protection': it didn't come off, but his overall approach was the first distinctively expressed ideology to have come from the complexities of Australian politics. It survived in various disguises and under diverse names until the 1980s. Cleaned up, and redesigned to fit a new age, some of it would still be useful.

As far as ideas went, the period between the two world wars was the meanest time in the Commonwealth's first hundred years. No one spoke any longer of Australia as a social laboratory. As prime minister in the 1920s, Stanley Bruce developed economic plans, but their basis was to increase exports of foods and fibres to Britain and to buy British manufactures in return; as prime minister in the 1930s, Joseph Lyons said the essential Australian policy was to 'tune into Britain' (in particular, the Bank of England). Australia had become more colonial-minded. For conceptualisation, what was most remarkable was that the rhetoric of Billy Hughes echoed on. As the Little Digger, he had become a principal myth-maker of the Great War and its imperial message: 'This Australia of ours could not stand, could not progress, could not exist, unless it was an integral part of the Empire.' When the voice of Australia spoke as part of the Empire during the Great War 'she spoke in trumpet tones that were heard and heeded throughout all the earth'. And his brew of anti-Labor poisons bubbled on for decades. ('The Labor Party is committed to a policy of communism that proposes to set up a replica of the Soviet government of Russia ... When the clouds of war were darkest if Labor had had its way victory would never have come to us.')

It was not until 1941 that a new voice of the future was heard on the wireless and in the newsreels – the confident, resonant, native voice of Labor leader John Curtin, a voice developed in his youthful years as a soapbox orator, where he learned the lesson that unless you reach your audience they will walk off and listen to someone else. Curtin's leadership developed by two accidents. The enabling accident was the political incompetence as a wartime leader of Bob Menzies, who was unable to look as if he was head of a wartime government, too lost in the rhetoric of imperial loyalty to speak simply to Australians about their own hopes and fears, so unconvincing as a politician that he lost the numbers in his own party and was replaced, after a short interregnum, by the once pacifist Curtin. A 'no' man in Billy Hughes's Great War conscription campaigns, Curtin was a reformed alcoholic, not at all sure of his talents, nor of the full support of his party. The next accident was that a few weeks later the Japanese bombed Pearl Harbor and invaded Malaya. His 'Australia looks to America speech' was attacked as anti-British, but in the first six months of the Japanese war he went on making strong, clear speeches about Australia's self-reliance and its fight for survival; his simple Australian presence, along with what seemed to be the competence of his administration, outlined a new kind of Australia. That kind of Australia did not go away.

23

10 STEPS TO A MORE TOLERANT AUSTRALIA

D.H. wrote this 2003 book in response to rising levels of xenophobia.

The pleasures of tolerance

Living in the world

I'VE JUST BEEN LOOKING AGAIN AT THE VIDEO OF THE opening of the Olympic Games in Sydney in 2000. Three years later, some of it now seems a bit schmaltzy but it still stands up, in my view, as the most confident, ebullient, creative and, in a sense, sophisticated mass-market presentation of Australia the world has seen. With a Newspoll survey at the time showing that 87 per cent of Australians interviewed found it 'fantastic' or 'very good', there seems little doubt that it went down well at home. But as far as can be made out, it also went down well overseas.

Why was that? It couldn't have been because people watching it knew that those men running around in strange headgear were Sid Nolan–inspired Ned Kellys, or that those funny-looking things on the ground were Victa mowing machines. Perhaps some Australian viewers missed these references as well. The success of the opening was partly because it was such an engaging arena performance, but mainly because it caught the verve and bounce that marks so many contemporary Australians (if at the moment lacking in almost all their politicians).

It wasn't a didactic experience, it was a mood set to dance, to some amazing backgrounds, including a tribute to corrugated iron as part of the Australian imagination and a collective tap dance through the Australian steel industry. But it also went down well because, in the democratic manner, it concentrated on ordinary people: in 12,000 characters there was only one immediately recognisable historical figure, Captain Cook, and he arrived on a contraption made out of three fantasy tricycles. And in focusing on all those dancing people, the visual message was one of reciprocity and variety, of inclusiveness. In all, it was a splendid idealisation of Australian potential of a new kind – still using a lot of the old stuff, but finding new meanings in it. Dinkum Aussieness brought up to date. And it was an Australia that was open to the world. Blacks, whites, yellows, Christians, Muslims, Hindus, non-believers. No xenophobia here.

Then, the following year, the *Tampa* election. And with that, the danger that Australians could get into the habit of seeing themselves as a virtuous, nervous but belligerent island in a threatening world. If we do that, we will bring misfortune upon ourselves, a curse of narrowness, aridity and isolation.

It would be disastrous for Australia's leaders to march us backwards into a narrow Anglo view of the world, back to some version of where we were fifty years ago, with the United States and the United Kingdom pretty well all that matter. Given the European basis of so many Australian institutions, and the origin of so many of our immigrants, continental Europe is still a discovery house for Australians with inquiring minds.

But for Australia, the countries of Asia also remain a special source of opportunities and enlightenment. For quite a time people from other countries could see the potential for Australia to be something of a bridge between the West and Asians. The idea seemed too patronising for many Australians with Asian experience, but it might be possible to make something of that ambition if it is a reciprocal process – them and us together.

*

When I was at high school, I learned that the great humanist Erasmus, at the age of fifty, was brought up short. He was northern Europe's most renowned scholar, and also its most renowned traveller – he became known as a citizen of the world – but he received a peremptory order to return to the monastery where he had begun his career as a monk and stay there for the rest of his life. He could make only one appeal – to the Pope. He made it, and he succeeded. He was famously told he might continue to 'live in the world'.

The quote is useful. To 'live in the world' (in the spirit, say, of the Olympic Games opening ceremony) is the opposite of the insularity that could dry us out. We can be grateful that there are many Australians who live in the world. Some move out and never return, but others regularly get around the world, or work in other countries for extended periods, still making Australia home. Many, many others live in the world by following what's going on out there – in politics, art, engineering, whatever interests them, perhaps just the simple pleasures of variety. For many tolerant Australians the world is open, with all its opportunities. The old cringe towards Britain has gone, as has the cringe towards an unknown land thought of as Overseas, where anything we could do, they could do better. Now there's a more cosmopolitan and sophisticated attitude, and using the positive and liberal sides of globalism, people – at least those with the right kind of education and experience – can move where there are new opportunities or new experiences. Out of this there may come a different way of doing things. Not just one determined by money markets, international corporations, mass culture, United States weapons or terrorists' bombs, but changed attitudes resulting from the intermingling of peoples.

In this process a more tolerant Australia could be an enlightened performer. A tunnel-visioned, let's-safeguard-our-borders obsession gets us nowhere with this. Or, to put it more exactly, it gets us nowhere as far as would-be immigrants with education and the right experience are concerned, although it has a tragic connection with the millions of refugees who don't have the desirable education and experience.

It may be hard for most present Australians to understand how closely we lived within our own borders when I was a boy, protected from 'the tinted races' by officials who kept an eye out even for over-swarthy Mediterraneans. The main way we saw the world was as members of 'the British race'. The images shown in the Olympic Games opening ceremony would have been seen then as un-Australian – even the Man-from-Snowy-River sequence would have been an outrage, since some of those people on horseback were sheilas. It was a time when the export of an Australian movie about bushrangers was banned because it would give people the wrong idea about Australia. For almost everyone, travel beyond our borders was unknown.

The New Improvement

'The challenge for our leaders is to bring out the best in us by advocacy and example,' said Ted Roach after he resigned as chairman of the Council for Multicultural Australia in protest at the dishonest tricks of the *Tampa* election campaign. A return to the Australia of a bipartisan truce against the exploitation of xenophobia would mean that political parties could go back to competing over issues worth competing over. Of course, in the nature of political parties, they may make a mess of it, but if the xenophobic wedge goes it becomes politically easier to talk practical, forward-looking stuff, instead of engaging in recurrent, furtive exploitations of nastiness.

One kind of sense that might be talked would show the bounce, confidence and generosity of the Olympic Games opening ceremony – and of many individual Australians. It could look to the past, to the English spirit of 'improvement' that came early and buoyantly to Australia. This spirit was an optimistic faith that things could be done, that material and social progress could be made, that the mind, to some extent, could be improved. Of course many things also went wrong, but perhaps, in a tolerant, creative Australia, with its xenophobia under control, what we might think of as the New Improvement would fare better.

The New Improvement could revive what used to be an essential part of Australian patriotism – the belief in a national development, to which people contributed as producers and from which they took out, if in unequal proportions, as users. National development had many follies, especially in its degradation of land, its strangling of rivers, and its lack of innovation in manufacturing. Perhaps this time, old follies could be avoided. Farmers who understand science-based technology now recognise that in order to preserve their way of life they must also preserve the land and the rivers which support it.

Big programs would have to be a basic part of a new national development program – although another name is needed, since 'development' is now, for many Australians, a dirty word. Perhaps National Advancement Program. Its schemes could include such things as renewed infrastructure, renewable energy, and conserving energy with new technology. Add some support, not necessarily monetary, for the many new small manufacturing firms that show enterprise. Invest in intellectual infrastructure, particularly universities, lifelong education and mind-broadening programs. There should be a new inclusiveness in the economy, as in the society at large.

Of course, this will cost money. Why not float National Advancement bonds and sell them to finance programs of general public benefit in a commonwealth of citizens and producers? War bonds helped win wars; National Advancement bonds could help win a better life for Australians.

Liberty and the right to be different

The Games opening ceremony portrayed the variety of Australian life as something pursued for its own sake. This was idealising, of course. The Australian steel industry wasn't a happy tap dance (although the movie *Bootmen* showed how well tap dancing fitted the then steel city of Newcastle as an art form). But in proclaiming benign variety, one should rejoice. And it can be somewhat more inspiring than the pedestrian statement made about cultural diversity by the Council for Multicultural Australia in 2002, when it noted that Australians need to act to maximise 'the social, economic and cultural dividends of our diversity'.

In speaking of variety, we are speaking of all the many beliefs, ways of life, hopes and fears in Australia, and most of the time we don't examine our lives as part of a 'national dividend'. We are conscious of them as lives that are being lived and, in varying degrees, we follow them for their own sake.

Early in 2003 the Australia Institute issued a research report announcing a new minority, a previously invisible class that it called the downshifters. A sizeable minority of working Australians, the report showed, are now giving up the 'national dividends' kind of mindset and sacrificing income to concentrate instead on wellbeing and a better way of life. The report suggests that nearly one person in four between the ages of thirty and sixty has in the last ten years voluntarily taken a pay cut, by changing careers or reducing working hours, in order to spend more time on family life and wider interests.

Thinking about this brought back to mind John Anderson, Professor of Philosophy at Sydney University when I was a student there, a distinctive voice and an intellectual influence a number of us never forgot. I can imagine him addressing members of the Free-thought Society, which he founded not long after arriving in Sydney from Glasgow. In one of his more poetic moods he is speaking of liberty. It is typical Anderson. 'Liberty is the ability to take things artistically, to pursue them for their own sake,' he says. 'It cannot be supported except by itself; there is no other motive for it than these free activities already in existence, in others and in one's own self.'

With this he defied the utilitarianism that permeated Australia, and still does, and he took liberty beyond rights, negotiations with the state over declarations on freedom of thought, and so on, and opened it out into the complex, more fallible, random and human aspect of pursuing things for their own sake. He was concerned with one of the most creative parts of human beings, one that exists only if it is used.

This feeling for freedom was backed by another Anderson phrase, the idea of 'ways of life', an expression then out of fashion that Anderson made his own (although the same phrase was used by the Liberal Party in its 1946 charter). It was then an illuminating reminder of the sheer contrariness of people in society, and it was given momentum by Anderson's concept of 'conflict' pluralism, whose most memorable wisdom was: 'Don't ask of a social institution what end or purpose does it serve, but rather of what conflicts is it the centre?' In fact, this made too much of conflict – 'differences' would be a wider and more useful word. But Anderson was concerned with contrasting pluralism with solidarism, a term coined by French educationalist Ferdinand Buisson to express the belief in a tight unity and fundamental sameness in society. Anderson cursed solidarism regularly and almost ritualistically: there was no overall social unity, no general interest – or if there was one, exclusive insistence on it favoured mediocrity. That's overdoing it, but we learned how to look at society not as one big granite monolith, immobile; we saw the uncertainties of many different institutions and movements and ways of life. Not only that, when we looked at people we were to imagine them moving between institutions and movements, and changing as they did.

It was a great start in life to be robbed of the illusion that to speak of a nation was to speak of a single entity. All nations have within them mixes of different ways of life, faiths (secular and religious), ethnic backgrounds, regional loyalties, material standards, enthusiasms, occupational groups, along with an enormous range of differences in personality. In this mix some win, some lose, some keep safely out of sight. Talking about a nation as if it were one entity is an insult to the people you are talking about. Even if you know none of the details, at least imagine that things aren't entirely what they seem, or are made to seem by those on top.

*

Consider for a moment the 50,000 volunteers who got behind the Olympic Games and helped give the idea that the Games belonged to everybody. How did they get there? Why were they so enthusiastic and successful? The answer goes back to 1974 and the formation of the Volunteer Centres, which in 1997 were given a national co-ordinating body, Volunteering Australia. Today one Australian in three gives more than four hours of volunteer service a week. If you want to put a figure on it, the Australian Bureau of Statistics estimates the value of what they do at almost $20 billion a year. The volunteering movement puts it higher, but these activities go beyond economic indicators. They move into a co-operative world of friendship, the productive spirit, and the sense of liberty in doing one's own thing.

Consider also the 12,600 Australians who performed in the opening ceremony. These were 12,600 Australians who belonged to a variety of groups and who came together in a sense of community that wasn't abstract, but was made up of people doing things for their own sake. With xenophobia under wraps, Australia would be a place where people enjoy the right to develop in their own way the particular meaning they give to existence.

For some people in prosperous societies such as Australia there was once a period of hopeful prophecy that began somewhere in the late 1960s, with the shift from an economy fundamentally concerned with producing goods to one whose main dynamic was providing services. The prophecy held that this would mean a nourishing spread in cultural and recreational pursuits, which could incidentally become new dynamos of economic growth. This could be one of the bases of a new policy of national development and a more inclusive economy.

It has indeed been happening. What are now called regional centres have looked to the founding of universities for growth, as their predecessors looked to butter factories or abattoirs. The idea of a cultural centre has become one of the recognised agenda items of regional councils. Byron Bay, once a failed fishing settlement dominated by a smelly abattoir, now runs what may be Australia's best writers festival, whose living base is in its own community. The Pioneer Women's Hut at Tumbarumba has become one of the best small-community museums in the world, the women of Tumbarumba telling their own story as well as that of pioneer women generally.

Why not look to the regions for creative variety? They're a reasonable size, they're comprehensible, and they're remarkably diverse. The old phrase 'the bush' has gone through a big revival, keeping pace with the number of politicians who wear Akubras, yet its old meanings have almost entirely lost their material base and their social structure. The idea of regional centres, in all their variety, is a much more valuable way of looking to the future than nostalgia about a stereotype called the bush. Especially if people begin to tell their own stories, by whatever means, big or small, giving not only themselves something to think about, but visitors as well.

But 'the regions' must also include the urban regions. A good example is the Liverpool District in Sydney's west, where the Casula Powerhouse Arts Centre is a symbol of a reciprocating, co-operative Australia celebrating the variety of its ways of life. The original powerhouse building was put up from a United States do-it-yourself kit in the early 1950s, instantly despoiling a relaxation and picnic area a few kilometres from Liverpool (now a city, then a centre for producing vegetables, milk, eggs and chooks for Sydney). When it closed as a powerhouse a couple of decades later, it almost instantly became a facility for vandalism and clandestine sex, and it remained like that for years, until Liverpool Council held a referendum on what was to be done with it. The people spoke.

The powerhouse was turned into a regional arts centre, with exhibition galleries – appropriately named the Turbine Gallery and the Boilerhouse Gallery – a theatre, workshops, studios, a meeting space, all designed after consulting the locals and helping them get what they wanted. The rebuilding produced something the local communities could feel they owned.

The work of the Casula Powerhouse was based on the assumption that its partners were to be found in the many local communities. Its launch in 1994 was celebrated with appearances by the Liverpool Marching Girls, the New South Wales Fire Brigade Band, a classical-music trio, an aerialist, a local rap group, a didgeridoo performance and Cook Island dancers, and its scope has since become even wider. Before the centre puts on a show, it calls for community expressions of interest, in the belief that if people can put their own values and cultures on show, they increase both their own self-esteem and esteem from others.

The Powerhouse has had exhibitions featuring local Dutch women and their experiences arriving in Australia after the Second World War; an exhibition by young Arab-Australians depicting the in-betweens of the two cultures; an exhibition recalling the experiences of local veterans of the Vietnam War, both Australian-born and Vietnamese-born; *Just Sensational: Queer Histories of Western Sydney* portrayed aspects of male and female same-sex life in western Sydney from the convict days to Mardi Gras; there was an exhibition which examined how the local tragedy of the gang-rape and murder of Anita Cobby affected the lives of friends and neighbours.

The Casula Powerhouse provides reminders of Australia's variety, and of how cohesion can come from recognising difference. Its exhibitions underline the fact that our wellbeing depends on having confidence in how we live in the world, on reciprocal tolerance, and on a climate in which xenophobia is contained.

How widely can we unveil that Australia? It's all around us. Just waiting for us to open our eyes.

24

MIND, BODY AND AGE

From Griffith Review: Making Perfect Bodies, *delivered as a speech at the Sydney Writers' Festival in 2004.*

People of my age can look back at a time when bodies, as part of the public spectacle, weren't seen as they are now. Then, it was intimations of the dangers of the body that were imprinted on the mind: in ads for patent medicines; in posters on railway stations listing precautions against drowning; in fading placards warning against the unhygienic habit of 'expectoration'; in pages on the sufferings of syphilis, leprosy and masturbation in books such as the four-volume *Household Physician* we had at home; and in the lectures of my grandfather, who had run away for a while to be a lad in a drovers' gang. His lectures specialised in remedies for the bites of venomous spiders and snakes, especially the death adders that lay around on bush tracks looking like dried sticks. I am still likely to keep an eye out for suspicious sticks on a suburban nature strip.

Then, there were no significant cults of 'the perfect body', a body that could overcome the imperfections that God or natural selection had worked into it. That was an ambition unimaginable until the discovery of antibiotics and then the development of bioengineering, cosmetic surgery and now genetic engineering. For women, there were ideals of facial beauty in the face-cream ads and, for men, ideals of the authentically Aussie face, exemplified in the aviator Kingsford Smith ('Smithy'), but as for a 'perfect body' – the full works – if it meant anything more than approximating to the proportions of a classical statue, for men it meant having biceps as big as Chesty Bond's, perhaps obtained after answering a 'Be Strong' ad for a home exerciser or spending time at some (usually scungy) gym. Women were not expected to 'be strong': the proper physical function for female bodies was motherhood (exemplified in the ample, motherly bosom), although 'uplift' and 'cleavage' began to come in during the Second World War. Some of the realities of bodies were to be seen on beaches but with so much fatness and skinniness spread out to dry on the sand there wasn't much in the way of classical perfection – except in the ideal of the lifesavers, the 'bronzed Anzacs', whose bodies and minds were being prepared, it was believed, for the next war.

Much of the body was not seen at all. Now, any child in front of a television set is likely to see a baby's head emerge from between a mother's thighs but it wasn't until my late boyhood that I saw a grown woman's navel – on the midriff of a dancer undulating on the platform outside a travelling tent show in a country town. If there was any broad body-belief, it was that bodies with black, brown or yellow skins denoted cultural and moral inferiority, but nothing could be done about them. Among the rest of us, the striving (if there was any) was not in the attainment of a perfect body but in keeping moderately healthy (a different matter), with occasional interest in what to eat (both fruit and breakfast cereals were coming in) and with getting plenty of fresh air (sleeping on verandas in summertime was healthy and hiking had come in as a minority enthusiasm). The heroic pioneering public health reforms of water supply, drainage and sanitation had been achieved and personal cleanliness was now getting a run. Campaigns from the soap companies enticed people to wash their underwear more regularly ('the change-daily habit') and wash under their arms and, by inference, between their legs, although for most people one bath a week was still enough body-washing. Bodies might not be expected to be perfect but, increasingly, they were expected not to smell.

*

We can have a sense of the body 'as a whole', but in limited ways: mainly in its satisfaction of bodily appetites, in particular, in co-operative sexual activity or in physical exchanges of affection – touching, stroking, hugging; or simply in feeling a glow of health or feeling hungry or feeling the heat or cold; or in sociability when we come together, with all these other bodies, in a reconciliation march or at a grand final (confrontation is one of the ways bodies work); or in dancing; or in companionship and friendship; or, sadly, in occasions such as the Nazi rallies when good was found in sound Aryan bodies and evil in the filthy bodies of the degenerate races. We can also have a feeling for our bodies in solitude. But while the body 'speaks' in appetites and feelings it becomes urgently real to the mind when it is identified by a part that goes wrong. That is what the body is made up of – parts. The parts that are now going wrong for me are the lungs, in a complex and continuing form – a stiffening among the alveoli, the 300,000 microscopic sacs that are the body's oxygen–carbon dioxide interchanges, essential for life. My lungs are now the principal most continuous reminder of my body. Through the doctor's stethoscope I can hear their distinctive crackle. When I have the flu I may hear them squeak, rustle, gurgle.

*

If we are going to talk about the possibility of 'perfect bodies', care should be taken not to talk about the possibility of 'perfect minds'.

The phrase 'perfect body' can have a sort of meaning: it gives a simple standard for bodies. Even though some of it is illusory, you can write down criteria and tick them off. But there are no generally applicable criteria for a 'perfect mind'. Minds are not standard. They work in all kinds of different ways. Religious and political sects can try to make us think the same way about the same kind of things, but unless humans are to be ants (there are, of course, theories that this is exactly what they should be) it is essential that there be myriad differences – if you like, 'imperfections' – in minds.

*

Can an illness be good for the mind? One example of how it can is the insights that can come from the turning of things upside down from having a fever. My most recent fever produced a sleepless near-hysteria at night – partly about not going to sleep and partly that I might forget to go on breathing. But during the day, between patches of languid reading and stretches of deep sleeping, I had a comfortable, reflective lassitude with a tranquil sense of indifference – indifference to the affronts and failures of the past, acceptance of folly as part of the human condition and the need for this as a way of seeing things. I downloaded Erasmus's *In Praise of Folly* from the web. That these insights might have come too late was also a matter of comfortable indifference.

To extend the point: there have been a few periods when I thought to use sickness and hospital experience as a way of turning myself into what I had decided would be a better person. The first of these periods began when, at the age of twenty, after spending some time in hospital after being hit in the face by a tree branch while travelling in the back of an army truck, I wrote off letters to friends predicting that now that some sense had been knocked into me they could expect improvement. When I was let out of hospital I looked slightly different: slanted and scarred, the right eyelid could seem angry while the left was level and steady. That seemed an instructive juxtaposition. But what I was looking for was an improvement based on putting behind me my undergraduate follies along with an impetuosity worthy (as I saw it) of the recklessness of the heroes of Stendahl's two great novels. How could I learn patience? After months of asking people, 'Do you think I've changed?' the most encouraging answer I could get was that I seemed to have begun relying more on humour than sarcasm and wit.

It was thirty years later that the occasion seemed to come up again – thirty years in which I scarcely saw a doctor but in which, in a triumph of mind over body, I could occasionally swell ennui into a psychosomatic symptom. (This was always based on dissatisfaction with the job I had at the time, even if by ordinary standards, so far as jobs go, I was usually seen as 'successful'.) It is 1972: now aged fifty, I am again sure that change will come upon me. I am to be under the surgeon's knife. My right eye is to be operated on – an event I see as possibly cataclysmic (like any other operation) but also perhaps revelatory, giving me time off for another go at reflection. As it turns out, the event is theatrical. I wake up in the blackness, both eyes bandaged. I am suffocating. I feel I am about to die. When I try to call for help all that comes out is a melodramatic groan, as from the grave. Then I begin to rise from the dead. There are voices. Hands touch me. There is the friendly whisper of oxygen. Later, when I come to back in my room, they tell me I had a 'laryngeal spasm', a sudden closing of the larynx, that can kill if it keeps the windpipe blocked. (The surgeon is sure that my ludicrous over-smoking prompted the spasm.) I think about this throughout the year and also talk, month after month, about how I have given up smoking – one of the hardest things I have ever done, a body-discovering experience if ever there was one. There is no immediate revelation but after several months of brooding and a general trying things on for size I resign from editing the *Bulletin* and join the staff of the University of New South Wales. Three years later I again find new life from a hospital – when I plan a book about the dismissal of the Whitlam Government, while recovering from surgery on a detached retina.

*

Last year, someone began a review of a book I had just published by saying that I was a 'retired octogenarian'. ('Retired' meant having left salaried employment. Obviously, since I had just written a book, I hadn't retired as a writer.) I suddenly felt alien. Was this me they were talking about? I have accommodated myself to the fact that I 'look old'. And I even showed tolerant indifference to the woman who, walking on the wrong side of the pavement, bumped into me and said, 'You silly old fool.' I know that, because of my deficient lungs, I now appear to the world, and indeed am, someone who is walking slowly, but one can take an intelligent interest in enforced slow walking – comparing the degree of slowness today with yesterday, examining performance on a slope, contemplating the effect of heat and humidity.

There was another change in public performance when I began using a walking stick because of a slight stagger and occasional stumble. There can be a sense of skill and style in using a walking stick. One can imagine one is brightening up the street somewhat, with dexterity in using it as rudder on the flat and as alpenstock on slopes, and versatility in switching to shooting-stick mode when stopping for a rest – not to mention the swinging of the tip with every second or third step to show who is in control. Yet, to the uninformed eye, I can seem an old man lost. For some years (having earlier realised that sitting in a bus looking at people can be as good as a visit to a portrait gallery), I have been standing still looking at street scenes 'turning them into paintings'. Several times, while I stand on the pavement, imagining a painting, a stranger has come up and asked if I know where I am, as if I need to be directed back to the nearest nursing home.

Body parts wear out. Hearts, lungs, eyes, brains can all falter, but is there such a specific thing as 'feeling old'? Tiredness, yes. Pains, yes. Disabilities, yes. Lost functions, yes. But the pains of the old are not necessarily any worse than the pains of the young, although the old are more likely to have pains more often, just as they are more likely to be frail more often. Despite my lungs, I consider myself in good health. I can't walk quickly, or for long distances, but these seem small inconveniences compared with the trials of my wife, many of whose joints have been attacked by osteoarthritis. She has had two hip replacements, but in other eroded parts she suffers discomfort every day. She survives through good spirits, a desire to enjoy life, weekly hydrotherapy, daily arm, leg and breathing exercises and anti-inflammatories, and, sporadically, an intelligent deployment of bionic exercise bike, electric massager, heat pad, massage pillow, Japanese wheat-husk pillow, peanut-shaped small pillow, pain killers, ointments and vitamin tablets.

*

Old people are closer to death than most but it is possible to become indifferent to the fact that one will die. There is the question, however: what does one do in the meantime?

Reflection on one's life is available to anyone who can manage it – at any time, of course – since you're living a life, why not take an intelligent interest in it? (My particular obsession at the moment is to examine my life as an example of both the failures and the successes of enthusiasm.) One friend of mine, quiet and cultivated, has been re-reading books. Recently we had a talk about why he thought *The Faerie Queene* stood up much better as a yarn than *The Lord of the Rings*. Another friend, a few years younger than I am, who has been writing on foreign policy for years, is now doing so from a new perspective – which, as it happens, matches my new perspective. (For some years we were out of sync although close before that.) Now the two of us talk about foreign policy over the telephone, he sends me clippings; we have had a couple of lunches, just the two of us (to me, one of the essentials of an intellectual life). Another friend, who retired a couple of decades ago as a senior civil servant and now lives in a country town, has lent his talents to a local land-reform movement. He regrets that, years ago, he didn't become a local member of parliament.

With luck, for those who have cultivated it and do not become demented, the mind is a better bet in old age than the body. There can be forgetfulness or slowness but there are no necessary stupidities among the aged. Some might be 'a bit out of touch', but it may be only on matters of fashion, and old people who have kept their wits, freed of the provincialism of the present, can know things other people don't know. Among the young there can be low energy and concentration, and there is not necessarily any particularly youthful liveliness of mind (in certain ways some people are born old). What can happen among the aged is a loss in previous enthusiasm, an atrophy of the senses of wonder and discovery, and the energy to carry things out, although these are failings that mark many people throughout their lives, and it doesn't have to happen in old age. The last time I saw Bill Wentworth, then aged ninety, was at a Gleebooks launch. When it was over he came up to me in a full steam of enthusiasm and wonder – no preliminaries: he at once rushed into outlining two plans, one for solving Sydney's traffic problems, the other for solving one of Australia's principal economic problems (I have forgotten which). There was nothing dotty about what he was saying. It was based on the same concerns for knowledge and argument as he had used, for example, when he was such a successful supporter of rail unification or when he was the pioneer minister for Aboriginal affairs in the Fraser government. He was showing more enthusiasm and wonder and knowledge about public issues than most of his younger fellow citizens could summon.

For those lucky enough to have a reasonably well-packed and curious mind and the determination to use it, age can give more perspectives from which to consider changed circumstances. But perhaps only if you've had some practice at it in your earlier life – only if, as things have come up, you've sometimes considered whether they should alter what you think. That's part of what can be meant by keeping your mind young. Keeping up with what's going on doesn't necessarily mean tagging after the latest, although it may mean knowing about it, and it doesn't mean just picking up a few vogue words. I have always tried to translate them into my own language in a kind of test of what they are 'saying' (sometimes this is remarkably little). If you're old, you need enough body parts left working to sustain at least fits of mental, even creative, energy and you need to have retained at least most of your memory, and to have acquired the patience to go around hunting for bits of it that may hide themselves from you.

As I was writing this I recalled a Latin reader containing extracts from great Roman writers that we studied in fourth year at high school. Among other things, it contained an elegy Catullus wrote to his lover's deceased linnet, Pliny the Younger's report on the destruction of Pompeii and a cheerful scene describing dolphins frisking around a boat. It also had a passage from Cicero's reflections on age. Among detailed musings on the possible satisfactions of old age, he said he could admire the young man who had something of the old man in him, but also the old man who had, within him, something of the young man.

25

DYING: A MEMOIR

Largely dictated into a tape recorder, D.H.'s last book was written up (and co-authored) by his wife, Myfanwy. It was published after his death in 2007.

Faith

(i)

A FEW WEEKS BEFORE MY EIGHTIETH BIRTHDAY, a friend sent me an email saying he had a problem he would like to discuss. He thought that perhaps we could talk about it at the rather large party that was to be held to celebrate my transition into old age. The problem, he said, was that throughout his life he had been somewhere on the left. But what did 'the left' mean now? Was there, in fact, still a left? And if there was, what was it? And where was it?

I explained that we would need a long, two-person lunch rather than a hundred-person party to discuss that. He didn't live in Sydney, so we agreed to hold this discussion over for a visit after the party.

The party came and went, but things were brought to their conclusion when I was interviewed on a television program a few weeks later. It was a program concerned with faith, and after first discussing death, I began by saying that everyone has faiths of some kind – without them we can't think or act. I also said that faiths are in no way exclusive to religion. The distinguishing attribute of religion is not faith but belief in the supernatural. And I added that some of humanity's most evil acts were as likely to be committed by people of religious belief as by those without it.

I then said that, having abandoned religion as a high-school boy, I had got by since then on secular faith alone; and that my increasing nearness to death had not increased my nearness to belief in the supernatural, which remained as remote as it had been for most of my life. Asked what that faith was, I said it was the faith of a secular, liberal humanist. I then explained very briefly what I meant by that.

The next day, I received another email from my friend, who had watched the program. 'No need for lunch now,' he wrote. 'I know what I am. I'm a secular, liberal humanist.'

(ii)

Before I go into what I had said to convince him, let me record that modern states have seen a decline in the once universal belief that without religion societies fall apart, a belief once shared by some atheists, who held the view that without religious practices and religious faith (at least for other people) the social order would disintegrate. Advances in scientific knowledge and practice, in managerial techniques, in administrative systems and in acceptance of diversity have all helped erode this belief. Even private prayer may now be in the process of being supplanted by stress clinics and counsellors.

However, a secular, liberal humanist needs to have a healthy respect for religious belief. One reason is that although religion is still often thought of as essentially conservative, it can also be one of humanity's more disruptive forces. Religious practice frequently goes with strong, sometimes fanatical, convictions, and these can produce conflagrations. New religions, or rewritings of old ones, can turn things upside down culturally, socially and politically.

The workings of what was seen as divine purpose have provided some of the great conflicts of history. The blaze-ups from the Reformation in Europe had states seeing themselves as divinely favoured ('God is English,' said one of Elizabeth I's bishops). Protestant versus Catholic religious conflict during the British civil wars caused more slaughter than did the revolution in France. In central Europe, the Thirty Years War culminated in depths of devastation and muckiness. Religion can go mad.

It is odd that there should be such confidence in it as an unshakeable conservative force, when in the past religious traditions have been drawn into the cause of so many radical social movements. Today, Muslim fundamentalists attempt to remake their religion into something that is more austere while engaging, to the horror of many of their co-religionists, in the excitement of jihads, with their promise of manly adventure and rewards. This path may have justification in a fundamentalist interpretation of history, but retreats to the past can be as radical as visionary advances into the future.

With the doctrine of Hindutva, Hindu nationalists want to transform the secular aspirations of India into a Hindu-dominated state. Then there are the consumer-society religious groups, especially in the United States and Latin America, where much of the serious content of religion has been gutted, leaving it promising lots of financial rewards and instant gratification. Sing, dance, fill in a form, pass over your money, and you'll be dining with your loved ones on the fast food of paradise. At the same time, the biblical fundamentalism of these sects can pose a threat to the scientific basis of the social order. And if they are wedged into the political system as a society-within-a-society, they can effect political schisms.

Look at the religious right's influence in the United States – in its opposition to abortion and stem-cell research, in its vaguely defined 'moral values', in the war on drugs, in demands for stricter divorce laws, in opposition to sex education and contraception, in bias towards orthodox sexuality and a hatred of homosexuals, in the resubmission of women, in creationist attacks on theories of evolution, in something thought of as Judeo-Christian standards and the slant that is put on them. And in lashings of Americanism and 'American values', whereby some of the things I like about America become crowded out.

What is wrong is not that people hold certain views but that so many of them, given half a chance, would impose them on others. If literalists, fundamentalists and creationists were to make the rules, it would shatter the social order in a modern industrial state.

(iii)

So what was it I said in that television interview that convinced my friend? First, the secular aspect: we should begin by recognising that the people who developed humanism during the Renaissance did so within a context of religious belief. And there is still much to value in what they had to say. Just one example – a quote from that wise, amusing book by Erasmus, *In Praise of Folly*. 'By terrorisation, we drive men to believe what they do not believe, to love what they do not love, to know what they do not know. But that which is forced cannot be sincere.'

It goes without saying that many liberal-humanist values are shared by people who are religious, but politically humanism is a secular movement. A modern secular humanist State is not an atheist State, but one where upholding a belief in the supernatural (apart from some exceptions) is considered to be outside the function of the

State. Perhaps it is more exact to say that the relationship of religious institutions to a liberal-democratic State is that of lobby groups – lobby groups with special and strong privileges, but of weakening, if still very significant, force.

To describe a secular democracy as Judeo-Christian is a contradiction. So far as the structure of the modern secular State is concerned, Greco-Roman would be nearer the mark, but a better, if somewhat pedestrian, phrase is the sociologist Max Weber's 'legal rational'. A country such as Australia is a legal-rational State in which the basis of authority comes not from God or king, but from the acceptance of rational rules and procedures.

Given that faith needs a focus, faith in the economic would seem to dominate us now. For balance, humanists might consider – as well as opposing any undue religious influence – the desirability of developing a greater civic faith, a faith of openness, accessibility and shared discourse, expressed in the language of common citizenship and based on maintaining the rule of law and equality under the law. They might consider the desirability of strengthening a liberal electoral democracy based on universal adult suffrage, and on freedom of speech and opinions, and on the ideals of a fair and tolerant society devoted to the welfare of its people. Something to be taught in schools.

As for the liberal aspect, this word is a reminder of the great ideals of freedom of speech, and freedom to pursue one's own way of life as long as this doesn't harm others. The ideal of equality under the law for all citizens, irrespective of faith, opinions, race, skin colour, ethnic or national origin, gender, age, sexual orientation, place of residence or marital status. It is also a reminder of the ideal of tolerance, but for this to work, one has to approach tolerance with a certain coolness. We cannot think that we are all likely to love one another, or even respect one another. Imagine instead that, despite a strong dislike for what others believe, we can live in peaceful coexistence.

In speaking of reciprocal tolerance, we mustn't expect too much. Reciprocal tolerance doesn't mean that we should compromise our beliefs and habits – unless they are overtly intolerant. It means that we accept non-violent coexistence, living together as citizens on publicly equal terms. It means that we accept differences between groups (within the law). We might consider some of their ideas dangerous, but we acknowledge that they are not criminals. They may be dismissive of us, but they accept our equal civil status. We might consider our beliefs to be absolute, as others consider theirs to be. All we can do is agree to differ, and, if a decision on action is needed, to find a compromise. What is the alternative? Look at history. Look at the news. Do most of us really want that?

Spinoza, the great begetter of the cause of tolerance, said it directly: 'To tolerate a group who follow a system of belief or a way of life is not a question of liking, or approving, or agreeing with them. It is a question of accepting their right to be there.' We shouldn't, as some people do, dismiss tolerance as patronising. It's a two-way process. You tolerate me. I tolerate you.

And humanist? A book I wrote in 1988 had a chapter with the title 'Liberal Humanism Is Our Only Hope'. It was based on the idea that, in many ways, there was already a strong Australian belief in humanism, but it was a humanism without doctrines. It was now time, my book suggested, for some doctrines. So what could these doctrines be, our 'core' values?

A good start would be the liberal-democratic values listed above, along with encouragement for the development of human potential, both individually and communally, and toleration and co-operation as ideal social forms. Such doctrines are not in conflict with the ways most of us structure our lives, or with beliefs in family, sociability, fair and reasonable material conditions, productive work, and the catharsis of leisure activities such as sport, music, films, theatre, books, art, and other pursuits that entertain or enlighten.

If all that sounds too optimistic, here's another thing to remember: Hope should be our guide – it is as fine a guide to probability as fear. Idealism may be the only practical path we can take.

SOURCES

1. *The Education of Young Donald* extracts are from Donald Horne, *An Interrupted Life*, HarperCollins, Pymble, 1998, pp. 2–10, 53–78, 104–18, 161.
2. 'John Anderson and the Andersonians', *Observer*, 29 November 1958, pp. 652–53.
3. 'A Time of Sadness', *Observer*, 20 September 1958, pp. 487–88.
4. 'You Made What You Liked of Me, Boys' from *An Interrupted Life*, pp. 304–05.
5. Donald Horne, 'Some Cultural Elites in Australia', *Angry Penguins*, 1945, pp. 133–34.
6. Donald Horne, 'The Great Crisis of the Golden Age', *Daily Telegraph*, 19 June 1948, p. 7.
7. 'Ambition' can be found in the Donald Horne Papers, Mitchell Library, Sydney, MLMSS 3525, add-on 1871, box 3 G26.
8. Donald Horne, 'The Metaphor of Leftness', *Quadrant*, vol. 6, no. 3, 1962, pp. 59–66.
9. Donald Horne, *The Lucky Country*, Penguin, Ringwood, 1998, pp. 5–13, 233–47.
10. Donald Horne, *But What If There Are No Pelicans?*, Angus and Robertson, Sydney, 1971, pp. 165–73.
11. Donald Horne, *The Story of the Australian People*, Reader's Digest, Sydney, 1985, pp. 245–55.
12. Donald Horne, *Money Made Us*, Penguin, Ringwood, 1976, pp. 181–86, 53–61.
13. Donald Horne, *Death of the Lucky Country*, Penguin, Ringwood, 1976, pp. 9–17.
14. Donald Horne, *Ideas for a Nation*, Pan Books, Sydney, 1989, pp. 67–78.

SOURCES

15 Donald Horne, 'A Story of What Might Have Been', from the 1986 William McKell Lecture, presented to the Australian Labor Party, Sydney, 2 December 1986.

16 Donald Horne, 'The Importance of Symbolism: Australia Should Become a Republic', Donald Horne et al, *The Coming Republic*, Pan Macmillan, Sydney, 1992, pp. 26–29.

17 Donald Horne, *The Intelligent Tourist*, Margaret Gee Publishing, McMahons Point, 1992, pp. 112–20.

18 Donald Horne, *The Public Culture*, Pluto Press, London, 1994, pp. 3–9, 208–13.

19 Donald Horne, 'The Politics of the Australian Tribe: A Confidential Report by an Anthropologist from Outer Space' in David Headon, Joy Hooton & Donald Horne (eds), *The Abundant Culture*, Allen & Unwin, St Leonards, 1995, pp. 133–40.

20 Donald Horne and Myfanwy Horne, *Dying: A Memoir*, Penguin, Camberwell, 2007, pp. 184–86.

21 Donald Horne, *Into the Open: Memoirs 1958–1999*, HarperCollins, Pymble, 2000, pp. 36–46.

22 Donald Horne, *Looking for Leadership: Australia in the Howard Years*, Penguin, Ringwood, 2001, pp. 100–09.

23 Donald Horne, *10 Steps to a More Tolerant Australia*, Penguin, Camberwell, 2003, pp. 143–58.

24 Donald Horne, 'Mind, Body and Age', *Griffith Review*, no. 4, 2004.

25 Donald Horne and Myfanwy Horne, *Dying: A Memoir*, pp. 241–50.

INDEX

Abundant Culture: Meaning and Significance in Everyday Australia, The (D. Headon, J. Hooton, D. Horne eds) 236
Age xxxv
Age of Improvement, The (Briggs) 187
aircraft industry 148
Aitkin, Don 10
Altman, Dennis xlv
'Ambition' (Horne, unpublished) xx, 84–92
American Museum of Natural History 217
anarchism xxii, xxiii
Anderson, John
  academic standards 65
  anti-planning 8, 68, 78
  becomes contradictory xxiii
  Freethought Society xvi–xvii
  Horne and xi, xiv–xviii, xxv, xliii, xlv, 62–3
  on liberty 271
  pluralism 272
  'Servile State, The' xvii, 78
  'ways of life' xxxi, xxxviii, 271–2
Andersonians xx–xxii, xxiv, xxxi–xxxii, xxxv, xlv, 62–5, 69
Angry Penguins xviii, 75, 153
anti-Communism xxii, xxiv, xxxi–xxxii, 8, 97–9, 102–3
anti-intellectualism 109–12
Anzac Day 29–30, 32, 38, 108, 122
Armstrong, David xxx
Arts Action xli
Asia, engagement with 122, 124, 146–7, 267

Askin, Robert xxx
Attlee, Clement 91
Auden, W.H. 67
Australia Council x, xxix, xl–xli, xliv–xlv, 4, 11, 205, 230
Australia Institute 270
Australian xxviii, xxxv
Australian Committee for Cultural Freedom xxii, xxiv, xxx–xxxi
Australian Constitutional Commission 4
Australian Diplomatic Corps xix
Australian Financial Review xxxv
Australian Labor Party
  attacks by Billy Hughes 263
  belief in economic growth 152–3
  control of profits 164
  defeat 1949 154
  dismissal of Whitlam Government 172–9
  election results 197
  formation 190
  1960s 158
  1974/75 159–60
  shortcomings 206
  socialism and 98
  Whitlam achievements 261
Australian Legend, The (Ward) xxviii
Australian People, The (Horne) xxxvi, 4, 141–54
Australian Quarterly xxvii
Australian Republican Movement xxxiv, xlii
Australian Society of Authors 4
Australian Ugliness, The (R. Boyd) xxvii
Australian Woman's Mirror 251

INDEX

Australian Women's Weekly 150
Australia's Home (R. Boyd) xxvii
Avenue of the Fair Go, The (Horne) xxix, xlii, 5

Bagehot, Walter 119, 124
Bandler, Faith xxxiv
Baume, Michael xxiii
Beazley, Kim 258, 261
Beddie, Brian xxiv
Beresford, Bruce xxiii
Bergson, Henri 190
BHP 148
Blainey, Geoffrey 12
bodies, attitudes towards 276–9
Bootmen [movie] 270
Bourke, Max xxxvi, 11
Boyd, Ben 167–8
Boyd, Robyn xxvii
Bradman, Don 31, 51
Brecht, Bertolt 88
Briggs, Asa 187
British allegiances 32–5, 38–9, 208–9, 263, 267
British freedoms 189
Bruce, Stanley 263
Bryce, James 190
Buisson, Ferdinand 272
Bulletin xxvi–xxvii, xxx–xxxii, xxxiv–xxxvi, 4, 9–10, 100, 108, 171, 251–6
Burns, Arthur xxiv
But What If There Are No Pelicans? (Horne) xxix, 4, 129–37
Button, John xlii
Byron Bay 273

Cairns, Jim 159
California Magazine 214
Calwell, Arthur 120, 123, 156
capitalism 94–100, 103, 170, 183
Carmichael, Joel 88
Carpenter family 47, 53–4

Carroll, Vic xxxv
Cassell's Book of Knowledge 47–8, 50, 55
Castles, Francis 197
Casula Powerhouse Arts Centre 274–5
  Just Sensational: Queer Histories of Western Sydney 275
Catholicism 186, 190
Centenary of Federation xli
Change the Rules! : Towards a Democratic Constitution (Encel, Horne & Thompson eds) xxxiv
Chesty Bond 277
Chifley, Ben 147, 151–4, 259
Chipp, Don xxxiv
Christesen, Clem 76–8
Christianity 35–8, 186
Christmas 25–6, 32, 108, 237
Churchill, Winston 141, 145, 260
Citizens for Democracy xxxiii–xxxiv
Clark, Manning xxvii, xxxii, xxxvii, 60, 185–7
Cobby, Anita 275
Coleman, Peter xxiv, xxxi, xlii, 108
colonial Australia 184–93
colonial exploitation 181–5
Coming Republic, The (Horne) 5, 207
Commonwealth powers 150–2
Conference-ville (Moorhouse) xxxv
Confessions of a New Boy (Horne) xi, 4
conservative xvii, xx, xxi, xxiv, xxix, xxx, xxxi, 8, 9, 12, 82, 102, 171, 199, 201–2, 255, 286–7
Constitution 240
Council for Multicultural Australia 268, 270
Country Party 159
Cox, Eva xxxiv
Crean, Frank 158
Crossbow 101
cultural rights 230–5
culture xxxviii, 11, 227, 246–7
Curtin, John 144, 147, 263–4

295

INDEX

Daily Telegraph xiii–xiv, xix–xxi, 8, 79, 162–3, 167, 252
Daly, Fred xxxiv
Darwin, Charles 188
Deakin, Alfred 196, 258, 262–3
Deamer, Adrian xxxv
Death of the Lucky Country (Horne) xxxii, xxxiv, 4, 171–9
Denbigh xiii, 39–40, 42, 45, 55–6
Depression, the 20, 31, 41, 50, 152–3
Dickens, Charles 9, 51–3
Discipline and Punish (Foucault) 184, 225
Dissertation on Roast Pig, A (Lamb) 56
downshifters 270–1
Dutton, Geoffrey xxviii, 120
Dying: A Memoir (Horne) xii, 5, 246, 285–91

Eastman, George 214
economic growth 155–61, 241
Education 75
Education of Young Donald, The (Horne) xi, 4, 8, 62, 66, 17–60
elections as festivals 237–43
Eliot, T.S. 67
Encel, Sol xxiv, xxxiv
'Endless Seminar, The' (Davis, essay) xlv
Enlightenment, the 186–7
equality 105–6, 190, 289
Erasmus 267, 279, 288
Evatt, H.V. 145–6
expressionism 153

Fahey, Warren xxxiv
faith 285–91
festivals, Australian 236–7
Fitzgerald, Robert 66
Forbes, Sandra xxxv
Foucault, Michel 184, 225
Founding of New Societies, The (Hartz) 183, 192

Four Corners xxxv
Fraser, Malcolm 171, 177–8, 258, 262, 284
fraternalism 105–6, 124
Friedan, Betty xxxv
Froude, J.A. 109
fundamentalism 287–8

Galbraith, John Kenneth 165
Gans, Herbert 225
General Theory of Employment, Interest and Money (Keynes) 156
God is an Englishman (Horne) xxxvii, 4
Golden Age 79–83
Gorbachev, Mikhail 223
Gorton, John xxxii, 258
Gramsci, Antonio 12, 197
'Great Crisis of the Golden Age, The' (Horne) 79–83
Great Museum, The (Horne) 4, 213, 222
Green, T.H. 262–3
Greer, Germaine xxxii
Gribble, Diana xii, xlv
Griffith Review xliii, xlv, 276
gross national product 155–6, 241

Hall, Sandra xxxiv
Hansonism 260
Hardy, Frank xxxi
Harries, Owen xxxvi, xlv
Harris, Max xxviii, 75–6
Hartz, Louis 183, 192
Hawke, Bob 258
Hayden, Bill 177
Hayek, Friedrich xvii, xx
Hindutva 287
His Excellency's Pleasure (Horne) xxix, 4
History of Australia, A (Clark) 185
History of England, The (Macaulay) 187
History of the British Nation, The xiii, 47, 50–3

INDEX

Hitler, Adolf 85–6, 92
Hitler's Table Talk (Hitler) 85
Hobsbawm, E.J. 192
Holt, Harold xxxii, 258
Honi Soit xvi, xix, xxiii, 3
Hope, A.D. 66, 68
Horne, Dave (father) xii, 3, 8, 18–24, 28–30, 33, 37–8, 52–5, 57–8
Horne, Donald
  on achievement 89–91
  acknowledged as 'elder' xliii
  advertising career xxvi, xxx, 3
  on ageing 281–4
  alcohol xxii
  amateur dramatics 56–7
  on ambition 84–92
  anti-Communism x, xx, xxii, xxiv, xxx–xxxii, 8, 97–9
  anti-'progressive' 8
  Australia Council x, xxix, xl–xli, xliv–xlv, 4, 230
  Australian Constitutional Commission 4
  Australian Diplomatic Corps xix, 3
  Australian Society of Authors 4
  awarded Order of Australia xliii, 4
  birth xii, 3, 8
  Bulletin xxvi–xxvii, xxx–xxxii, xxxiv–xxxvi, 4, 9–10, 254–6, 281
  career at University of NSW xxxvi–xxxix, xlv, 4, 10, 281
  chancellor, University of Canberra xlv, 5
  childhood xiii, 17–44
  conscription xv, 3
  conservative xx–xxi, xxv, xxx, 8–9, 12, 171
  Daily Telegraph xix–xxi, 3, 8
  death xliii
  on destruction 91–2
  on dominance 89
  editor xxi–xxii, xxvi, xxxvi, 9, 254–5
  education 45–55, 59
  on excitement 87–9
  grandfathers 20, 24–5, 39, 51, 54, 276
  grandmothers 50–1
  Honi Soit xvi, xix, 3
  Honorary Doctor of Letters xliii, 4–5
  Ideas for Australia 4
  intellectual x–xi, xxvi, xli, xlv
  joins Conservative Party [UK] xxi
  leaves Packer xxvi, xxxvi
  on the Left 93–103
  lung disease 278, 281
  marriage to Ethel xxi, 3
  marriage to Myfanwy xxiii, 3, 9
  memorial service xliv
  move to England xxi, 3, 9
  National Living Treasure xliii, 12
  Newsweek International xxxvi, 4
  Observer xxiii–xxvii, 9
  orator xxxix–xl
  pessimism/optimism xiv, xvii, xxv–xxvi, xliii, 9, 49–50
  Quadrant xxx–xxxi, 4
  'radical conservative' xviii, xx, 8,
  republicanism xxxiii–xxxiv, 207–9
  satire 79–83
  scepticism xii, xxiv, xxx, xliv
  small-l liberalism xii, xxxi, xlv, 8
  student journalism xvi
  Sydney Sun xxi
  timeline 3–5
  'unintended consequences' xvii, xxv, 8–9
  university student xiv–xv, xviii–xix, 3, 8, 62–5
  Weekend xxi–xxii, xxiv, 3, 9, 254
  writing style xix–xx, 11–12
Horne, Ethel xxi, 3
Horne, Flo (mother) 3, 18–19, 21–2, 25–6, 36, 50, 52–3, 55
Horne, Julia xxvii, 3

INDEX

Horne, Myfanwy (née Gollan) xii–xiii, xxviii, xxxiii, xliv, 3, 9, 11–12, 251, 282, 285
Horne, Nick 4
Howard, John xlii, 258
Hughes, Robert xxiii
Hughes, W.M. (Billy) 206, 263–4
Hull, Andrea xli
humanism 189, 286, 288–90

Idea of Progress (Pollard) 187
Ideas for a Nation (Horne) xlii, 4, 180–93
Ideas for Australia xli, 4
immigration xxiv, xxv, 147–8, 152, 261–2
'Improvement' 187–8, 269
In Praise of Folly (Erasmus) 279, 288
In Search of Billy Hughes (Horne) 4
Indonesia 147
industrialisation 148–9, 152
inflation 158–61, 164
Inglis, Ken 122
intellectual infrastructure 270
Intelligent Tourist, The (Horne) 5, 213, 213–21
International Refugee Organisation 147
Interrupted Life, An (Horne) 5
Into the Open (Horne) xi, 5, 251–6
Iraq 247

Jackson Wain xxvii, 3
Japan 43, 51, 114–15, 141–6, 247
Jefferson, Thomas 187
Johnson, George xxi
Jorvik Viking Centre 218–19

Keating, Paul 207–8, 258, 260
Kelly, Ned 192, 265
Keneally, Thomas xxxiv
Kerr, Sir John xix, xxxiii, 172, 174–7
Keynes, J.M. 156–8, 161, 191
Kingsford Smith, Charles 31, 50–1, 277

Knopfelmacher, Frank xxx
Kramer, Leonie xxx–xxxi
Krygier, Richard xxiv, xxx–xxxi

Labor Party, *see* Australian Labor Party
Labor's Role in Modern Society (Calwell) 156
labour force 184–5, 188
labour law history 195
Lamb, Charles 56
land rights 262
landscape painting 153, 192
Lang, J.T. 206
Lenin, Vladimir 88, 91, 223, 227
Liberal Party 153–4, 159, 172–5, 177, 179, 271
liberal-democratic society 96, 103, 228, 230, 234, 289–90
liberalism 196, 262, 286, 288–90
libertarianism xvi, xxii, xxxi
liberty xxxi–xxxii, xlv, 32, 187, 271
Lippmann, Walter 213
Looking for Leadership (Horne) xlii, 5, 257–64
Lucky Country Revisited, The (Horne) 4
Lucky Country, The (Horne) 104–25
 final chapter 113
 overview 104
 publication xxiv, xxviii
 quotations from ix
 serialised in the *Australian* xxviii
 success xxviii
 Tribune critique xxxi
 writing xxvii, xxviii, 8–9, 11
Lynn, Jack 63
Lyons, Joseph 263

Macarthur, Douglas 143
Macaulay, Thomas Babington 187
MacCallum, Mungo xlv
Mandle, W. 192
Manning, Peter xlv

manufacturing, post war 148–9
Marx, Karl 96
mass culture 103, 191, 232–3
'mateship' 40, 193
Mayer, Henry xxiii–xxiv
McAuley, James xv, xxii, xxx, xxxii, 4, 66–9
McCallum, Doug xxiv
McCalman, Janet 188
McClelland, Jim xxx, xxxv
McMahon, Bill 258
Meanjin 76–8, 75, 114, 153
Medibank 261
'Meeting Soviet Man' (Clark) 60
Menzies, Robert 93, 120, 123, 146, 164, 179, 258–9, 262, 264
'Metaphor of Leftness, The' (Horne) 93–102
Métin, Albert 190
Mills, Deborah xliv
'Mind, Body and Age' (Horne, essay) xliii, 276–84
'mixed economy' 96, 99–100, 156, 191
Money Made Us (Horne) 4, 11, 155–70
Moorhouse, Frank xxxiii, xxxv, xliv
Morris, Meaghan xxviii–xxix, xxxv, xxxviii, 10
multiculturalism 262
Murdoch, Rupert xxvi, 163, 251
Murray, Les xxxii, xxxiv
museums 215, 217–21
Muslim fundamentalism 287
Mussolini, Benito 227
Muswellbrook
    Anzac Day 29
    golf links 22
    Horne's childhood xiii, 3, 8, 17–18, 24, 56
    Muswellbrook District Rural School 45, 47
    population 41–2
    snobbery 39

Nation 120
Nation Review xxxv
National Council for the Humanities xli
National Country Party 174–5
National Summit of Ideas xli
National Trust xliii
nationalisation 151
nationalism xli, 107
nation-defining 180–93
'New Australians' 148
New Guinea, defence of 143–5
New Hellas restaurant xlv
'New Protection' 196, 263
New Writing 75
Newsweek International xxxvi, 4
Next Australia, The (Horne) 4
Nield, Bruce 63
1988 and All That (Shaw) 189
Nolan, Sidney 265

Oakeshott, Michael xxiv
Observer xxiii–xxvii, 9, 62, 66, 86–8, 251
O'Grady, Desmond xxiii
Olympic Games (Sydney 2000) 265–6, 270, 272–3
100 Years in Yosemite (Russell) 214
Overland 60
Owen Stanley Ranges, Battle of the 144

Packer, Frank
    Australian Woman's Mirror 251
    Bulletin xxvi, xxxv, 251, 255
    Daily Telegraph xiii–xiv, xx, 162–4, 167–8, 252
    Observer xxiii, 9, 251
    ownership of business 165, 167–9
    profit motive 162–4
    recalls Horne to Australia xxi
    Weekend 9
Palmer, Vance 114–15
parliament 243–5

INDEX

Partisan Review 99
patriotism
   national development 269–70, 273
   national mirages 224–7
   Russia 222
   USA 224
Pearson, Noel xliii
Penguin xxviii
Penton, Brian 8
Perkin, Graham xxxv
Permit, The (Horne) xxix, 4
Philosophy Journal 64, 78
photography 213–16
Pioneer Women's Hut, Tumbarumba 273–4
Pocket Bookshop xxxv
political leadership 257–64
Pollard, Sidney 187
Popular Culture and High Culture (Gans) 225
Porter, G.R. 187
Portrait of an Optimist (Horne) xi, 4
Prices Justification Tribunal 164
Pringle, John xxxv
Prior, Ken 256
profit motive 162–70, 241
progressive 49, 93-4, 100, 114, 124, 194
public culture 227–9
Public Culture, The (Horne) xii, 11, 222–35
Public Opinion (Lippmann) 213
Public Service 150–1
public works 152

Quadrant x, xviii, xxiv, xxx–xxxi, 4, 93

racism xxiv, 194, 254, 256, 260, 268
Raymond, Bob xxiii, xxxv
Reagan, Ronald 224
realism 215–19, 221
Reid, George 196
religion 35–8, 186, 190, 286–8

republicanism xxxi–xxxiii, 207–9
Rerum Novarum (Pope Leo XIII) 190
Right Way Don't Go Back (Horne) 4
Roach, Ted 268
Road to Serfdom, The (Hayek) xvii
Rolfe, Patricia xxxv
Roosevelt, Theodore 259
Ross, Lloyd 76
Russell, Bertrand 109
Russia 222–4
Russian Revolution, The (Sukhanov) 88
Russians, The (Smith) 222
Ryan, Peter xxxii

Santamaria, Bob xxx
Sayle, Murray xix
Schlesinger, Arthur Jr 99
Schultz, Julianne xliii, xlv
Scott, Walter 187
secularism 188–9
'Servile State, The' (Anderson, article) xvii, 78
sexism 150, 194
shareholders 165–6, 168, 170, 208
Shaw, George 189
shipbuilding 148
Short, Laurie xxx
Singapore, fall of 141–2
Slessor, Kenneth 66
Slim, William 144
Smith, Hedrick 222, 224
Sneddon, Billy 159
snobbery 39
Snowy River Scheme 152
social welfare 151, 161, 191, 195, 262
socialism 88, 95–100, 103, 173, 190, 204
'Some Cultural Elites in Australia' (Horne) xix, 75–8
Somerville, Oliver 63
South Sydney Junior Leagues Club 104–5
Southern Exposure (Horne) 4

300

INDEX

Soviet Union 222–3
Spann, Dick xxiv
Spencer, Herbert 190
Spender, Stephen 67
Spinoza, Baruch 187, 290
sport 109, 191–2
Sport in Australia (Mandle) 192
'stagflation' 158
Stalin, Joseph 224
Stendahl 280
Stewart, Douglas 66
Stewart, Harold 68
Stonier, Brian xxviii
'Story of What Might Have Been, A'
 (Horne) 194–206
Stretton, Hugh xix
Struggletown (McCalman) 188
Sunset Strip 160–1
'supremacy of the economic' 183
swagmen 192
Sydney Mail 50–1
Sydney Morning Herald xxxv
Sydney Push xxii–xxiii
Sydney Sun xxi
Sydney University
 Freethought Society xvi–xviii, 63–4, 271
 Honi Soit xvi, xix, xxiii
 Literary Society xv, xviii, 63–4
Sydney Writers' Festival xliii

Tampa election 266, 269
Tanner, Les xxiii, xxvi
tariffs 31, 195, 261–2
technological change 103, 111, 113, 115–18, 122, 124
10 Steps to a More Tolerant Australia (Horne) 5, 265–75
Theodore, Ted 204–6
Thompson, Elaine xxxiv, xxxviii, xlv
Threepenny Novel, The (Brecht) 88–9
Tocqueville, Alexis de 190
tolerance 103, 107, 125, 231, 267–9, 275, 289–90
Tony's Bon Gout restaurant 171–2
tourism 214–16
Town Life in Australia (Twopenny) 189–90
travel writing 216–17
Tribune xxxi
Trouble with Economic Rationalism, The (Horne) 5
Tucker, Albert 153
Turnbull, Malcolm xxxiv
Twopenny, R.E.N. 189

unemployment 151, 157–61, 226
union movement 98, 188, 190
United Australia Party (UAP) 153
United Nations 146
 General Assembly 146
 Security Council 147

Vietnam War xxx
Viking museums 218–21
Volunteering Australia 272
volunteering movement 272–3

Walsh, Richard xxxv
Ward, Barbara 111
Ward, Russell xxviii
Waugh, Evelyn 9–10
'ways of life' 271–2
Weber, Max 289
Weekend xxi–xxii, xxiv, 3, 9, 254
Wentworth, Bill 283–4
White Australia policy xxiv–xxv, 261
White, Patrick xxxii–xxxiii
Whitlam, Gough
 achievements 261–2
 condemned by McAuley xxxii
 dismissal xxix, xxxii, xxxiii, 158, 172, 174, 176–9

Whitlam, Gough (cont.)
    economic management 159
    election loss 1975 171
    orator 258
    Prices Justification Tribunal 164
Wilson, Thomas 101
Winner Take All (Horne) 4
Wolfsohn, Hugo xxiv
women
    discrimination against 261
    roles during wartime 149–50
    wages 149–50

Women's Employment Board 149
'work' 226, 241
Working Class and Welfare, The
    (Castles) 197
World War I xii, 28, 30
World War II xv–xvi, 141–6, 264
Wran, Neville xxxv, 206
Wright, Judith 66

Yeltsin, Boris 223
'You Made What You Liked of Me, Boys'
    (Horne, poem) xv–xvi, 70–1

www.ingramcontent.com/pod-product-compliance
Lightning Source LLC
Chambersburg PA
CBHW031427160426
43195CB00010BB/637